light color sound

light color sound

Sensory effects in contemporary architecture

Alejandro Bahamón
Ana María Alvarez

W. W. Norton & Company
New York • London

Light Color Sound

Published by Parramón Ediciones, S. A.,
Roselló i Porcel, 21, 9th Floor, 08016,
Barcelona, Spain

Originally published in Spanish as LUZ COLOR SONIDO:
Efectos Sensoriales en la Arquitectura Contemporánea

Printed in China

Graphic Design: Mídori
Electronic production by J. Lops
Production manager: Leeann Graham

Library of Congress Cataloging-in-Publication Data

Bahamón, Alejandro.
[Luz color sonido. English]
Light color sound : sensory effects in contemporary
architecture / Alejandro Bahamón, Ana María
Alvarez.
p. cm.
Originally published: Luz color sonido : efectos
sensoriales en la arquitectura contemporánea.
Barcelona, Spain : Parramon Ediciones, 2010.
Includes bibliographical references and index.
ISBN 978-0-393-73337-2 (hardcover)
1. Senses and sensation in architecture. 2. Architecture,
Modern—20th century. 3. Architecture, Modern—21st
century. I. Alvarez, Ana María. II. Title. III. Title: Sensory
effects in contemporary architecture.
NA2543.S47B3413 2010
720.1—dc22
2010018278

ISBN: 978-0-393-73337-2

W. W. Norton & Company, Inc., 500 Fifth Avenue,
New York, N.Y. 10110
www.wwnorton.com
W. W. Norton & Company Ltd., Castle House, 75/76 Wells
Street, London W1T 3QT

0 9 8 7 6 5 4 3 2 1

Cover:
Dexia Tower
LAb[au] Architects
Photo: © LAb[au] Architects

Contents

6
Introduction by Ana María Alvarez

11
Points of view

12
Light, color, sound . . . The art of systems | LAb[au]

18
New 42nd Street Studios | Platt Byard Dovell White Architects

20
Entirely an interior job | Bart Lootsma

24
Good waves | Michela Mezzavilla

28
The sound of space | Christopher Janney

32 | light

34
Star Place | Kao-hsiung, Taiwan
UNStudio

46
Le Prisme | Aurillac, France
Brisac González Architects

58
Dexia Tower | Brussels, Belgium
LAb[au]

68
Nelson-Atkins Museum | Kansas City, MO, United States
Steven Holl Architects

80
Tire Shop | Zurich, Switzerland
Camenzind Evolution

90
Watercube | Beijing, China
PTW Architects

100
Spots | Berlin, Germany
realities:united

110
Kubik | Barcelona, Spain
Modulorbeat

118
Urban oasis | Various European cities
Chetwoods Associates

126
Center for Contemporary Artistic Creation | Córdoba, Spain
Nieto Sobejano Arquitectos and realities:united

134
New 42nd Street Studios | New York, NY
Platt Byard Dovell White Architects and Vortex Lighting

144
GreenPix | Beijing, China
Simone Giostra & Partners Architects

156
Club Nox | Recife, Brazil
Metro Arquitetura and Juliano Dubeux

168
Luxembourg Philarmonic | Luxembourg, Luxembourg
Christian de Portzamparc

178 | color

180
Didden Village | Rotterdam, Netherlands
MVRDV

190
Atrium—University of Jussieu | Paris, France
Périphériques architectes

202
Fire station | Houten, Netherlands
Philippe Samyn and Partners

214
Montreal Congress Palace | Montreal, Canada
Tétrault, Dubuc, Saia et associés, and Hal Ingberg

222
Els Colors kindergarten | Manlleu, Spain
RCR Arquitectes

234
The Reece School | New York, NY
Platt Byard Dovell White Architects

242
Parque Explora | Medellín, Colombia
Alejandro Echeverri Restrepo

254
Netherlands Institute of Sound and Vision | Hilversum, Netherlands
Neutelings Riedijk Architecten

266
Agora Theater | Lelystad, Netherlands
UNStudio

276 | sound

278
Windshape | Lacoste, France
nARCHITECTS

288
Sonic Forest | Zaragoza, Spain
Christopher Janney

298
Center for the Dramatic Arts | Taipei, Taiwan
B+U

310
Low Rez / Hi Fi | Washington, DC
Höweler + Yoon Architecture

318
Chant de bambous | Chaumont-sur-Loire, France
N+B Architectes

324
Kofmehl | Solothurn, Switzerland
ssm architekten

332
References

334
Directory of Architects

INTRODUCTION

Ana María Álvarez

What is the sensory experience of architecture in this new technological era? How is architecture perceived? Can we speak of sensual pleasure when we contemplate building?

Our perception of architecture has been focused on sight and touch, leaving smell, hearing, and taste to one side. Buildings are created as striking images of instantaneous persuasion, as a photograph that produces a single description of an object, devoid of any dimensions or details. The last few years, however, have started to give rise to projects that investigate—from both the architectural and the technical viewpoints—the application of artificial light, color, and sound. Buildings of an interdisciplinary nature are being created to link and fuse art, architecture, and technology—projects in which the involvement of artists or the experience of an engineer are basic to the design and development.

Experimentation with light, color, and sound permitted the emergence of architecture that controls the sensations and perceptions of onlookers. These buildings act as an instrument of communication, totally connected with the senses; although color and light are perceived with the eyes and sound with the ears, all five senses react to them. Architecture is experienced with the entire body through the perception of the qualities, materials, and scale of the space: the constant interaction of all the senses articulates reality.

Amid today's constant bombardment of information, the choice of techniques and materials distinguishes a project and seeks to alter the way it is perceived. The achievement of sensory effects via architectural elements requires a long process of exploration, suggestion, and revision that will be different for every project. The impact of one building cannot be repeated or copied or transferred to another. The more provocative the stimulus for onlookers' perception, the freer the creative power and the greater the incitement to participate in the development of their environment. Effects of light, color, and sound are highly distinctive in architecture and render a building unique, giving rise to image-projects that represent a brand or insignia of communication.

Although every building is a declaration of intent (the creation of lasting experiences), its close connection with the current state of technology means that, while being fixed, it is also ephemeral and capable of being adapted and transformed according to the spectacle or context: architecture made to last as long as is appropriate and necessary. This ephemeral quality reflects the cultural moment of its creation. It triggers the need for new reading and, above all, the avoidance of an immediate impact that could make a building instantly obsolete. In this respect, the sensations produced by light, color, and sound are dependent on a building's setting, so the effects produced by its architecture turn it into an urban landmark. These values serve as a means to creating both aesthetic and functional effects: to make streets and squares stand out or become uniform, or to distinguish, articulate, or animate a building.

Architecture communicates specific ideas about our relationship with the world. The desired effect for a building to have on its surroundings is structured around the human body and senses. The projects featured in this book focus on the role of elements in a building that remain unseen: technical installations that make light, color, and sound a reality. The chosen examples constitute a small selection of strategies applied by architects from all over the world in order to make sensory effects the central theme of their design. The presentation of each project closely examines its formal language and its role in the configuration of the modern landscape.

These projects are complemented at the start of the book by five commentaries, entitled Points of View, which endorse the importance of sensory effects in contemporary architecture. They express the vision of professionals and academics who stress the roles that light, color, and sound have played over the course of twentieth-century architecture and in the design of their own work.

LIGHT

The development of architecture is closely linked to that of artificial light, although it was only at the end of the twentieth century that architects began to treat artificial light as an integral element of the design process, rather than a functional system or a cosmetic extra. Buildings themselves became light sources, not only fulfilling the basic needs of visibility but also creating an effect, an atmosphere, a condition.

The use of light was previously confined to areas devoted to entertainment and commerce: Times Square in New York, Sunset

Strip in Las Vegas, the Shinjuku district of Tokyo, and London's Piccadilly Circus. In the early twentieth century, light accentuated the structure of buildings and made them expressive at night (through movement and rhythm). Both night and day began to be considered in the design process, in order to give equal importance to a building's nighttime and daytime appearances. So, the interior began to be reflected on the exterior by means of light: glass that would allow natural light to seep inside during the day became gleaming lanterns that would illuminate their surroundings at night.

In these circumstances, artificial light is more than just a functional medium. Architecture is transformed at nightfall. The appearance of forms and materials changes under natural or artificial light; surfaces look different and set up contrasts between day and night (for example, solidity by day, transparency by night). In projects whose design is based on light, the facade ceases to be an enclosure or a boundary between inside and outside to become a distinctive surface in its own right.

The surroundings of the buildings on display in this section are totally transformed, as the scale of their forms and spaces is altered. A building is not merely lit up, it becomes a veritable spotlight. White or colored lights or audiovisual elements can be used, rendering a building a huge screen that reflects the origin of the architectural design.

COLOR

Color tends to highlight parts of a building; it can emphasize them, make them invisible or transparent, or conceal them. Once color is separated from its customary role, it becomes the guiding element of a design. So, the sensations produced by color in architecture depend upon its setting, history, atmosphere, light. Extremely complex effects can be created by taking advantage of new technologies and techniques. Color can be used to emphasize forms: if the color of a well-known shape is changed, our perception of it also changes and it is no longer so easy to recognize.

Color is also a memory. The memory of the cities we visit is often associated with specific colors: Paris is gray, New York blue, Tokyo red, Lisbon white. Color is a fundamental part of a city's skin, and it alters moods and perceptions. It has its own intrinsic properties, over and above being a layer on a surface. It transforms the experience of objects or, more precisely, it alters their state: reality itself is affected by them.

Color was fundamental in the conception of some key projects in modern architecture, albeit as a complementary element in their composition—for example in works by Le Corbusier such as La Tourette Monastery, in Charles Eames's own house, and the tower and home of Luis Barragán. During the last three decades of the twentieth century color took on a leading role instead of being a complement—the Pompidou Center by Renzo Piano and Richard Rogers, the total white of Richard Meier's buildings, the optical illusions with colored light in the first projects by OMA.

Although color is perceived with the eyes, all five of our senses react to it, so it is a means of expression by which an architect can illustrate the spirit of what he or she wants to convey. As a basic element in architectural composition, the relationship between the colors in a project establishes an alphabet: a building emits messages.

As regards the use and effects of color, the striking qualities of the projects described here demonstrate that it has ceased to be merely a decorative element and has become instead a means of emphasizing dimensions and defining the volume of spaces. Color underlines a project's artistic nature by dissolving the limits between physical and imagined space. It highlights a building's theatricality. Color makes a building stand out from its context, turning it into something unexpected and often surreal.

SOUND

Like color, sound in architecture is a memory. Visual impressions are related to a sound which, ultimately, acts as the link across time between the project and the viewer. The echo of architectural space stays within the subject as an unconscious experience. This is how cities and buildings are remembered and related to specific sounds.

The constructions presented in this book are examples of experimentation with sonic architecture: their very structure, in interaction with their surroundings, produces or contains sounds. They are striking for their capacity to create sound with architectural elements and to make architecture on the basis of sounds. These projects cover not only buildings specifically designed as concert halls but also ones that resonate on their own or invite viewers themselves to produce sounds by touch.

points of view

12
Light, color, sound... the art of systems | LAb[au]

18
New 42nd Street Studios | Platt Byard Dovell White Architects

20
Entirely an interior job | Bart Lootsma

24
Good waves | Michela Mezzavilla

28
The sound of space | Christopher Janney

LIGHT COLOR, SOUND . . . THE ART OF SYSTEMS

LAb[au]

This opening section reviews a group of twentieth-century avant-garde works that reveal a link in current artistic practice between relevant media and advanced technologies. The artists' method was based on establishing systems and processes in creating artifacts, as well as on the emergence of an art of systems, or parameter design.

‹ SYNESTHESIA ›

In the Bauhaus era, Wassily Kandinsky applied principles of musical composition—particularly those of Schoenberg—to his painting, and this led him to develop his theory on synesthesia, as formulated in *Concerning the Spiritual in Art* (1912). He described synesthesia as a phenomenon of transposition of experience from one sensory modality to another. Rather than transposing musical and color harmonies through frequencies of light waves and sound waves, Kandinsky first investigated two essential problems: dissonance and temporality. His synesthesic approach cannot therefore be understood in terms of simple correspondences such as tone-color relationships, but rather in terms of compositions based on visual and sonic patterns in "collaboration and opposition" that reveal tension and emotion within an interplay of colors, forms, and shapes. During his Bauhaus period, he focused on research in methodology along the same lines as Johannes Itten with his color indexing and Paul Klee and Josef Albers with their "fugue" paintings, which transposed the rules of musical composition onto painting. The Bauhaus method marked a rupture with the fine art tradition by considering aesthetics in the context of technological and social change derived from the Industrial Revolution. This in turn challenged the very concept of art itself.

Similarly, Piet Mondrian studied the problem of the visual perception of movement in his apparently static compositions. By using the perceptual effect of a rhythmically moving raster, he sought to add to the two dimensions of painting not just a third dimension of depth but also a fourth dimension of time, as a visual suggestion of movement. The synesthesia of movement in visual rasters remained a central theme of Mondrian's experiments, culminating in *Broadway Boogie-Woogie* (1941–42), which depicts the city of New York in an abstract interplay of color surfaces and geometric structures seen from a skyscraper while listening to jazz. In this painting, colored areas correspond to sounds with a definite pitch, whereas areas with no color correspond to sounds without any definite pitch (which Mondrian referred to as "noise"). The primary colors have their analogues in the pitches of the standard scale, recalling Isaac Newton's analysis of the spectrum in terms of the seven tones of the Western scale.

Other relationships in Mondrian's scheme are the visual notion of size, corresponding to dynamics or acoustic amplitude, and position in space, corresponding to position in time, recalling the flow of cars through a maze of city streets or the complex interplay of rhythms in a jazz improvisation. By combining the time-sequenced parameters of music with the visual aspects of painting, Mondrian explored the perceptive and cognitive modalities of pictorial space. Rather than fulfilling his intended aim of constructing a universal language, however, his greatest legacy was the establishment of a system of assignments (signifiers), a methodological approach based on the perceived parameters of a medium in the creation of art.

‹ OEUVRE TOTALE ›

Light, color, rhythm, image, sound; the basis, the data for a new performance; we can call it electronic play. . . .
—Le Corbusier, *Le Poème électronique.* Les Editions de Minuit, 1958.

As an illustration of parameter design using a historical but non-digital example, the design of the Philips Pavilion for the 1958 Universal Exposition in Brussels—the *Poème électronique* by Le Corbusier and Iannis Xenakis—can be understood as an instance of new building techniques but also as a contemporary expression that extends architectural principles to music and cinema. The superimposition of a hyperbolic external shape, conceived by Iannis Xenakis, on the internal shape of a "cow's stomach" conceived by Le Corbusier, constitutes more than just a contradiction of one of the main architectural principles (inside = outside/form follows function); it also represents a deconstruction of architecture's traditional language and presages today's media-based design approach.

On the one hand, the application of new static construction principles based on hyperbolic mathematical functions—which were also the basis for the two musical compositions by Iannis Xenakis played as an interlude in the pavilion, *Metastasis* and *Concrète PH*—can be seen as a rational way of relating space, music, and construction through science. Both of the musical scores represented a completely new concept of music that went beyond tone and notes to draw on mathematical functions and physical behavior. In the case of *Concrète PH*, the hyperbolic functions established a temporal system for the evolution of sound, but also a spatial vocabulary for music, such as density,

Exterior of the Philips Pavilion for the Universal Exposition in Brussels, 1958. Eindhoven Druk Bv. Courtesy of Bart Lootsma

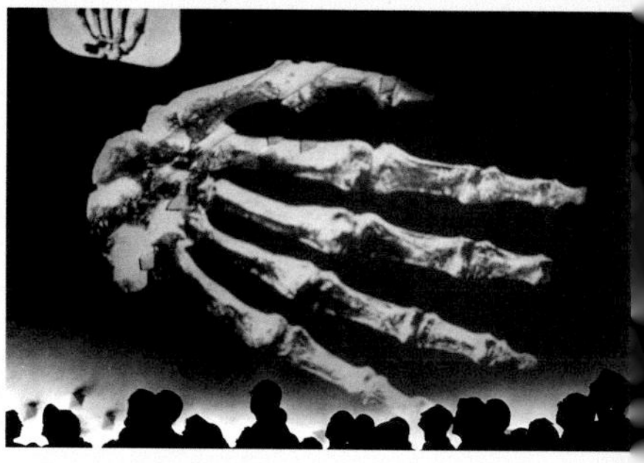

Skeleton's hand from Sequence 3, "From Darkness to Dawn," *Poème électronique* © Philips

growth. . . . The application of mathematical functions as a sonic and spatial entity is a major theme of Xenakis's entire work, best exemplified today by his "Polytopes" series and the theory of granular synthesis.

On the other hand, the internal shape of the pavilion created an organic space of "flows," an imaginary cave covered on the inside with projected images displaying the history of man and technology, which can be seen as a cultural approach acting on the semantic level of form. The footage by the Italian filmmaker Philippe Agostini included time-based color sequences that made the entire inner space float in a single color; the same principle can be found in the book put together by the graphic designer Jean Petit, where transparent slides were inserted in between the pages to sequence and structure the composition. This abstract color play reinforced the sequential, rhythmic perception in the same way as the musical score *Poème électronique* by Edgard Varèse, which was commissioned for the pavilion and is now considered one of the first electronic music compositions. The spatial projection of synchronized images and colored light was enhanced by a sonic "spatialization" of the pavilion, involving 425 speakers distributed all over the internal shell to immerse the listener in sound. The result was a groundbreaking environment, an "*oeuvre totale*": the pavilion featured audio and visual materials as integral parts of the architectural design, a "*machine à spectacle*" achieved by electrical technologies that connected the different levels of perception in a completely new way.

These two apparently opposite design approaches form a single vision in their perception of the correlation between space, color, and light; this vision embodies the interrelationship of technology and aesthetics in the construction of sign forms, which was the essential theme of the Philips Pavilion design. From this point of view, the pavilion design expresses the positivist view, and the aim of the 1958 Expo to place technological progress at the center of a new society after "point zero." In the Xenakis/Le Corbusier example, space was related to form, light, and sound on both a parametric and a cultural level.

‹ CYBERNETICS ›

By programming and combining the non-material elements of space, light and time as well as the concrete forms deriving from them (such as architecture, film, video, dance and literature), Nicolas Schöffer has sought to bring together various disciplines that have been separated since the Renaissance. His work involves contemporary technology, such as the computer. He foresees a "collective choreography" of the visual and sonic spaces of cities, involving the creative interaction of artist and public.

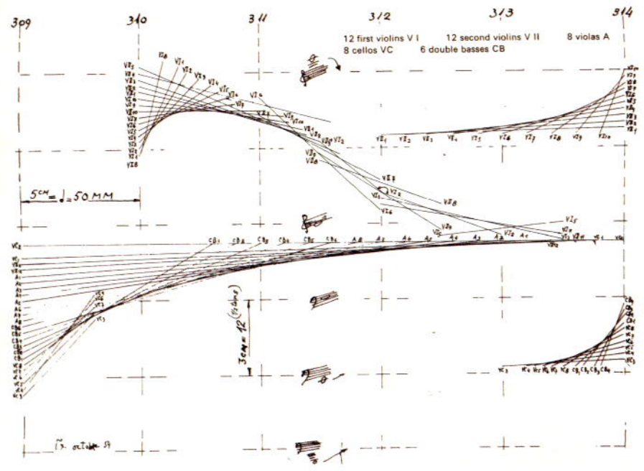

Diagram of a glissando from *Metastasis*, Iannis Xenakis, 1954

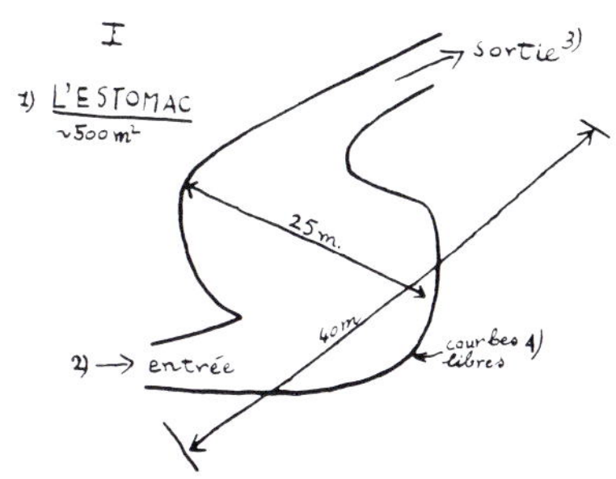

Conceptual sketch by Iannis Xenakis from the Philips Pavilion
© Philips Technical Review

Nicolas Schöffer, *Cysp 1*, 1956

Nicolas Schöffer, *Chronos 10*, 1978

—"Sonic and Visual Structures: Theory and Experiment," Nicolas Schöffer (1912–1992), in Leonardo, 1983 http://www.olats.org/schoffer/savs2.htm.

At almost the same time as the *Poème électronique*, Nicolas Schöffer's first cybernetic sculpture, set on the rooftop of Le Corbusier's Unité d'Habitation in Marseille, represented a second important step in the relationship between media and architectural art. *CYSP 1* consisted of metal blades and plates of various shapes and colors equipped with microphones and photoelectric cells. Within the sculpture's cylindrical base, an electronic device developed by the Philips company regulated the various motions triggered by information retrieved from the environment Variations and modifications in color (= light) and sound affected the movement's device to reflect the intensity of the changing parameter. For example, sharp sonorities or the color blue evoked agitated movement, while low sonorities and/or a red spark produced movement in the opposite direction and at low speed. *CYSP 1* was the first interactive sculpture to retrieve its data from its environment. The title comes from a merging of the twin principles of cybernetics and spatiodynamism, while translating them into rules of kinetics, light, and sound.

Every surface, however insignificant, can be transformed into a "Light Wall," thanks to colored and moving projections of a chronos or lux sculpture, brightened by colored spotlights and rotating slowly on its base. Some Light Walls are obtained by lumino-dynamic effects on screens of variable size. These effects can eventually be controlled, modified and diversified by the user-contemplater of the show.
—Nicolas Schöffer http://www.olats.org/schoffer/murlum1e.htm.

In his "chrono-dynamic" works, Schöffer explored electronically time-based programming that provoked visual effects by means of rotating mirrors and color light projectors, setting up reflections on a screen in front of the sculpture. The final light painting is the result of a programmed kinetic sculpture creating endless variations, with the additional factor that the visitor can step aside to follow the mechanics. Later on, Schöffer created—either alone or in collaboration with musicians such as Iannis Xenakis, and Pierre Schaeffer—scores for non-repeating musical compositions. These *sculptures à spectacle* were milestones in the development of an interactive and system-based art, whose aesthetic depended on the relevance of the system in question. This approach created a new relationship between object and subject, as evident in Schöffer's cybernetic tower in Paris—a "reflector" of the city's flux and life and his formulations of the cybernetic city. Today, his cybernetic vision can be seen as a precursor of the art of the sixties by extrapolating the technological progress of a growing post-industrial society into a general vision in which art has a major role in a new social order.

‹ DATA MAPPING ›

Direct connections persist between ornament and music, which mean that Ornaments are Music. If you look at a strip of film from my experiments with synthetic sound, you will see a thin stripe of jagged ornamental patterns along one edge. These ornaments are drawn music—they are sound: when run through a projector, these graphic sounds broadcast tones of a hitherto unheard-of purity, and thus, quite obviously, fantastic possibilities open up for the composition of music in the future.

—"Sound Ornaments," Oskar Fischinger, *Deutsche Allgemeine Zeitung*, July 8, 1932; http://www.oskarfischinger.org/Sounding.htm.

The "sound ornaments" of Oskar Fischinger constituted another important step in the art of systems. Yet instead of the synesthesis produced by the use of different media typical of the 1920s, his work introduced a totally new approach.

The precise process of interrelation achieved by mapping one medium onto another marked the structural and semantic foundation of an aesthetic that operated on the level of signs and codes, with the process determining the produced result. The process itself—and the system—became the creation, the level at which significance was produced. Fischinger created his "sound ornaments," or music, not with the usual background and perspectives of a musician but with those of a visual artist.

In the light of the methodological research undertaken by the avant-garde artists of the twenties—such as those of the Bauhaus as well as the Constructivists, who tried to integrate contemporary technological progress into the concept and production of artifacts—Fischinger's "sonic ornaments" stand in direct relationship to the experiments of Josef Albers, Wassily Kandinsky, Moholy-Nagy, and their contemporaries.

Lázló Moholy-Nagy's Constructivist movie *Black-White-Gray* used photographic techniques of positive and negative overlaying of images "to paint light in movement" by exploring his kinetic sculpture *Light Space Modulator*, whereas Fischinger directly mapped visual patterns onto music. The common ground of their work, however, was the technical exploration of the boundaries of cinema in search of a new visual and sonic experience. Thus, Fischinger's experiments in the 1930s presaged the aesthetic discourse of the second half of the twentieth century and, more particularly, the computer age.

His work had a great impact on composers such as Edgard Varèse, who met Fischinger in California shortly after his arrival in America in the late thirties. Indeed, a direct line can be drawn between the synesthetic approach of the twenties and thirties and the cybernetic works of the sixties: both were united by a quest for parametric and system-based art that explored the technologies of their time to establish a methodological approach to creating artifacts. These examples are just a small selection from the host of works that pioneered the aesthetics of the information age from the twenties and thirties.

Oskar Fischinger, *Sound Ornaments*, 1932.

László Moholy-Nagy, *Black-White-Gray*, 1932

‹ INFORMATION ›

The technological developments of the last few decades provide the basis for the shift from an industrial to an information society, where computation and communication technologies extend our very senses. The notions of body, matter, space, and time are increasingly defined by the unit of information, as its structures, processes, and systems introduce new extensions of space and time, such as networks, real-time immersion, and interaction, as well as new extensions of materiality (nanotechnologies and smart memory materials) and biology (gene technologies). This opens up a huge artistic endeavor that promotes the exploration of new cultural codes and semantics based on the notion of inFORMation.

One of the specificities of the digital medium is to reduce all information to a binary signal—be it a picture, text, space, or sound. All data is recorded as a binary sequence constituting the base of computation as defined by programming languages and communication through networks governed by transmission protocols. Thus the medium, through its processes, unifies information, on the structural as much as on the semantic level. To talk of digital media is the equivalent of placing this programmatic relationship inside a spatial and temporal structure between data, and therefore between the different types of textual, visual, and sonic data.

This interrelationship between different media nevertheless must be described through programming (structured language) by importing its own methods, processes, and codes. Consequently, such information mapping leads to systematic thinking in the production of artifacts. The "coding" acts as much on the structural as on the semantic/cultural level, corresponding to what were previously known as "signifiers"; but it also reveals operational aspects (a system has to run on a chosen technological platform) and an aesthetic relevance. When talking about the relevance of systems, it is therefore important to encompass the modalities of a medium, as much as its cultural and semantic inscription of a set system.

This review of a small selection of pre-digital artworks underlines the continuous quest during the twentieth century for an artistic method in setting sign systems, which of course rely on technology but also on the cultural environment. From this point of view, the twentieth-century avant-garde works outlined here were already projecting the potential for current artistic exploration within the digital realm, as well as framing our conception of aesthetic relevance by their general viewpoint.

LAb[au], Laboratory for architecture and urbanism: based in Brussels, founded in 1997 by Manuel Abendroth, Jerome Decock, Alexandre Plennevaux, and Els Vermang. This studio focuses on the creation of graphic material, audiovisual representations, and large-scale panoramas. Its work has been presented in various museums and at art festivals in both Europe and the United States.

NEW 42ND STREET STUDIOS

Platt Byard Dovell White Architects

Far from the emerging pastiche and "theme architecture" of its time, the New 42nd Street Studios building was conceived as a work in itself, rather than a New York State–mandated memory of past buildings and styles.

When we looked at the context and the program we were given, the idea of a collage gradually emerged as the most appropriate response. The project was demanding, including not just the basic elements—rehearsal studios and office space—but also a black-box theater, an entrance for the studios, a ground-floor retail space, and a major ground-floor presence for the Roundabout Theater Company, which, while not actually part of the new building, connects with it. In addition, we were required to incorporate an existing six-story facade and to create signage and lighting mandated by the state's "42nd Street Now!" plan. Rather than treating the signs and lighting as something to be applied to the building, as elsewhere on the street, we made them integral to the architecture, so they became central elements in an abstract composition. The entire building, in effect, is a three-dimensional collage, distilled from our understanding of the project's context and program—a collage in which we invented the various pieces and then assembled them in response to the character of 42nd Street.

The first component in the collage was the required incorporation of the existing six-story facade of the Selwyn Office Building. This was a determining influence in the design. We understood that we could play with depth to some extent and find ways to resolve the conflict between what already existed and what was proposed. A most important element was the armature—a suspended grid of perforated, ground, stainless-steel, louvered blades in front of the aluminum and glass curtain wall—serving as a screen for a continuous play of lights, while otherwise allowing for views both from within and into the building.

When the Selwyn facade collapsed in an extraordinary accident in December 1997, we were forced to rethink the entire arrangement of the front of the building. The Selwyn facade embodied something considered of significant historic value, and it served as a key piece of the collage. It also performed an essential direct programmatic role, which was to house a critical support space for the black-box theater and function rooms. What took its place is a smaller, layered glass lightscreen, penetrated by fins of dichroic, filtered glass that give a multicolored shimmer of light and color during the daytime. To the left of that, as you face the building, is the light "pipe"—another element in the collage—rising (175 feet, or 53 m) as a single column of light.

The lighting designer, Anne Militello of Vortex Lighting, brought with her the context of New York City theater and her experience of lighting shows both on Broadway and Off Broadway. The project team extended the approach and the use of materials to employing light at night, and Militello helped open up possibilities with the facade to capture the imagination of everyone involved in the project. The array of perforated stainless-steel blades became the screen—a medium for a fantastic show of computer-programmed lights designed by Militello. Using the immediate contextual reference on 42nd Street, the variation in changing lights matches the changing levels of street activity between slower weekdays and busier weekends. This light "performance" progresses through the entire week. But if the computer were stopped, and the lights remained static, we would still have something that looked like an art piece, in a theatrical and sculptural sense.

The New 42nd Street Studios are conceived as illumination in themselves. It is as if the building were a lighting fixture and a sign. In its totality, the Studios building ends up incorporating the mandated requirements for lighting and signage on 42nd Street, with the building as an object that proclaims a message through light.

Every other building on the block is about consumption, making available a product. They exist to offer you a play, a movie, a meal, a piece of clothing, or a souvenir.

The New 42nd Street Studios exists for the exhibition of the process of creating, offering a type of street theater.

The whole building articulates that idea, especially in the way it is opened up to reveal the process inside. You might not see people in the rehearsal studios at all times, because of the limitations of sightlines on the street, but you will get the idea that the process is happening in there—you understand that activity is going on. We wanted to express the building as a creative factory, engaging and exposing all the different components of the collage. Every single one of those elements was hammered out and very carefully considered. You don't get that opportunity in every building. We were very lucky to have New 42nd Street Inc. as a client.

PLATT BYARD DOVELL WHITE ARCHITECTS: architecture firm with over thirty years of experience in renovation projects in the United States. Work includes the enlargement of the Museum of Art in Saginaw; a building for the Congregation Shearith Israel on West 70th Street in New York, the Educational Alliance art school, also in New York; and the conversion of New York's Seventh Regiment Armory into an exhibition center. The firm has forty employees and is run by principals Charles Platt, Ray Dovell, and Sam White.

ENTIRELY AN INTERIOR JOB

The *Poème électronique* of Le Corbusier, Edgard Varèse, and Iannis Xenakis

Bart Lootsma

For more than twenty-five years, Le Corbusier's Philips Pavilion and his film *Poème électronique* remained his most mysterious projects—even though thousands of people had seen them at the 1958 Brussels Expo. The *Oeuvre complète* shows only three photographs of the pavilion, all taken from the outside, along with an early model. Shown inside the pavilion, Corbusier's film—with a musical score by Edgard Varèse and the musical "entracte" *Concrète PH* by Iannis Xenakis—was for a long time only available without the crucial color projections that accompanied it. The sole documentation was in the form of three different versions of the book on the *Poème électronique* made by Jean Petit for Philips, and some technical articles in *Philips Technisch Tijdschrift*. Magazines and newspapers that featured the Expo in Brussels in 1958 hardly showed the building, or, if they did, only the exterior since technical difficulties delayed the opening for weeks after the official ceremony.

After the Expo, the pavilion was destroyed. Thus, Le Corbusier's building became better known for its revolutionary shape, defined by an intriguing play with hyperbolic parallel surfaces, and for its exceptional construction from prestressed concrete, a mere 2 in (5 cm) thick, than for what it was really intended to be: the first immersive electronic multimedia environment to rely largely on computers.

Even when the project was finally developed by Le Corbusier and Varèse, it did not function in the way intended. Visitors to the pavilion were startled and irritated; moreover, methat there was a failure of synchronisation between the different apparatuses, and on top of that, the Philips technicians made unauthorized changes to the program at the last minute.

The prospect of developing a spectacle of light and sound was the main reason Le Corbusier accepted the commission for the Philips Pavilion. He characterized the building itself—the construction of which he left to his collaborator, the engineer and composer Xenakis—as "entirely an interior job."[1] "For this I require a fee, and not for a building that ought to cost very little money and that ought to be more of a hollow structure, made of poured concrete, utterly lacking in 'architectonic' radiance, as they say."[2]

In his first sketches for the pavilion, Le Corbusier was thinking primarily of something organic; the ground plan drawings resemble a cow's stomach. But Le Corbusier also had a more mechanical reference in mind, based on his admiration for the organization of slaughterhouses and factories: "It should appear as though you are about to enter a slaughterhouse. Then once inside, bang, a blow to the head and you're gone."[3] It was this blow to the head that interested Le Corbusier; even by today's standards, the *Poème électronique* is a raw and violent piece.

The visual component consisted of three elements: image projections; a program for light and color projections; and two plastic figures—a female nude and a geometric body, symbols of matter and spirit. The entire *Poème* lasted for 8 minutes (480 seconds) and consisted of seven image sequences. Each sequence had its own projections of colored light, an ambience that served to intensify or counterpoint the effect of the pictures and bring structure to the stream of images: "Ambiences that surround the

1. Transcription of a conversation between L. C. Kalff, general art director for Philips, and Le Corbusier, February 25, 1956.

2. Letter from Le Corbusier to Kalff, September 1956.

3. Bibeb, "Interview with Gerrit Rietveld," Vrij Nederland, April 19, 1958.

Philips Pavilion for the 1958 Universal Exhibition in Brussels.
Eindhoven Druk BV. Author's personal archives

500 viewers, penetrating them with psychophysiological sensations: the red, the black, the yellow, the green, the blue, the white. The possibility of evoking feelings, sunrise, raging fire, storm, indescribable illumination."[4]

‹ MOVING MURAL ›

Even though commentators such as the professor of architecture Marc Treib see the piece as belonging largely to a cinematographic tradition,[5] Le Corbusier conceived the *Poème* not so much as a film but as a giant, moving wall painting. In fact, he worked on it in much the same way as he worked on the *fresque photographique* that he introduced into the Pavillon Suisse in Paris in 1932. Le Corbusier had long been reluctant to employ murals in his work and only accepted them on walls that were not architecturally satisfying. There, murals could produce an explosive effect, opening onto another space. This was exactly what he wanted to achieve in the Philips Pavilion. The images of *Poème électronique* hardly took the form and structure of the pavilion into account. In the photographs we see them overlapping beams and clusters of loudspeakers. Indeed, the real "interior job" was the *Poème électronique*.

In Varèse's music, silence was to prevail for a moment precisely at the middle of the *Poème*, while the space filled with a hard white light. Although today the film is usually shown with the music, it is incomplete without the colored ambiences, which were only reconstructed in a digital version in 1998 by Willem Hering and Hank Onrust, based on the watercolors in Le Corbusier's original *minutage*. The image sequences consisted primarily of black and white photos with a strong signlike character, following one another in rapid succession and alternating with short strips of black and white film. Together, the images told the story of humanity, using art from all parts of the world, depictions of technological accomplishments, and war scenes (nuclear explosions in the fifth sequence), culminating in a series of images showing people in poverty, numerous babies, and examples from the architecture of Le Corbusier as an opening to the future. The relationship between image and color projections presages Le Corbusier's last paintings, in which drawing, the basis of the work, functions along with color as an independent system of forms obeying its own laws and interacting with the lines.

The independent handling of the figurative and non-figurative aspects of painting goes back to one of the fathers of experimental aesthetics, the French politician and professor Victor Basch (1863–1944). According to Basch, the aesthetic experience should be separated into its elementary parts: color, form, rhythm, and tone, each to be analyzed individually. Naturally, he was also persuaded of the reverse: that works of art could be created through the use of "scientific" knowledge. The theories of Basch exerted a great influence on Le Corbusier and his brother-in-arms in the early days, Amédée Ozenfant. Under the title "Discipline of the Arts and Sight," the latter wrote: "We do not know exactly how it works (but what do we know exactly?). Yet it is evident that, independent of each comprehensible treatment or evaluation, forms and colors are intense enough to influence our primary feelings." Using a series of examples, he goes on to show how color produces reactions in humans and animals that are intense enough to influence behavior,

4. Jean Petit, *Le Poème électronique le Corbusier* (complete, unabridged, Brussels, 1958).

5. Marc Treib, *Space Calculated in Seconds, The Philips Pavilion, Le Corbusier, Edgard Varèse* (Princeton, NJ: Princeton University Press, 1996).

Exterior of the Phillips Pavilion.
Eindhoven Druk BV. Author's personal archives

Installations hall. Eindhoven Druk BV.
Author's personal archives © Philips Technical Review

in a bullfight, perhaps, or in some working situation. He writes that: "In the Lumière Factories in Lyon, the laboratories where photographic plates were produced were lit ruby red: the result was that the male workers were in a constant state of arousal and became importunate. As for the female workers, they began having more children, as many as possible. Horrible! A calming green replaced the red and suddenly their birth rate dropped to around average."'[6] Le Corbusier probably did not expect such spectacular results from his *Poème*. Nevertheless, the Philips Pavilion was intended as a concentrated conditioning machine, based to a not inconsiderable extent on the composition of just these sorts of "color baths." The color projections were equally important, or maybe even more important than the images, precisely because they have this immediate psychophysiological effect.

‹ INTEGRATIVE ARCHITECTURE ›

The music by Varèse—a mixture of electronic sounds, recorded noises, and shreds of music produced in a studio in Eindhoven specially equipped for the purpose—likewise bathed the public in sound. Over three hundred loudspeakers were mounted on the walls of the building. The spatial orchestration of the sound was probably the most revolutionary aspect of the building. Not only could any fragment of music be played from any corner, but the sound could also wander along so-called *routes du son*. Thus the call "Oh, God" emerged from above the entrance, and a fluttering sound—the technicians called them "birdies"—reverberated horizontally around, while at the end a whistling tone shot up to the roof of the pavilion. In addition to the loudspeakers and the ten 120-watt amplifiers, two tape players were also required to control the sound, one with three tracks and another with fifteen, as well as an impressive battery of relay boxes and telephone switchboards, a precursor of the computer.

All of this equipment was installed in duplicate, in case of malfunction. Overall, the apparatus gave the service room the look of the command center for the first Sputnik launch. The plan was for visitors to stream past this room into the open air after enjoying the spectacle, while the view through a window revealed that this magical event had only been possible thanks to Philips technology. What was not revealed was the fact that the central Interlok machine, intended to synchronize all of the apparatus, had not yet been installed, so that the witnessed version of the *Poème électronique* was actually a matter of pure chance. This did not make much difference, for Varèse was aiming for a sense of "dissociation" in order to extract from the material "a power . . . deriving from contrast, a dynamic confrontation of the poles of tension, the visible and the audible rhythms."[7] But, as he confessed to "Mon cher Corbu": "I was unable—in the middle of the *Poème*—to achieve tranquillity. It has become the loudest moment of the piece."[8]

Now, in the early twenty-first century, we can assess the full significance of the Philips Pavilion (and not just because archives and documents long thought lost have since become available). The *Poème électronique* appears to have given birth to an architecture

6. Amédée Ozenfent, *Foundations of Modern Art* (London, 1931; 1952).

7. Odile Vivier, *Varèse* (Paris: Editions du Sevil, 1973).

8. Ibid.

A violet ambience.
Eindhoven Druk BV. Author's personal archives © Philips

Tribal sculpture from Sequence 2, Matter and Spirit.
Eindhoven Druk BV. Author's personal archives © Philips

Mask from Sequence 2, Matter and Spirit.
Eindhoven Druk BV. Author's personal archives

whose central concern is the evocation of atmosphere. The new electronic media, whose effects are simultaneously optic, haptic, and acoustic, thereby constitute an enrichment and enlargement of classical tectonics. It is as if a new chapter were being added to Gottfried Semper's *Stoffwechselthese*: the thesis that in the course of history, under the influence of technological progress, certain materials are replaced by others, while at the same time referring back to their original appearance.

Xenakis grasped this even more clearly than Le Corbusier and Varèse. He had already made a name for himself as a composer while still working in Le Corbusier's office as an architect. However, he had initially worked on the Philips Pavilion solely in the latter capacity—the exterior may safely be considered his work—until finally he was given the opportunity to compose a piece for the pavilion. It was to be played during the breaks when one group was leaving the building and another entering. In *Concrète PH*—a play on words alluding to *musique concrète* and the building material concrete, as well as to Philips and the scale for measuring acidity—the sound of smoldering wood coals was broadcast throughout the pavilion. This crackling noise must have given the visitor the feeling that the extraordinarily elegantly constructed prestressed concrete shell—a mere 2 in (5 cm) thick—was beginning to collapse, thereby engaging all five of the visitor's senses.

After the Philips Pavilion, Le Corbusier considered how he could incorporate the *jeux électroniques* (as he dubbed his invented art form) into buildings. But it was Xenakis who independently continued the tradition of the *Poème électronique* in his "Polytopes," spectacles of sound and light with architectural and even urban implications—or, conversely, architectural and urban projects with musical and visual implications—until later generations with new technological means could take over.

BART LOOTSMA, historian, critic, and curator in the fields of architecture, design, and visual art. He is professor of architectural theory at Leopold-Franzens University in Innsbruck and professor of architectural history, theory, and criticism at the Vienna Academy of Visual Arts. Lootsma is the author of *SuperDutch*, *ArchiLab 2004*, and *The Naked City*, and joint author, with Dich Rijken, of *Media and Architecture*.

GOOD WAVES

Michela Mezzavilla

‹ THREE ELEMENTS ›

In the last few years, I have had the good fortune to work as a lighting designer on major projects, both at home and abroad, collaborating with various professionals and friends. These projects have ranged from architectural lighting that involved both technical challenges and specific functional demands to ephemeral light installations that provided the opportunity to experiment with fantasy and the imagination; from projects with a huge budget to those where I had only a few sheets of paper and four fluorescent tubes to work with. The basic ingredients, however, are always the same: light, color, and sound, carefully allotted in suitable proportions to the different types of project. Natural light is free, but artificial light can still retain something of this democratic character. There is often no need to spend a fortune on equipment, as the true value lies in the appropriate placement of light sources, in the play of light and shadow, in the highlighting of color and texture.

Although each of these elements has its own rules and applications, in reality it is their mutual interaction that delights our senses and gives rise to a new perceptual dimension.

And yet, to be precise, since color is in itself already the result of the interaction of light in contact with a particular material, in objective terms, color does not exist! The real, original "raw materials" are light and sound. Both are distinctive, intangible elements that transcend materiality but interact in a very complex way with the material itself.

Both these physical phenomena can be explained as the result of waves that can be superimposed and can also interfere with each other; that can cover very large areas; and that pass simultaneously through different places. Light and sound possess truly exceptional physical properties, but—from the perceptual point of view—they are above all sensations, a sensory personal experience that is unique to every individual. Maybe this is why I like to imagine these waves as magical materials that are untamed despite the physical laws that govern them, and that always have something unpredictable about them.

‹ PRACTICE ›

In my architectural projects, light is generally "white, white, or white," in the words of a famous slogan. In effect, the application of colored lighting in this type of project is a very delicate matter, but not all whites are the same, as some are warmer and others colder. Using "white" light does not mean a rejection of playing with color—on the contrary, it means that the playing can become much more subtle. In the Bodegas Protos by Rogers Stirk Harbour + Partners, which is set in the Spanish town of Peñafiel, I configured light with different shades of warm white. The variations are minimal, lying between 4,400 and 5,300 degrees Fahrenheit (2,700 and 3,200 degrees Kelvin), but each shade was chosen to highlight a specific material, be it the wood on the ceiling, the exposed concrete of the structure, or the glossy stainless steel of the vats. This resulted in an overall scheme of controlled, calibrated architectural light; but at times one encounters surprises, such as a slither of water that gleams with light in the main patio, as if trying to match the nuances of the sky and the view of Peñafiel Castle. The building's lighting was organized around a number of settings, on the basis of the functions that each one had to fulfill and on the production cycle for wine. The light is generally warm and diffuse, but it explodes during the grape harvest, which is the high point of the production process. We could say that the light in Bodegas Protos is in tune with the sound of Peñafiel: the soothing silence of the open spaces of the countryside, the whistling of the wind, the calm of faraway views and abandoned villages. This leisurely rhythm is disrupted by an unrelenting frenzy just once a year, at the time of the harvest.

In other projects in which I have participated, sound was already a part by definition. When one enters the auditorium of the Palau de la Música Catalana in Barcelona, even when nobody is singing or playing, there is such a symphony of forms and colors that it is almost possible to hear it. The sculptures seem to be on the point of flying out of the walls and one's eyes dance from one color to another. In this triumph of the sensations, amidst all this exuberance, the most logical reaction would be to go, once again, for light that was "white, white, or white" and to concentrate on getting the tones, focus, and intensity right. In a rush of blood to the head, however, it occurred to us to illuminate the organ with colored light. In fact, the entire space was vibrating with a thousand touches of color, light, and shade; but, paradoxically,

Water and City Pavilion, Zaragoza Expo, 2008, for Studio Italo Rota and Nussli, with Pablo Martínez

Bodegas Protos, 2004–2008, for Rogers Stirk Harbour + Partners, Biosca & Botey

only the organ, shrouded in gloom, and gray, remained aloof from this visual music. So, we tried out this dubious effect and, to our surprise, a slight hint of blue unquestionably gave the organ new life and a brighter sheen, allowing it to harmonize better with its surroundings. In the Stettin Philarmonic Hall, however, nothing has been touched yet, it is a work-in-progress, but just a glimpse of the evocative images by EBV allows one to imagine its music. Seen from the outside, the building is a glass structure, resembling white ice, that emits cold light and sounds like Beethoven's Fifth Symphony. But in the interior hides a warm heart, a concert hall with lighting inspired by the great Austrian and Italian theaters, ideally suited to an opera by Puccini.

In all of these architectural lighting projects, sound and color have been underlying inspirational elements for me; in ephemeral installations, by contrast, I have been able to turn them into the indisputable stars. In creating lighting scenarios, however, I often find inspiration in music, which either accompanies the light or provides me with a script for its programming. The Water and City Pavilion at the Zaragoza Expo was a real challenge of low-tech. In the midst of a display of RGB LEDs and multimedia screens, we decided to play with a few simple, watertight projecters—albeit personalized by dichroic filters—that were arranged and focused to produce a motley array of colors on leaves of Lexan hanging from the roof. The idea was to reproduce the randomness of a nebula of light and color, a wispy, volatile effect that in our initial enthusiasm we combined with a musical selection in the style of Led Zeppelin, although we later opted for a more sedate, Satie-like rhythm.

In the work with the Grupo MCI (MCI Group), we did not play with color but with black and white. The underlying concept was the duality of positive-negative, on-off, repetition, and a rhythmic beat. We drew up a matrix of white LEDs against a black background, a screen with a very low resolution where lights would come on and reiterate the rhythm of a pure break beat. In *Tunnel of the Senses*, the idea was to work with the thresholds of perception. When the limits of space, light, and sound tend to disappear, the spectator's senses are heightened to the maximum, so we dreamed up a very low level of light accompanied by almost imperceptible sound. *The Vicereine's Dream* was an ephemeral installation for the Palau de la Virreina in Barcelona. Drawing inspiration from the story of the Viceroy and Vicereine, I imagined them searching in vain for the palace, which was engulfed by an imaginary forest.

Visitors enter a space with subtle lighting in shades of green, a building vibrating under the effects of light and sound. Further inside

Tunnel of the Senses, 2005, with Roberto Elueteri

The Vicereine's Dream, Barcelona, 2008, for Arquiset and Anoche

they come across presences, lurking shadows; they hear the patter of footsteps on the staircase and arrive in the main patio, which is being invaded by the forest, bearing with it the secrets of the two protagonists. In this patio, the soundtrack is the pure voice of nature itself, recorded in situ in the Amazon rain forest by the musician Carlos Barroeta.

Light, color, and sound are the means by which the building is transfigured and reveals its secrets. The most gratifying part for me was undoubtedly seeing how much people enjoyed entering this dimension that I had dreamed up and capturing those "waves," each in the deepest intimacy of his or her own perception.

I think that the magic of light and sound is enhanced when they are used together, as our perceptual dimension expands and our senses are amplified.

In these cases, we process information not only through sight or hearing but also through their mutual interaction. This can trigger metaphorical sensations and poetry, where, in the words of Valère Novarina, "something unexpected awaits us . . . through listening to the darkness, seeing through the ears, discovering once again the questions of children."

MICHELA MEZZAVILLA, architect and lighting designer, professor of IED in Barcelona and conference participant at various European universities, has collaborated on *Light Art*, projects of architectonic lighting, and light installations for Rogers Stirk Harbour + Partners, Jean Nouvel, Estudio Lamela, b720 Fermín Vázquez, and Patrick Genaro & Associates. She has written for *Lumínica, Constructiva, and De Architect.*

THE SOUND OF SPACE

Christopher Janney

‹ DISSOLVING THE PROBLEM ›

If I had learned to draw better, I would never have gotten into sound.

In the creative process, you cannot both observe and participate in an event. Your attempt to observe while participating will taint your perception; likewise, if you try to participate while being an observer, you lose objectivity. As a result, you have to decide to either watch or play, knowing that you cannot have full knowledge of both. Another way to look at this phenomenon is that you are either in the bubble or outside; prior to the event, you commit yourself to standing outside and observing, commenting, making a critique. You must remain in this realm to really observe what is going on. If you choose to enter the bubble, your conscious critique of the event distorts the groove.

In my world of improvisation, this means that after great preparation (Louis Pasteur said that "Chance prefers the prepared mind"), you have to let go of the conscious brain, surrender to the moment, step into the bubble, participate and be in the *now*.

For me, this duality also occurs in the brain, between the left and right sides. There are two very different thought processes going on, two different ways of perceiving: the cognitive and the intuitive. To shut out one requires a certain amount of self-discipline and practice. If you let the two mix, then you often get mush, confusion.

Perhaps this is my Piscean dilemma—the two fishes forever caught in a quandary of circular confusion. If I do A, I cannot do B, or vice versa. But I have also found that, in the end, the solution lies neither in A nor B, but in the invention of C, which, in turn, dissolves the A–B problem. This often requires turning away from the stated problem and looking elsewhere, in logically illogical places: combining physics with economics, or biology with structural engineering, or, in my case, architecture with jazz.

This may also be the solution to Heisenberg's dilemma. The answer is not in knowing the position and the speed simultaneously, but in approaching the problem from an entirely different perspective. Perhaps it is on one of the seven planes of consciousness discussed in ancient Indian philosophy. Or perhaps it is on one of the ten planes that string theory proposes. (Or the realization that these two conceptual models, the one in science and the other in philosophy, are, in fact, referring to the same thing.)

Bikers © PhenomenArts Inc.

Pisces © PhenomenArts Inc.

Psychologists tell us that our conscious mind makes up less than ten percent of our total brain. Intuition is the connection to the unconscious mind. To access more of the brain, you can't look it "straight in the eye"; you have to sneak around it, to "dance with the unconscious." It's definitely a partnering on all levels—physical, social, intellectual. The trick is to learn to dance ever closer to the fire without falling headfirst into the flames.

Lastly, I love reading artists' biographies. I love learning about what influenced a certain artwork or idea, because it is often not what popular opinion holds. For example, Marcel Duchamp's interest in the newly developed X-ray photography and in public carnivals influenced the layout of his seminal work, *The Large Glass*. Bob Dylan's "Like a Rolling Stone," considered one of the greatest songs in contemporary music, was first written as a lazy-tempo waltz. It is interesting to me to see how real life intercedes to alter artistic ideas.

All of which brings me to my work: having been trained as an architect and a jazz musician, I have tried to fuse these two seemingly unrelated disciplines. At times, I find I am attempting to make architecture more spontaneous, more "alive" in the moment. Other projects reverse the paradigm—trying to make music more visual, more physical.

‹ SOUND IS INVISIBLE COLOR ›

Designers solve problems. Artists ask questions.

While living in New York, I continued to read more books on art, go to galleries, museums, and performances, and soak up the art and architecture scene. This caused me to think more about the stability of the architectural profession versus the "what life" of an artist. For artists, I thought, there just wasn't any there there. However, slowly, art became a physical entity to me, particularly as I read more about Marcel Duchamp. One night, it struck me that art can be as present as a building; it just has an ever-changing, ever-transforming physical form. Sometimes it could be manifested in paint, sometimes in concrete; but when it is good, when you are looking at/listening to/touching/smelling/tasting it, it is a very tangible thing.

For me, it was Duchamp who continuously stripped away the utility and laid bare the essence. I read that Duchamp once said, "A title is like an invisible color." With his works *L.H.O.O.Q.* and *Fresh Widow* especially, I could see how the title framed or extended the idea, and

Turn up heat. © PhenomenArts Inc.

Sun clocks. © PhenomenArts.

how Duchamp was always pushing for synesthetic events—events where more than one sense was at work, be it the eyes and the intellect or, as in *With Hidden Noise*, eyes, sound, and concept. So, it wasn't too much of a leap when I realized that sound within a visual environment could also be this "invisible color," adding another new layer to the visual or architectural information. From there, it becomes an interplay of media, pushing the viewer/participant to the level of their choice.

‹ FROM THE OBVIOUS TO THE ABSURD ›

If you go where it's at, by the time you get there, it'll be gone. So go where it's not and keep your eyes and ears open.

When critiquing my own work, I like to see where it sits on this line. If it's too *obvious*, it's flat, boring. On the other hand, if it's so *absurd* that one can't understand it or any relationships within it, then, for me, it's in the ether. In discussions with my students, I asked for examples of each.

Where is a good spot on the line? Right of center for me.

It's more absurd than obvious, but it's not so absurd that you can't get a handle on it. There are "hooks" into it, whether it's the reality of stairs, or waiting on a subway platform, or looking out through transparent tinted glass at the real world.

But it has enough absurdity in it that it leaves questions, ignites curiosity, sparks imagination—a "musical stair" on your way to work? Waving your hand (and not saying hi to anyone in particular) in an impersonal environment like a subway; walking through waves of colored light and approaching the childhood dream of being "inside a rainbow."

Then there is the example when the obvious and the absurd are very close together, as in the case of some Minimalist art:
Robert Wilson's *Deafman Glance,* 1970
Carl Andre's *Equivalent VIII*, 1966
Steve Reich's *Four Organs,* 1970
Donald Judd's *Untitled,* 1969

This, to me, is what makes good Minimalist art so powerful. The good stuff is both boring and absurd but not absolutely one or the other. The counterpoint sparks a sense of imbalance, questioning, unresolved issues, curiosity, sometimes (mis) leading to thought—overload, "the less there is, the more there is to talk about."

Soundstair. © PhenomenArts Inc.

Sonic dream. PhenomenArts Inc.

‹ FOUR PEOPLE IN EVERY CONVERSATION ›

I tell students that it is easy to be complicated; the hardest task for an artist, or anyone, is to be clear and simple.

1. There is "the person" in your head.
It is very clear in your mind what you want to express.
It's such a good idea, too, and all the world needs to know it.

2. There is you, the person we see, "the person" who is speaking.
True, the words are coming out of your mouth,
but are they expressing exactly what is on your mind?

3. There is the other "person" in the room hearing words from your mouth.
Does he hear all the words, or is he listening for a moment
to the birds outside and missing a key word?

4. Then there is "the person" inside his head:
processing the words he is hearing and mixing them with
his own ideas, values, thoughts.

CHRISTOPHER JANNEY, an American architect and jazz musician, is currently giving the seminar "Sound as a Visual Medium" at the Pratt Institute architecture school, and since 1980 he has run his own multimedia projects studio, PhenomenArts. He has created various interactive installations with light and sound that seek to bring back greater spontaneity to architecture (Harmonic Runway and REACH:NY) and to make music more tangible (HeartBeat:mb with Sara Rudner and Mikhail Baryshnikov).

light

34
Star Place | Kao-hsiung, Taiwan
UNStudio

46
Le Prisme | Aurillac, France
Brisac González Architects

58
Dexia Tower | Brussels, Belgium
LAb[au]

68
Nelson-Atkins Museum | Kansas City, MO
Steven Holl Architects

80
Tire Shop | Zurich, Switzerland
Camenzind Evolution

90
Watercube | Beijing, China
PTW Architects

100
Spots | Berlin, Germany
realities:united

110
Kubik | Barcelona, Spain
Modulorbeat

118
Urban oasis | Various European cities
Chetwoods Associates

126
Center for contemporary artistic creation | Córdoba, Spain
Nieto Sobejano Arquitectos and realities:united

134
New 42nd Street Studios | New York, NY
Platt Byard Dovell White Architects and Vortex Lighting

144
GreenPix | Beijing, China
Simone Giostra & Partners Architects

156
Club Nox | Recife, Brazil
Metro Arquitetura and Juliano Dubeux

168
Luxembourg Philarmonic | Luxembourg, Luxembourg
Christian de Portzamparc

PRADA
PRADA
PRADA

Star Place

UNStudio | Kao-Hsiung, Taiwan 2008

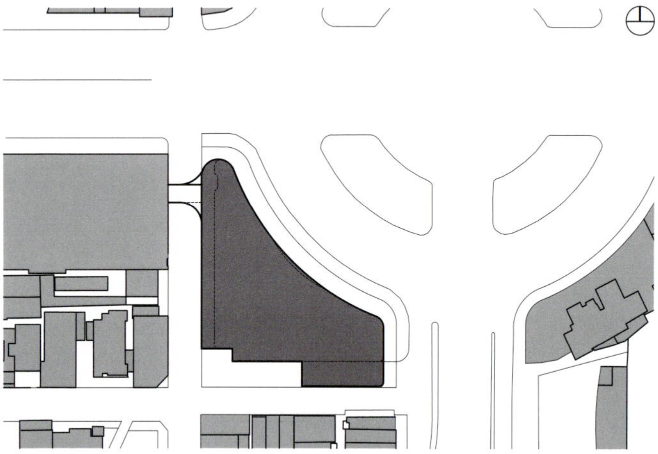

SITE PLAN

Kao-hsiung is Taiwan's second city in terms of both size and importance, as well as being the hub of its heavy industry. It is currently in the midst of a process of urban renewal and is seeking to emphasize its modernity in order to project the image of an attractive place in which to live. Starting from this premise, Kao-hsiung sought a large shopping area that would put its citizens center stage. The architectural firm chosen to take on this enormous task was UNStudio, founded by Ben van Berkel and Caroline Bos in 1999 to specialize in urban development and infrastructural projects.

Star Place is set on a triangular lot in front of a major road junction. The project established a clear relationship between the interior and exterior, both formally and functionally: the design of the exterior cladding sought to give the main facade greater depth, while linking up with the interior by means of the arrangement of spaces around a patio—through which pedestrians (and potential customers) can pass. The patio in turn is visually connected to the exterior by means of glass walls. The facades themselves constitute a veritable urban manifesto; the longest is concave and thus opens up the whole building to the city.

TYPE OF PROJECT **Shopping mall**

LIGHTING **UNStudio and Arup Lighting**

TOTAL SURFACE AREA **394,000 sq. ft. (36,600 m²)**

LOUIS VUITTON
LOUIS VUITTON

The design scheme of the facade reflects the activities generated inside the building. This explains why the top floors, which contain the eating areas, have been allocated fewer vertical wings (and even these have less depth), to provide greater transparency and open up views of the landscape.

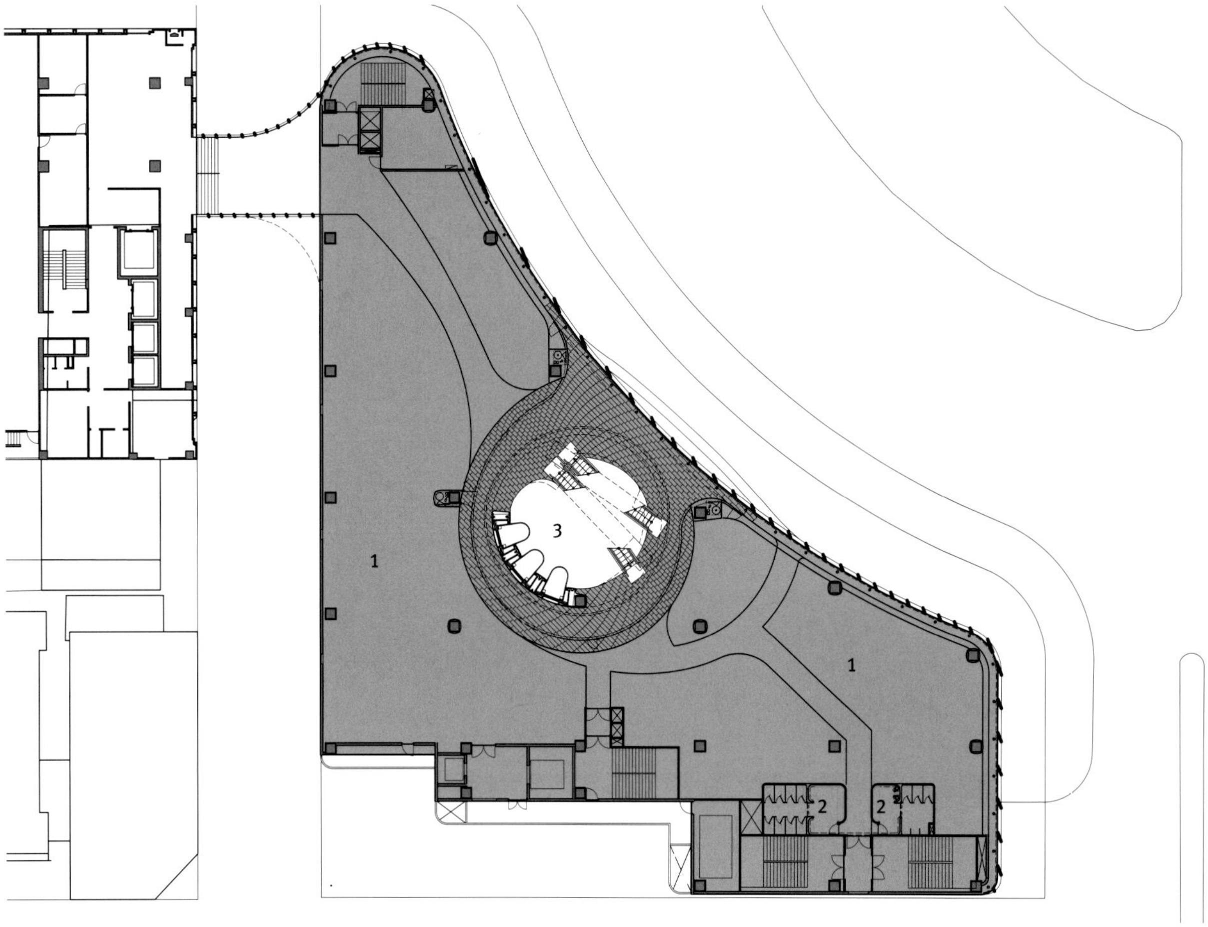

SECOND FLOOR

1. SHOPPING SPACE
2. SERVICES
3. CENTRAL SPACE

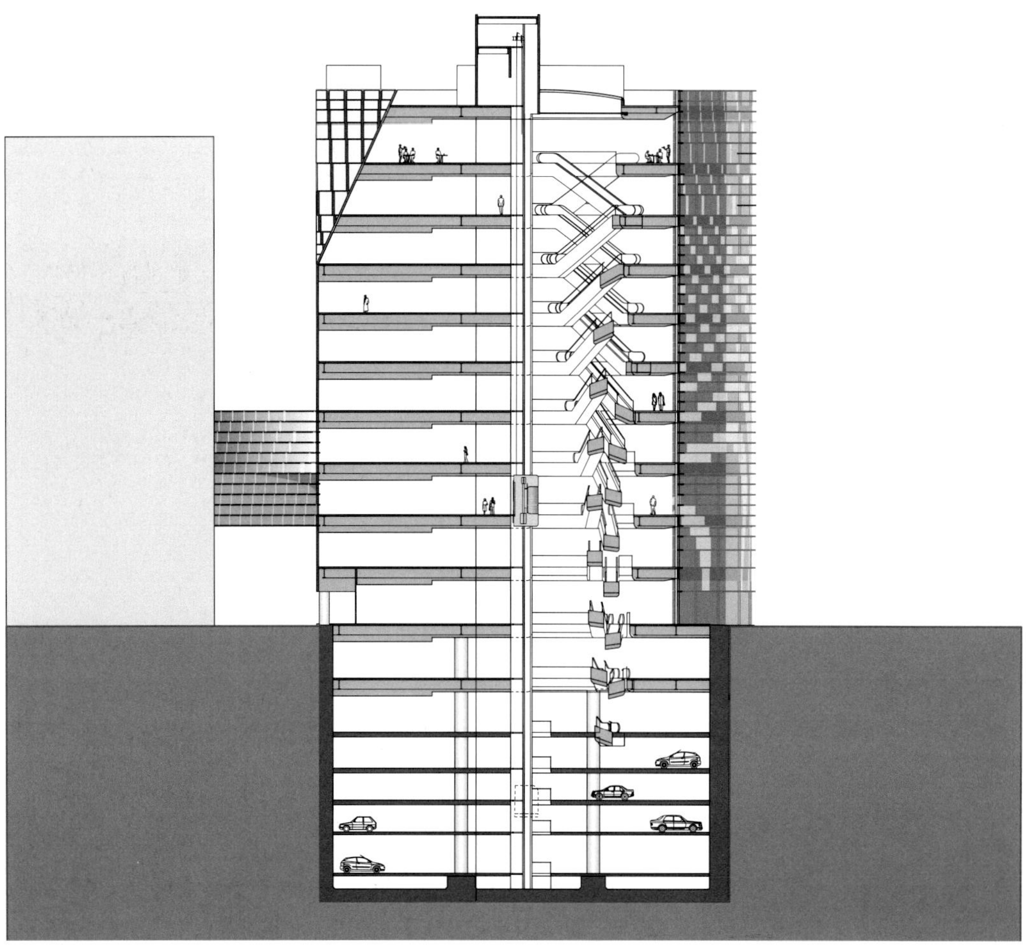

CROSS SECTION

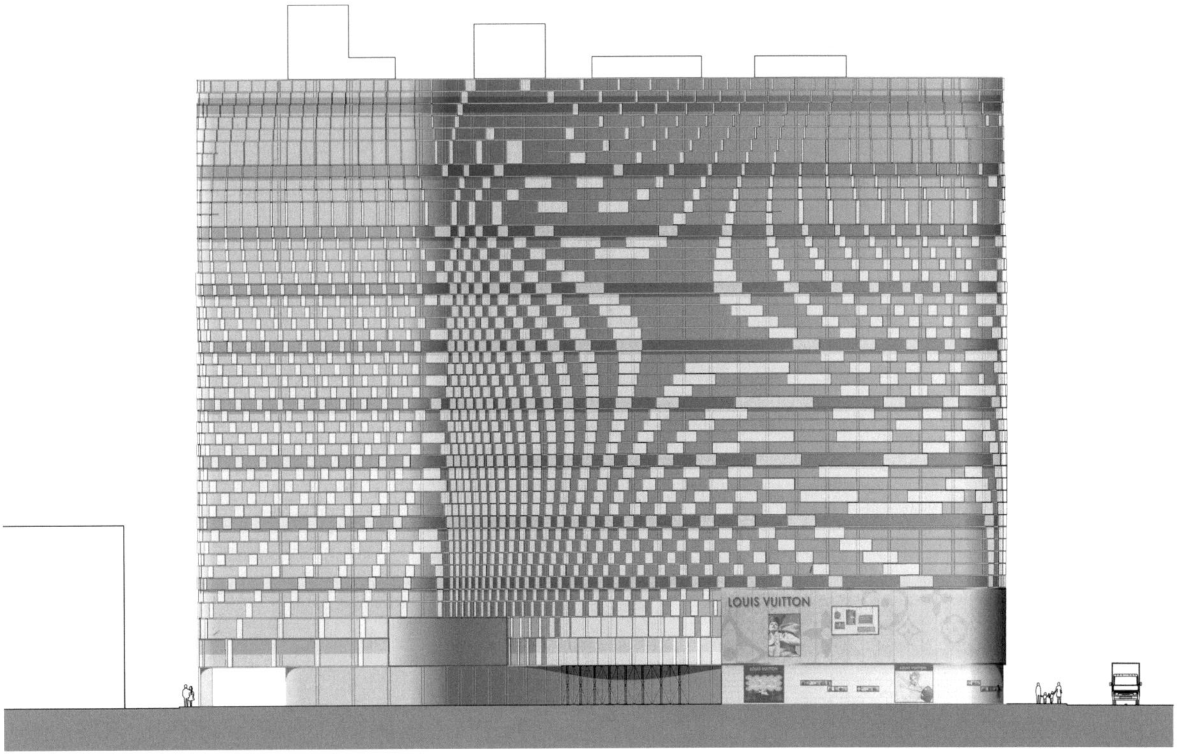

EAST ELEVATION

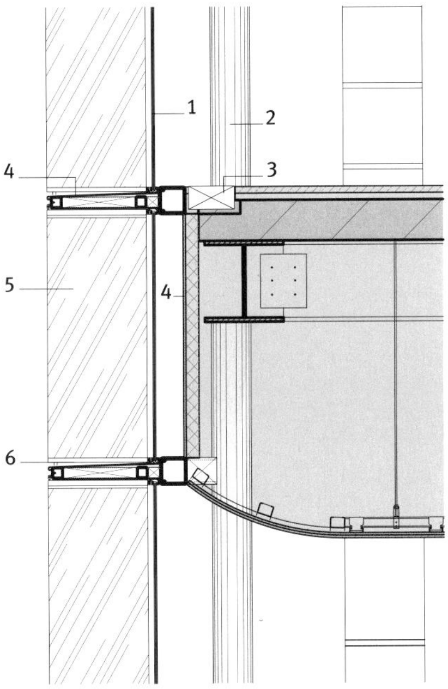

DETAIL OF THE SHOPPING SPACE

1. LOW-EMISSION TEMPERED GLASS
2. STEEL PILLAR Ø165
3. REFLECTOR
4. ALUMINUM PLATE COVERED WITH HIGH-RESISTANCE POWDER
5. WINGS OF TEMPERED GLASS
6. SHELL FOR LED

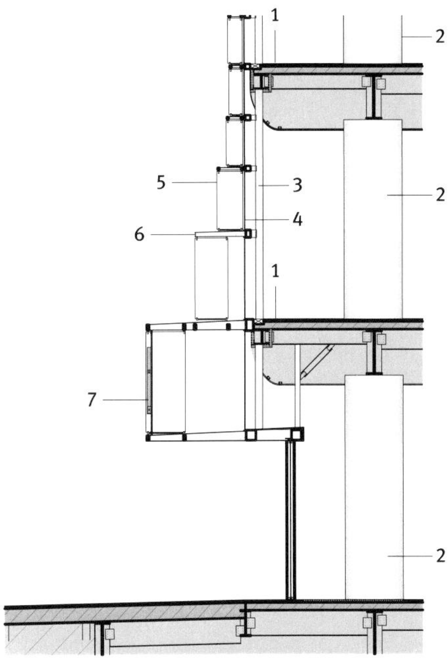

DETAIL OF THE MAIN ENTRANCE

1. STONE FLOOR
2. STAINLESS-STEEL FINISH
3. STEEL PILLAR Ø165
4. LOW-EMISSION TEMPERED GLASS
5. WINGS OF TEMPERED GLASS
6. ALUMINUM PLATE COVERED WITH HIGH-RESISTANCE POWDER
7. SIGN FOR THE STORE

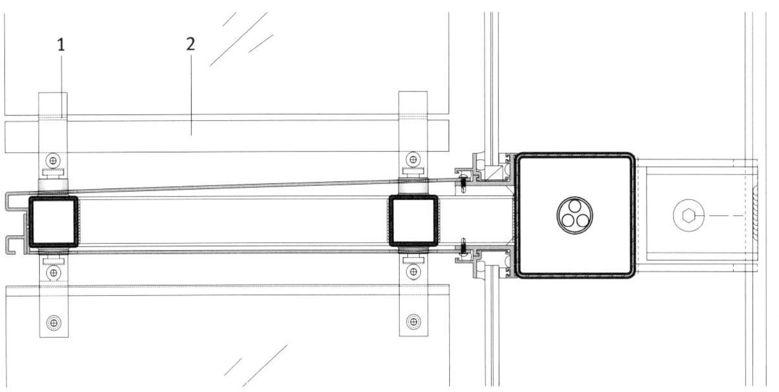

DETAIL OF THE HORIZONTAL STRIPS

1. STAINLESS-STEEL GLASS HOLDER
2. SHELL FOR LED

Before UNStudio became involved in the project, earlier plans were drawn up by Dynasty Design Corp and HCF Architects, and their basic scheme and structure were retained. The architects at UNStudio were intent on organizing large spaces with no columns, on the basis of the earlier project, and they left a huge central hollow running up all the building's twelve floors to create an uninterrupted visual and spatial flow. This central hollow, set on the edge of the main space, is a circular opening that appears to spiral up toward the roof. The optical effect is created by moving the position of the escalators by 10 degrees on each floor, resulting in a total rotation of 110 degrees from the ground floor to the ceiling.

The facade is made up of horizontal aluminum strips and vertical glass wings. The strips are set 3 feet (1 m) apart, so the ceilings of the stories cannot be distinguished from the outside. The wings are made of tempered glass with a low iron content to provide optimum clarity. A computer animation program was used to assemble these elements, and after an assessment by feng shui experts, a final design in the form of a red phoenix was chosen. The wings look white during the day as a result of the dots printed on both faces; at night, digitally controlled LED lamps set at the base of each wing produce changing effects of colors and forms visible from a distance.

LOUIS VUITTON
LOUIS VUITTON

LOUIS VUITTON

The central space is the main feature inside the building, and it works as a vertical display window. Around it, the circulation is bounded by glass walls that provide access to the stores. This circulatory space emphasizes the relationship between interior and exterior; similarly, the tiles in the interior reflect the radial pattern of the facade.

Le Prisme

BRISAC GONZÁLEZ | AURILLAC, FRANCE 2007

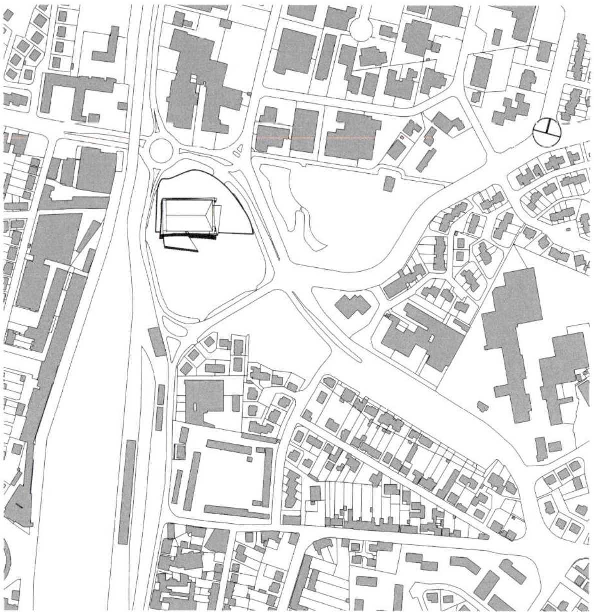

SITE PLAN

Aurillac is a town located in southwest Auvergne in the French Massif Central. *Le Prisme* is set in a square close to the main train station—an area in the process of renovation that will provide a link with the city's historic center. The building has spaces both inside and outside designed to host congresses, conventions, fairs, and a wide range of shows and concerts, as well as sports events. The stage in the main hall, which accommodates 4,500 people, can be dismantled and the seating removed, so a space that is normally fixed can be used flexibly.

The project, designed by Brisac González, won an architectural award. The building is meant to be seen from a distance as a solid entity with simple details. In order to take advantage of fine weather, the architect came up with a three-dimensional structure that reflects the rays of the sun. The pyramidal bricks in the curved facades create shadows that make the building stand out during the day.

The top part of this colorful facade is built with bricks specially manufactured in Portugal for the project. The wavy surface on the inner face of each brick creates a Fresnel-style lens that intensifies the light—whether natural or artificial—that falls on it.

TYPE OF PROJECT Multipurpose space for sports events, fairs, and shows

LIGHTING Brisac González

TOTAL SURFACE AREA 57,000 sq. ft. (5,265 m²)

PHOTOS © Hélène Binet

The effect created by the pyramidal bricks on the facade of the top floor changes from day to night. By day, sunlight is reflected by the lens in each piece; by night, different designs are projected by the lamps set inside the facades to correspond with activities taking place in the interior.

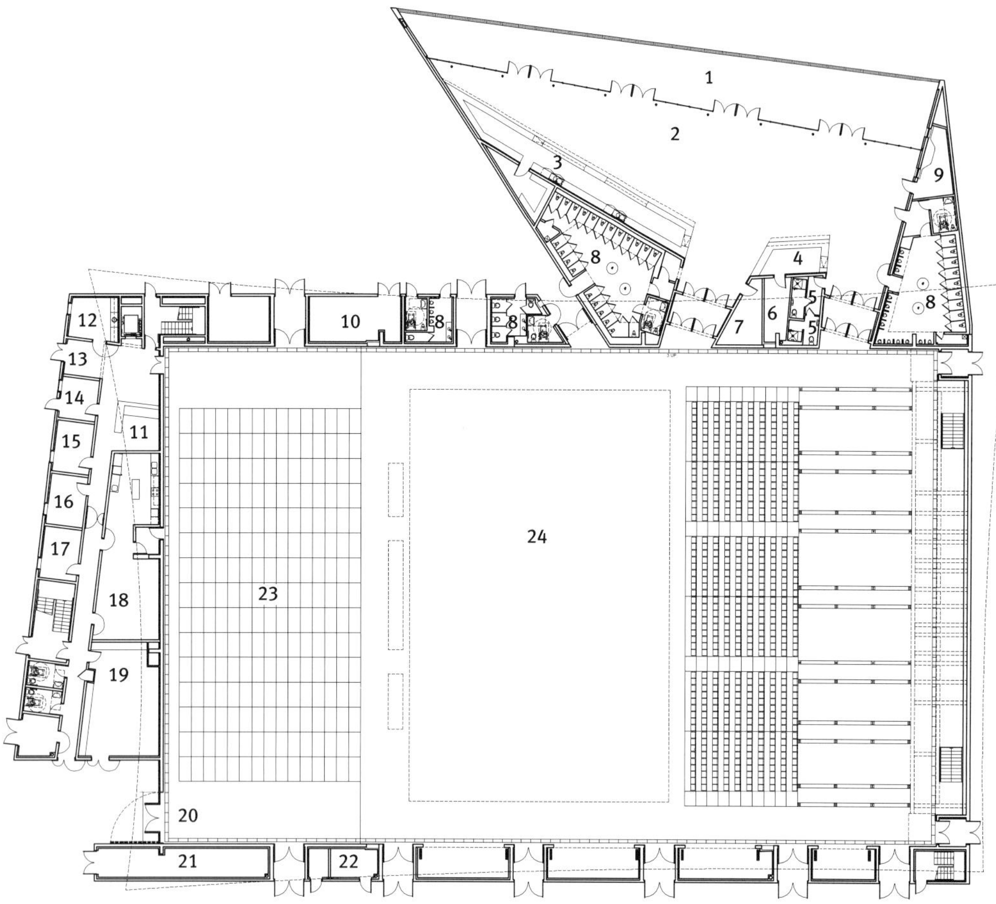

1. PUBLIC ENTRANCE
2. FOYER
3. BAR
4. COUNTER
5. BUILDING STAFF RESTROOM
6. PRODUCTION
7. STORE
8. PUBLIC RESTROOM
9. CONTROL ROOM
10. COMMERCIAL SPACE
11. RECEPTION
12. FIRST AID ROOM
13. STAGE DOOR
14. FIRE SERVICE
15. SOUND AND LIGHTING TECHNICIAN
16. PRODUCER
17. HALL MANAGER
18. CATERING
19. MULTIPURPOSE HALL
20. ENTRANCE FOR TECHNICIANS AND DELIVERIES
21. WORKSHOP
22. INSTALLATIONS
23. STAGE
24. DEMOUNTABLE BLEACHERS

GROUND FLOOR

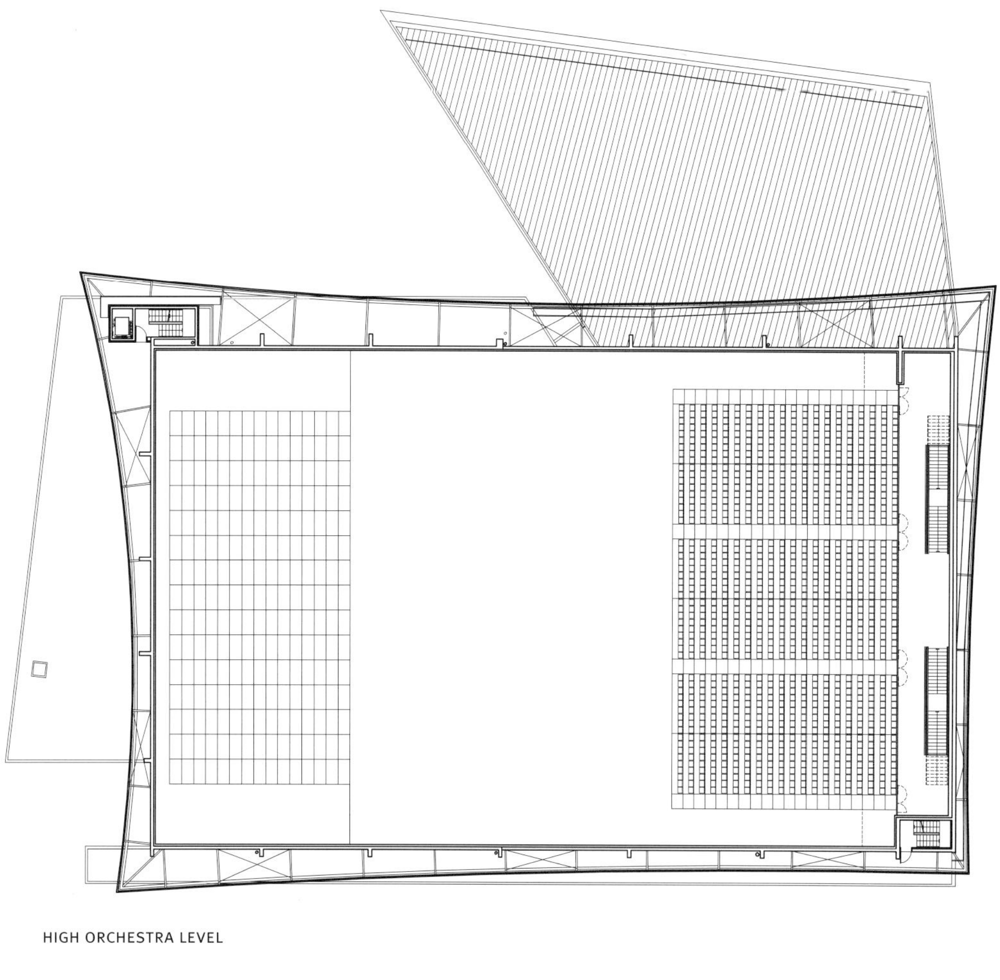

HIGH ORCHESTRA LEVEL

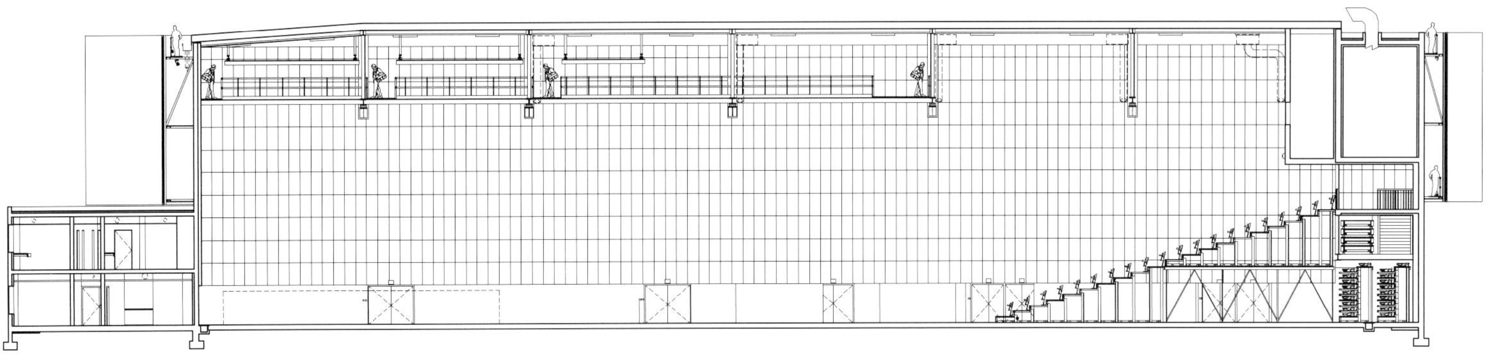

LONGITUDINAL SECTION

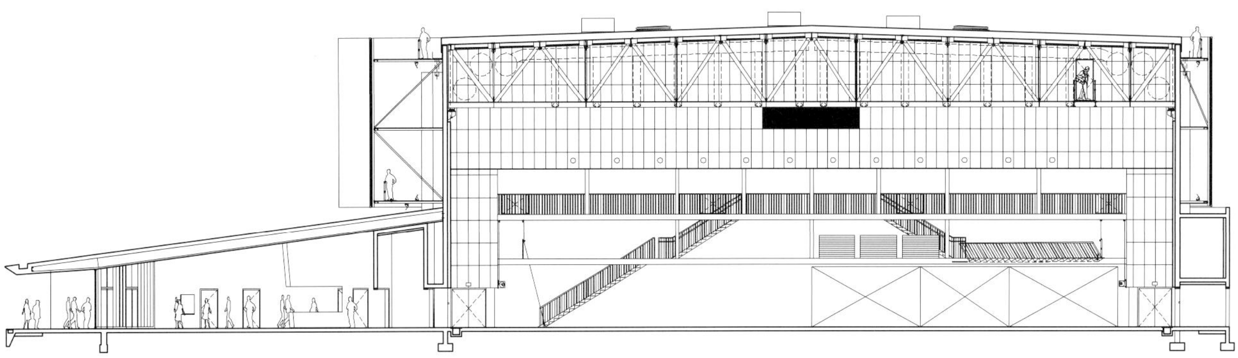

CROSS SECTION—FOYER

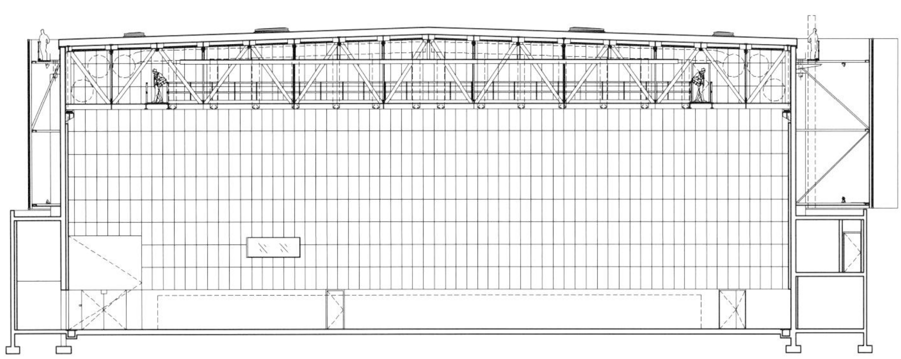

CROSS SECTION

The prefabricated panels that form the facade on the top floor measure 5 feet square (1.5 m). These panels are attached to the concrete structure, which was constructed in situ on a foundation slab. The concrete has been left exposed to view, with only a layer of black to insulate the sound. In all, 90 percent of the entire construction is of concrete.

DETAIL OF THE PANELS

1. POLYURETHANE
2. STAINLESS-STEEL HA6
3. GUTTER

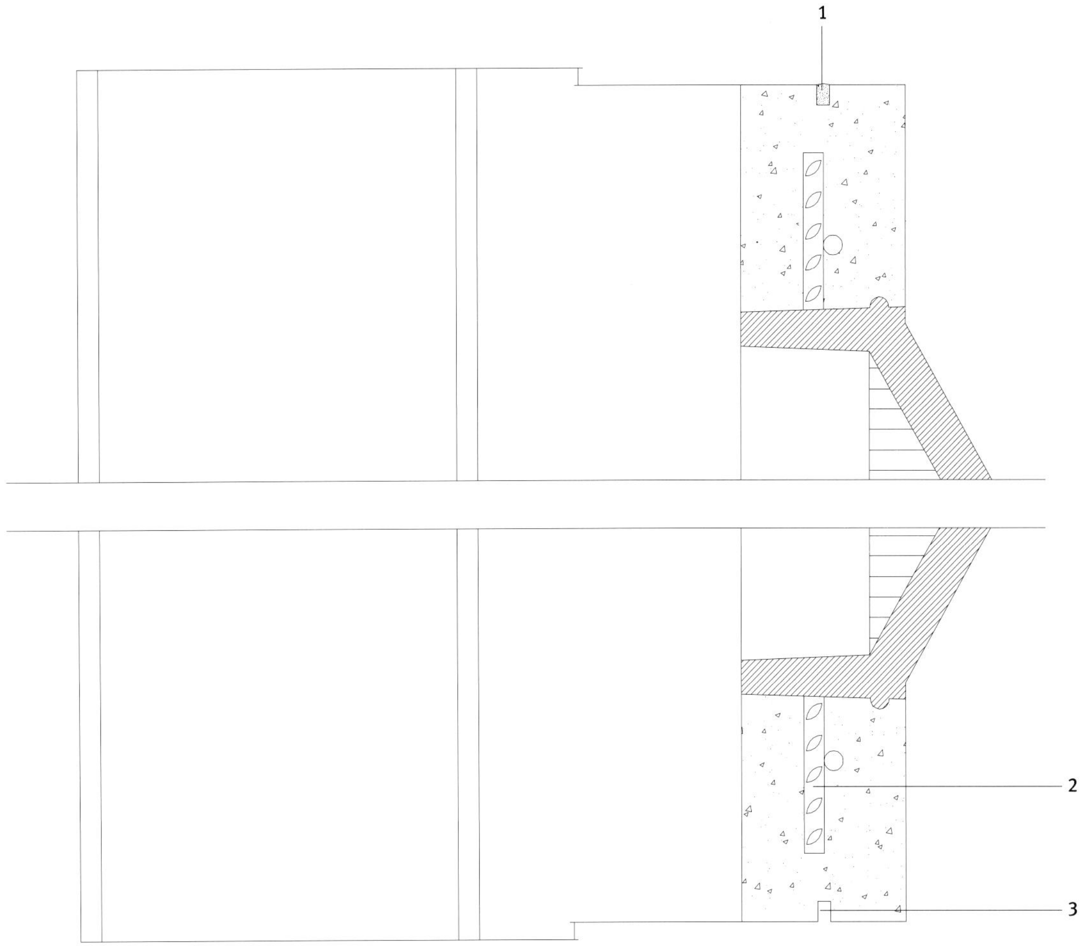

CONSTRUCTION DETAIL OF THE PANELS

1. STAINLESS-STEEL HA6
2. WASHER/STOPPER
3. SUPPORTING BRACE
4. CURVED STAINLESS-STEEL BAR
5. NEOPRENE WASHER

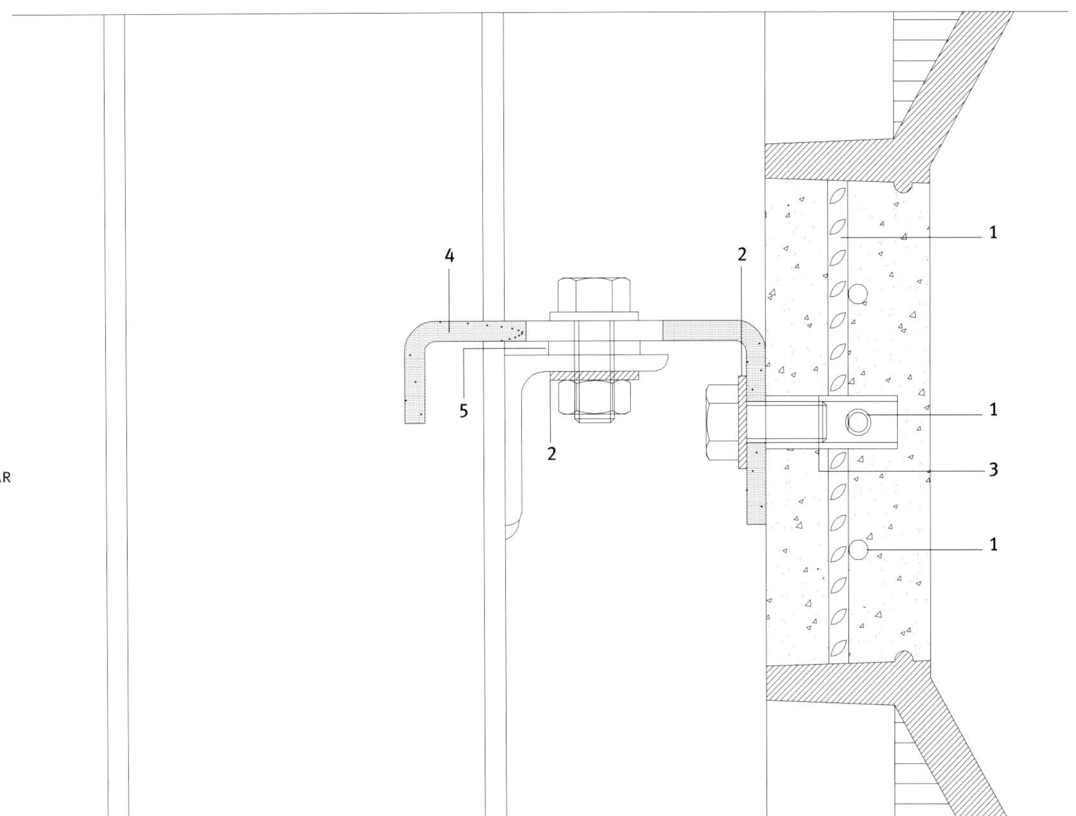

CONSTRUCTION DETAIL OF THE PANELS

The 25,000 pyramidal bricks are lit by artificial lamps set inside the building and on the top and bottom of the facade. The lighting can be modified by twenty-four different programs, with a range of one to eight colors. It is also possible to coordinate the program with shows taking place in the flexible space.

The building is made up of three horizontal strips of differing heights and textures that can be adjusted to various uses. The first strip (the ground floor), which contains the foyer, is 20 feet (6 m) high, and the waves on the facades mark the entrance into the building. The other two strips contain stores and installations for events. The position and articulation of the strips set up residual spaces arranged for machinery and technical services.

Inside, the geometry is uncluttered and a limited palette of colors contrasts with the exuberance of the exterior. The foyer, which is free of columns, is 131 feet (40 m) wide, 197 feet (60 m) long and 39 feet (12 m) high. These dimensions allow the small forklift trucks used to move equipment for events to maneuver freely. This space appears to be in one color, as the gray of the concrete floor is reflected in the white ceiling.

SORTIE

Dexia Tower

LAb[au] | Brussels, Belgium 2006 and 2007

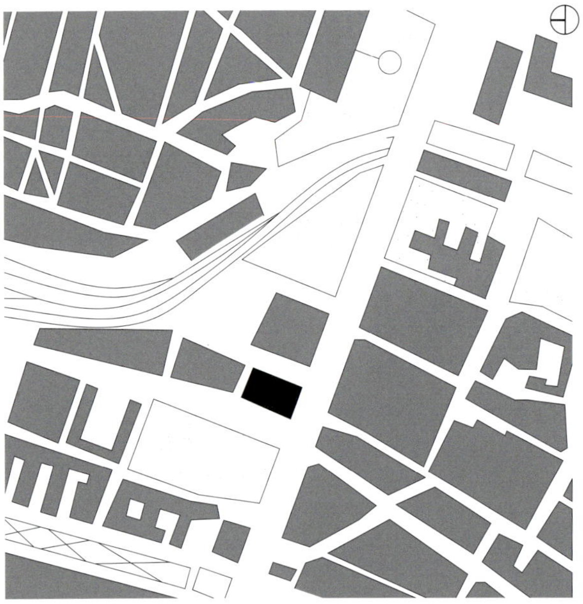

SITE PLAN

LAb[au] is a Belgian firm that works from a multidisciplinary perspective using methodologies derived from both art and science. It has focused on investigating technological progress and its fundamental role in the evolution of architecture, creating the computer applications needed to represent interactive graphic material and to design audiovisual installations. The work of LAb[au] involves first mapping out a lighting program in time and space before completing the basic design to support this lighting. The firm perceives lighting design as a means of communication—illumination as information.

The Dexia Tower, an office building in one of the busiest parts of Brussels, was designed and built in 2006 by Philippe Samyn and Partners, Architects & Engineers, in collaboration with M. & J. M. Jaspers-J. Eyers & Partners. Its facades are ventilated by means of double glazing, with a continuous, fixed outer layer and a mobile inner layer that can be opened to provide access to the space between the panes—a space fitted with rails with LED lamps in three different colors. Since 2006, LAb[au] has dreamed up three audiovisual installations embracing all 4,200 windows in the 475-foot (145 m)-high vertical expanse of the building. The most recent of these was *Who's Afraid of Red, Green and Blue?*, created in 2007, where the three colors were combined to reproduce other colors and turn the building's facade into a focus of light in the midst of the city.

TYPE OF PROJECT **Temporary installation**

LIGHTING **Barbara Hediger and LAb[au]**

HEIGHT OF FACADE **1,560 sq. ft. (145 m²)**

PHOTOS **© LAb[au]**

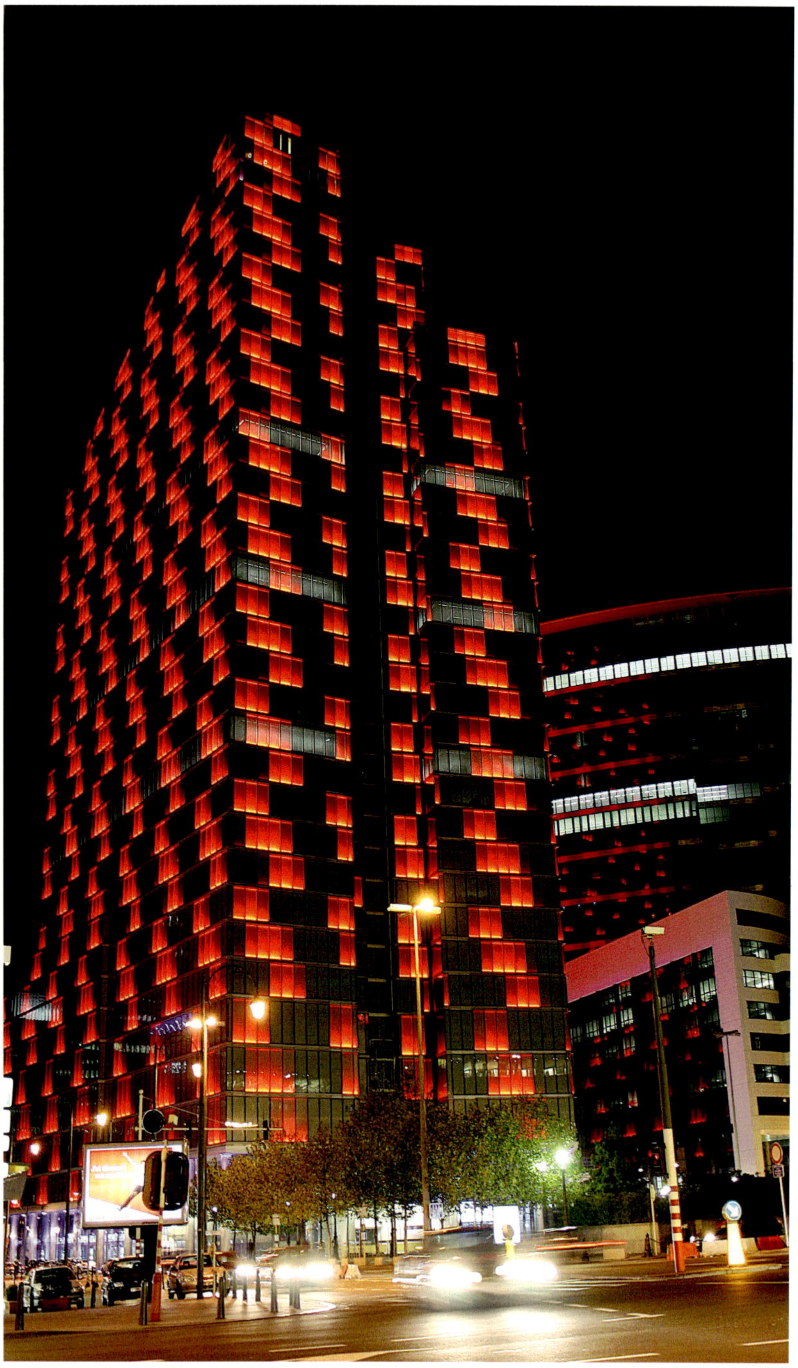

The projects presented as part of *Who's Afraid of Red, Green and Blue?* were based on a geometric language of dots, lines, and planes. The intensity of the light inverted the logic of daytime brightness and nighttime darkness by making midnight the time of greatest brightness, while the light level was more subdued in the morning.

This program involved a couple of graphic projects. The first represented time by means of a color code, with red symbolizing hours, green minutes, and blue seconds. The second displayed the weather forecast for Brussels, in collaboration with the Royal Meteorological Institute of Belgium, with colors and geometric patterns showing the temperature, cloud cover, rainfall, and wind patterns predicted for the following day. Earlier, LAb[au] curated an event called *Spectrlalum* one night in September 2007. This was a series of audiovisual and light pieces created by artists with an international reputation to mark the *Nuit Blanche* in Brussels. The idea was to relate the spectrum of light and sound to the tower's architectural form and its urban context.

The team's first installation for the Dexia Tower, in 2006, was an interactive art display called *Touch*, where a tactile screen allowed passersby to interact directly with the building. A unit mounted in the square in front of the tower recognized touch and gestures to generate a graphic language of dots, lines, and planes, resulting in a composition, visible on the building, that was then photographed and sent as a postcard from a Web site. The design of the interactive unit was based on the idea of a space that folded and unfolded, thus combining spatial elements with parameters of time, reflecting the sequencing and dynamism of the building's program.

TACTILE SCREEN

ONE FINGERPRINT = ONE DOT

COORDINATING SPACE WITH COLORS

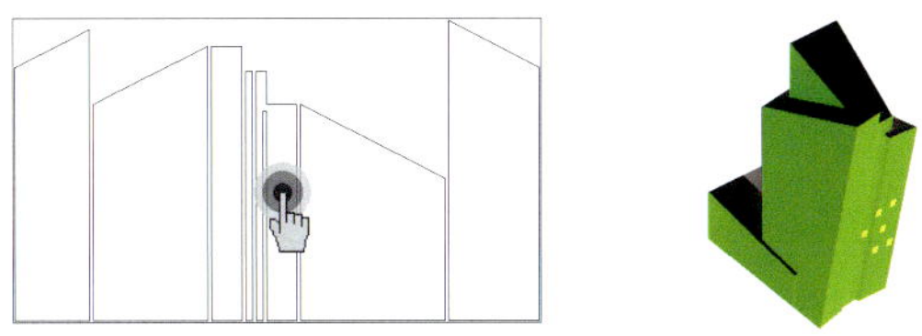

LONGER CONTACT = MORE DOTS

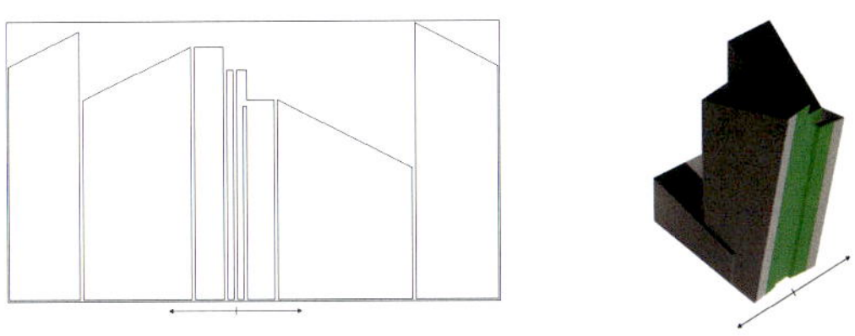

FACADE UNFOLDED

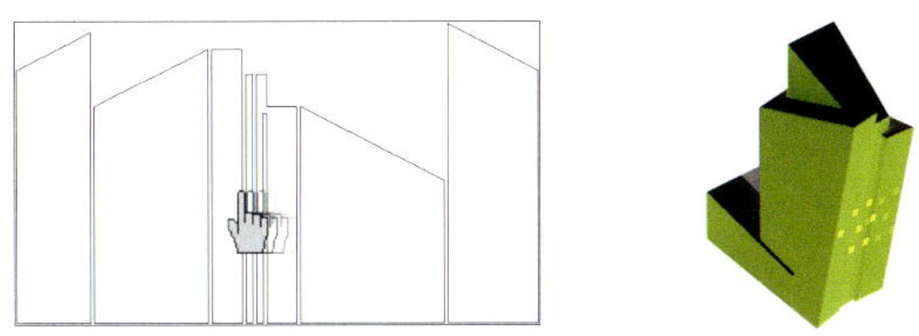

ADDED MOVEMENT = DOTS IN MOTION

1. FRAME
2. RAMP
3. TACTILE SCREEN
4. BENCH
5. SCREEN

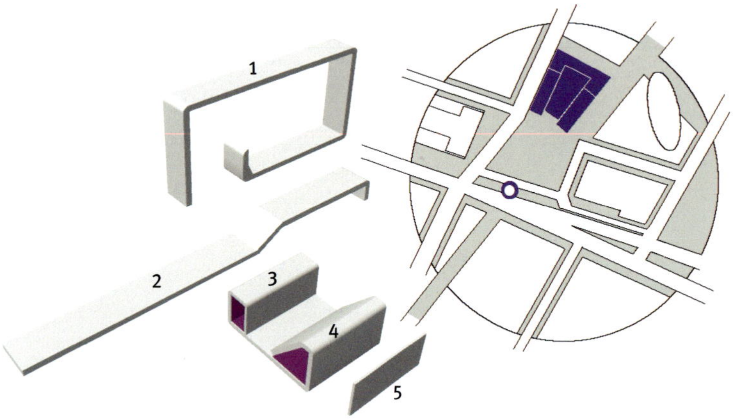

BREAKDOWN

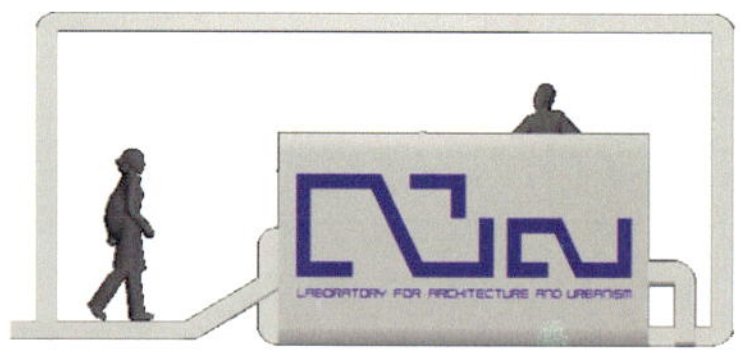

SOUTH ELEVATION

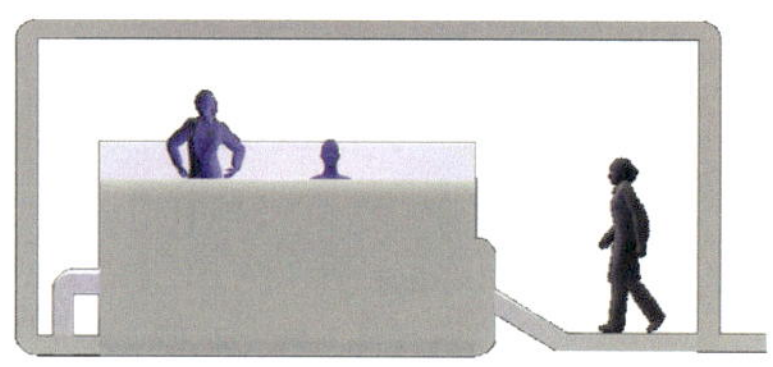

NORTH ELEVATION

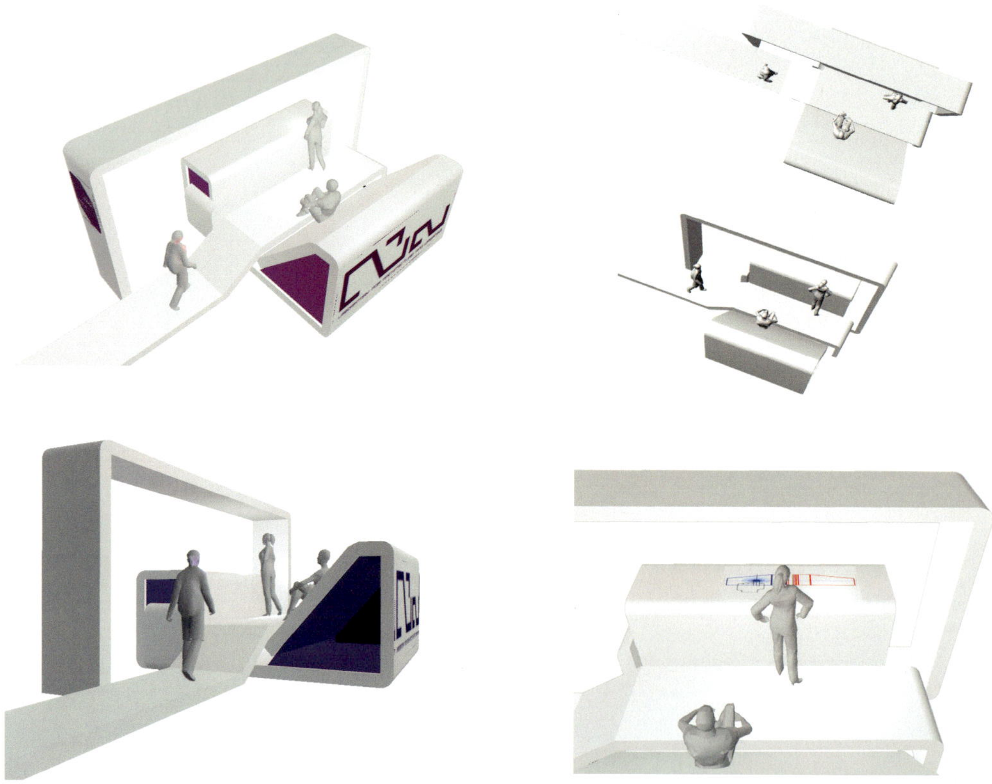

PERSPECTIVES

Touch required 15 miles (25 km) of DMX cable (from the ground floor to the 39th floor) to connect the circuit in the 4,200 windows on the building. Moreover, twenty-two blue lights and forty 3-watt LEDs were specially made for the columns. The ninth floor was equipped with a central computer that could isolate or mix colors on the different levels, according to the size of the design that was created.

Nelson-Atkins Museum

STEVEN HOLL ARCHITECTS | KANSAS CITY, MO, 2007

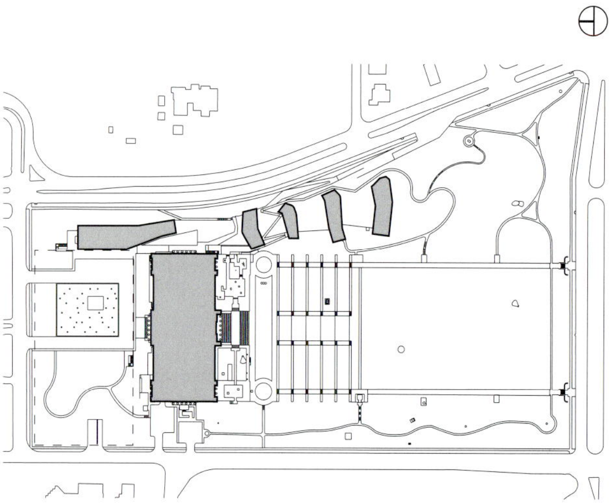

SITE PLAN

The Nelson-Atkins, founded in 1933, is one of the best known museums in the United States. In 1999, Steven Holl's architectural firm was the winner of the international competition for designs for the Nelson-Atkins's enlargement and renovation. The architects set five "glass lenses" along the east side of this historic building, next to the 18-acre garden. The new towers provide a surface area of over 161,000 sqare feet (15,000 m^2)—increasing the size of the museum by 55 percent.

The new glass lenses follow the rolling contours of the terrain while the paths weave through the sculptural garden in dynamic, fluid movements. The architects wanted these new elements to set up a contrast with the existing volume by means of their transparency and lightness, their penetrability, the interrupted circulation, and the views of the surroundings.

The original entrance via the north side was enhanced by the creation of a large stone square and a reflecting pool. At one end, the biggest tower serves as a foyer leading on to both the old building and the new galleries in the other towers. The new underground parking lot is lit by special glass fixtures installed in the bottom of the pool.

TYPE OF PROJECT **Art museum**

TOTAL SURFACE AREA **415,000 sq. ft. (38,597 m²)**

PHOTOS **© Roland Halbe**

The color, geometry, and placement of the extension to the Nelson-Atkins Museum contrast with the classical architectural composition and materials of the original building.

The lens structures were made with U-Glass, an extremely rigid component of translucent glass in the form of an elongated U, with a texture similar to printed glass. It is self-supporting, so that straight and curved partitions can be put up without any need for metal supports.

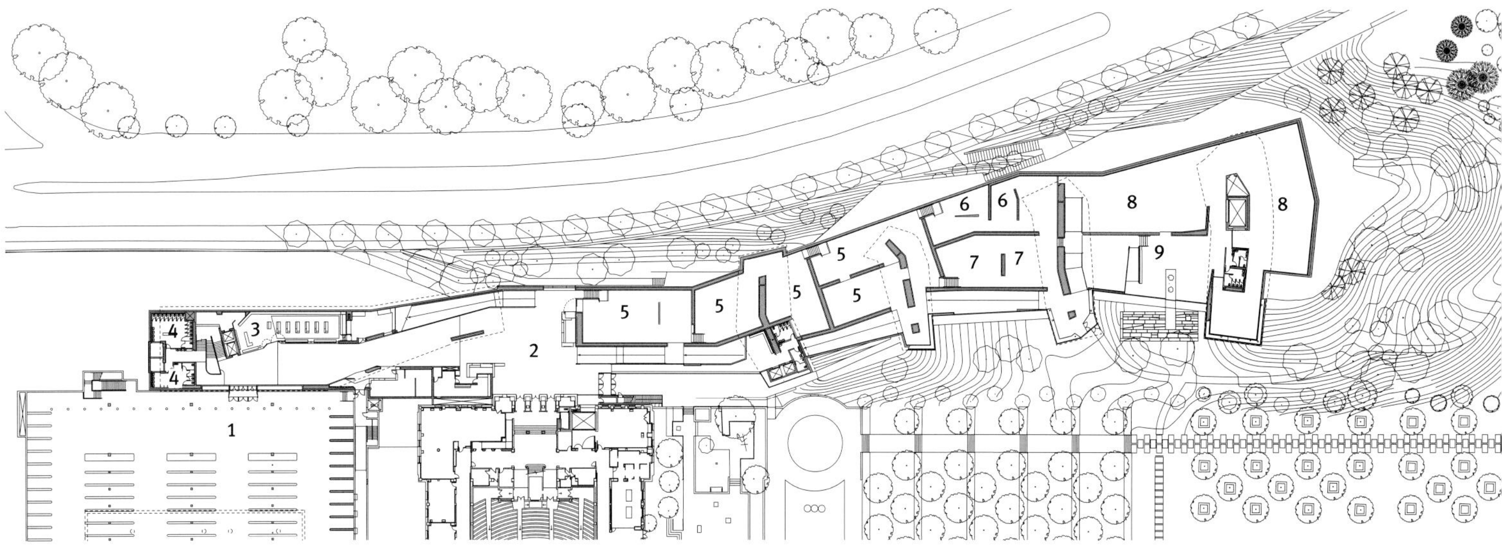

GROUND FLOOR

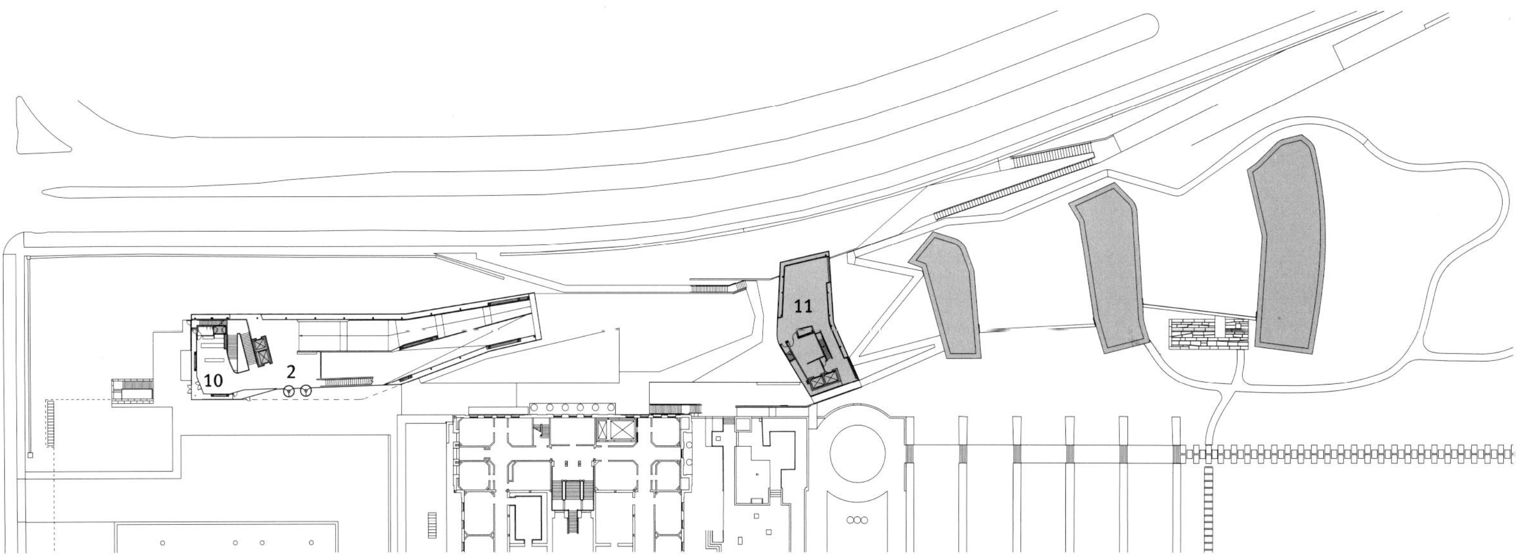

SECOND FLOOR

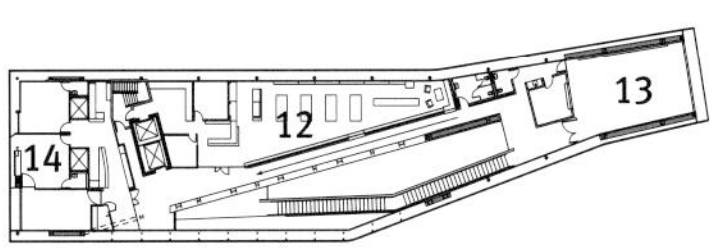

THIRD FLOOR

1. PARKING LOT
2. LOBBIES
3. STORE
4. REST ROOMS
5. CONTEMPORARY ART GALLERY
6. PHOTOGRAPHY GALLERY
7. AFRICAN ART GALLERY
8. SPECIAL EXHIBITIONS
9. NOGUCHI GALLERY
10. CAFÉ
11. EVENTS ROOM
12. LIBRARY
13. MULTIPURPOSE HALL
14. OFFICES

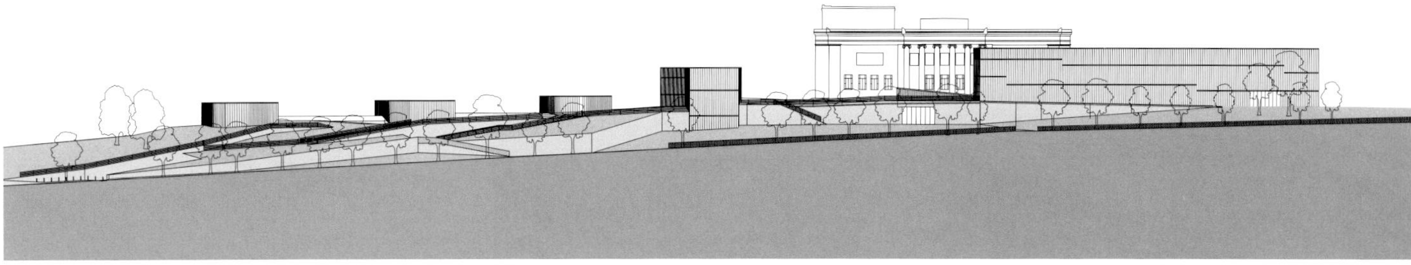

EAST ELEVATION

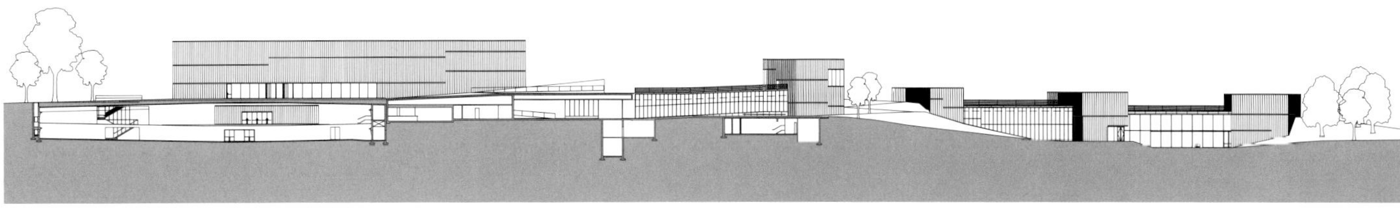

WEST ELEVATION

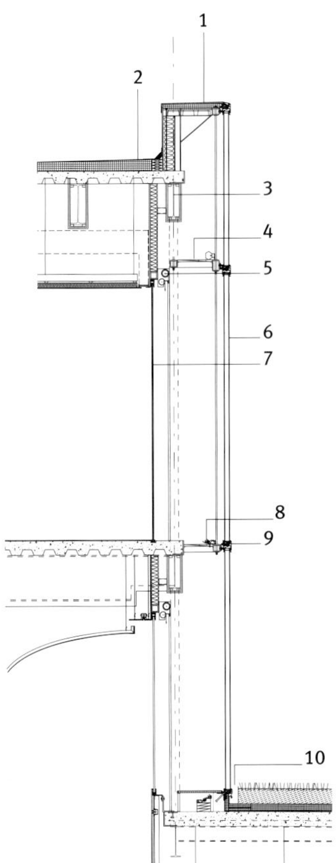

CONSTRUCTION DETAIL

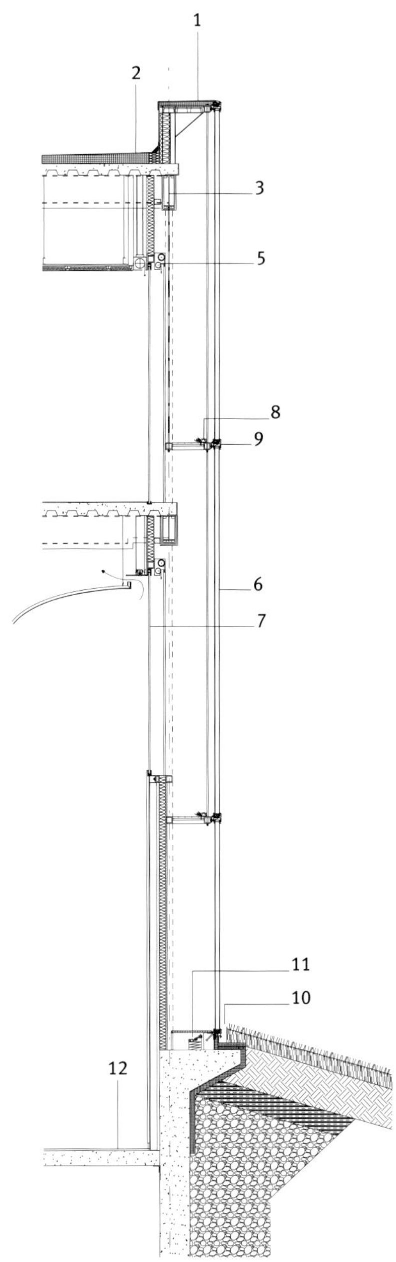

CONSTRUCTION DETAIL

1. ALUMINUM TOP
2. RUBBER WATERPROOFING
3. STEEL STRUCTURE
4. MAINTENANCE WALKWAY
5. CONTROL OF SHUTTERS
6. DOUBLE GLAZING WITH LOW IRON CONTENT
7. LAMINATED GLASS
8. LIGHT
9. INTERMEDIATE GUTTER
10. SMALL STAINLESS-STEEL GUTTER
11. FIXED LIGHTS UNDER REMOVABLE GRILLE
12. WOODEN FLOORS

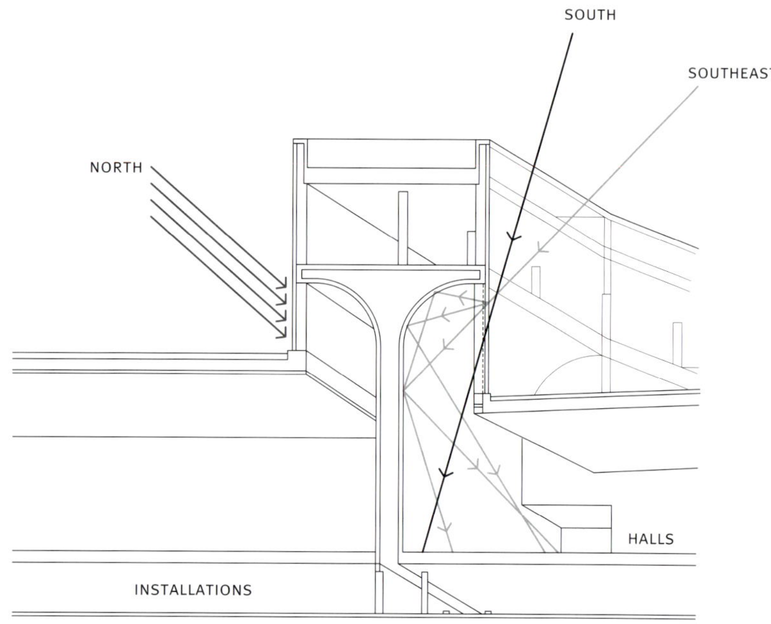

DETAIL

The new galleries were designed to follow the continuous movement of the terrain, in order to open up the views on to the gardens unexpectedly. As a result, visitors end up confusing the circulation and the exhibition amid the various levels and vistas. Similarly, the roofs of the towers echo the contours of the exterior topography.

The facades of these glass lenses serve as large lanterns providing information about the events and activities inside the museum. In keeping with traditional ideas about restricting the entrance of natural light—due to the deterioration of artworks through exposure to ultraviolet rays—the galleries were situated underneath the towers, and a glass filter was also installed to block harmful rays.

In structural terms, the galleries were conceived as a distributor of light and air, giving rise to a "breathing T" that supports the glass and gathers together the ventilation ducts, while its curved sides reflect the natural light into the interior. Furthermore, the double glazing of the facades makes it possible to retain air heated by sunshine in the winter and expel it in summer.

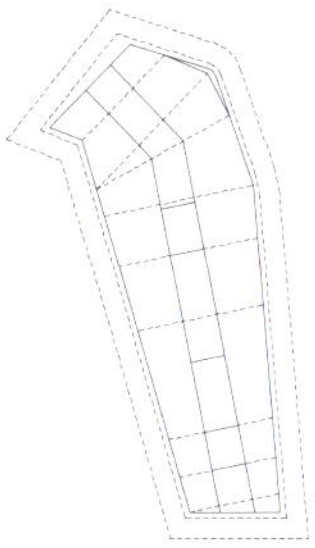

PLAN

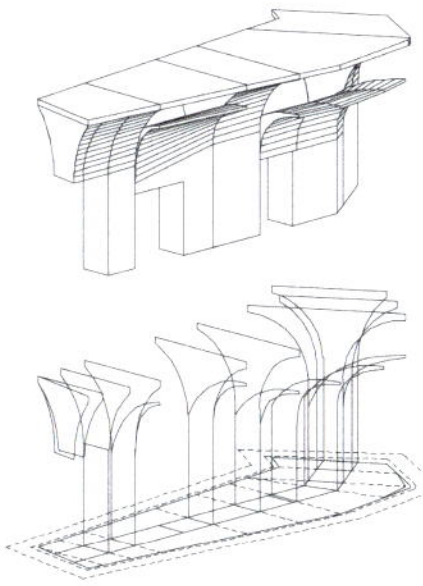

AXONOMETRIC

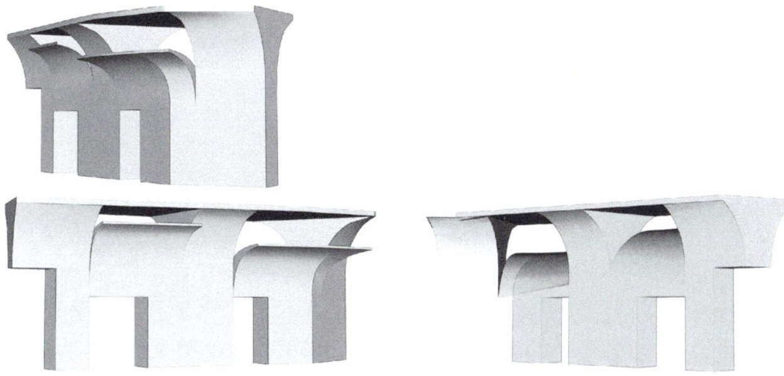

PERSPECTIVES

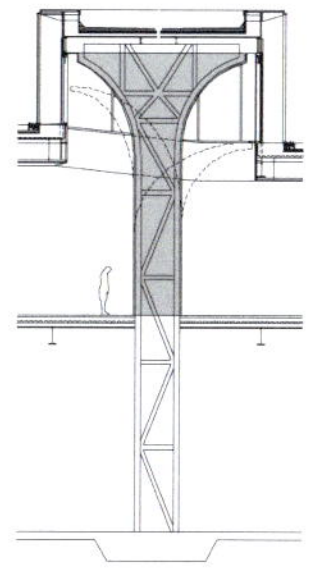

SECTION

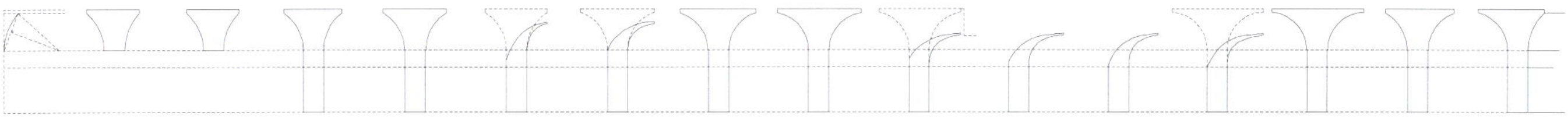

DIAGRAM

William T. Kemper Galleries

Tire Shop

CAMENZIND EVOLUTION | ZURICH, SWITZERLAND 2003

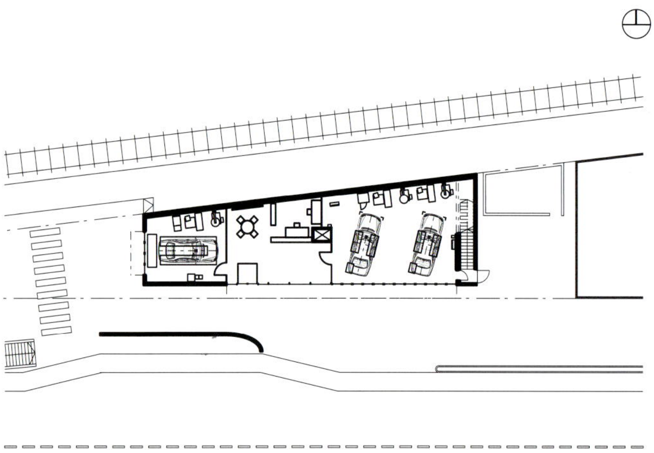

SITE PLAN

The Tire Shop, set on the border between the center of Zurich and the suburban residential belt, was conceived as a cultural reference point marking the entrance to the city. The area where the building is located reflects socioeconomic developments that have affected the region, with its gas stations and cut-price and 24/7 stores that serve the continual flux of people between the city center and the outskirts. This constant activity and mutation was the primary inspiration for the building.

The glass facade on the upper floor is a 2,153-square-foot (200-m^2) interactive surface designed to give opportunities to young artists, sponsored by tire manufacturers, to present their work outside traditional art galleries. In this way, the store becomes a space that displays art for vehicles driving through the area and pedestrians waiting for trains, while creating a way to blur the usual boundaries between art and commerce.

The facade is clad with glass on the ground floor to protect the metal panels on the walls from the rain; on the upper floor, the metal panels are set back from the glass facade to create a 20-inch (50-cm) gap in which artworks can be installed. This area is lit with fluorescent lights embedded in the ceiling.

TYPE OF PROJECT **Tire shop and art promoter**

ART INSTALLATION **Martina Issler**

TOTAL SURFACE AREA **2,700 sq. ft. (252 m²)**

PHOTOS **© Martina Issler, Peter Wuirmli**

dahin, wo ferne naht
fernwärts. heimwärts

dahin, wo ferne naht

The placement of the building and the use of distinctive nighttime lighting make this project a cultural monument on the outskirts of the city. The architects believe that urban areas of the future will be distinguished by this type of cultural landmark rather than by their acknowledged historic monuments.

The materials used—concrete, steel, glass—blend in with the other buildings in this constantly changing environment.

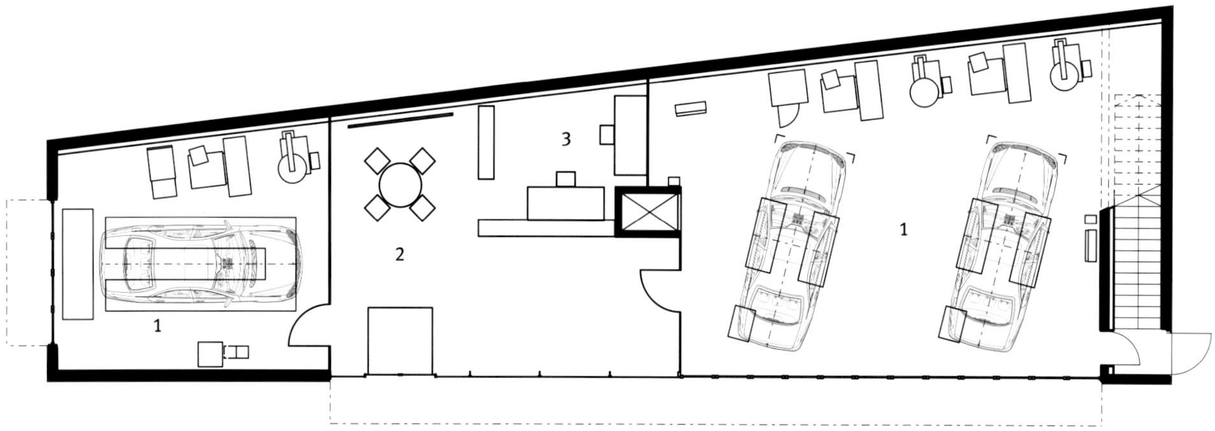

GROUND FLOOR

1. WORKSHOP
2. SALES ROOM
3. OFFICE
4. STORAGE AREA

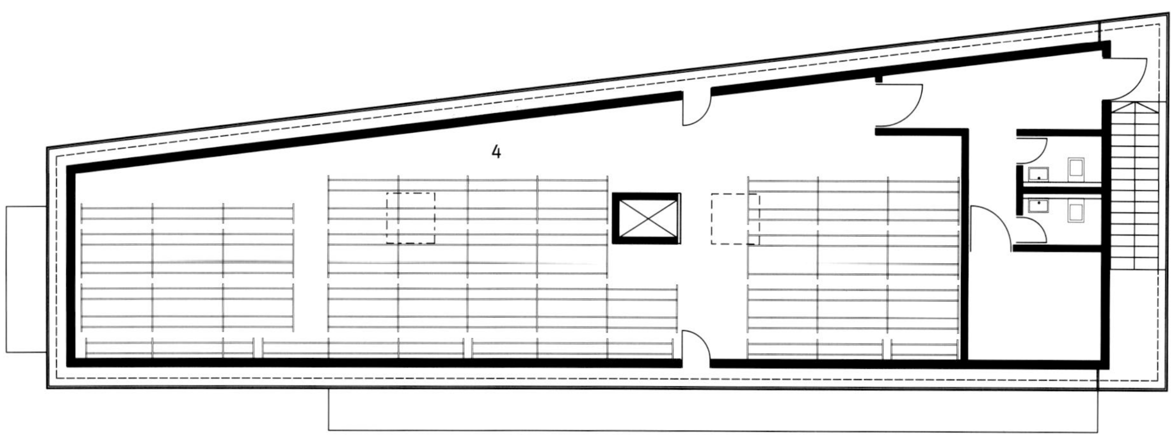

SECOND FLOOR

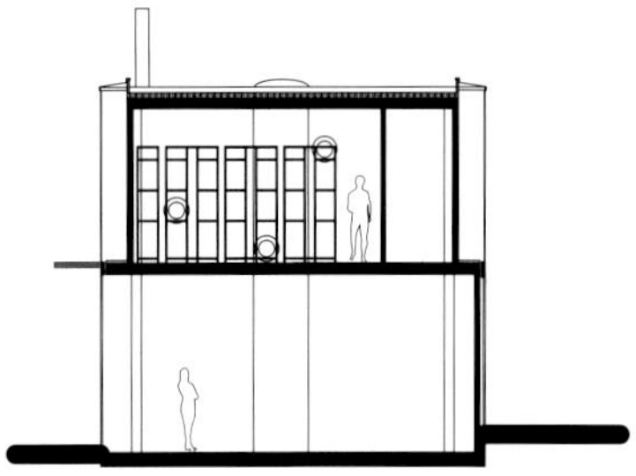

CROSS SECTION

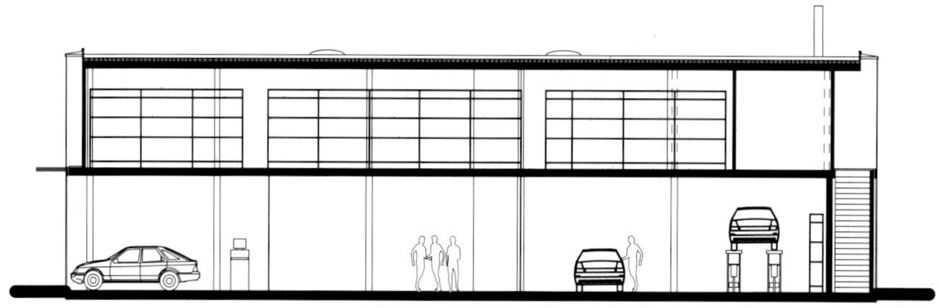

LONGITUDINAL SECTION

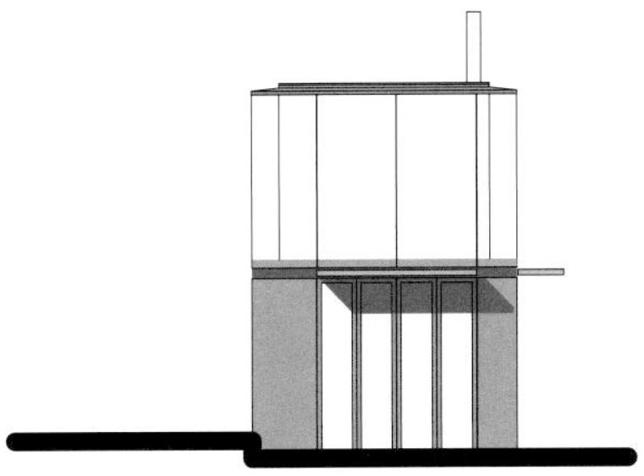

SOUTH ELEVATION

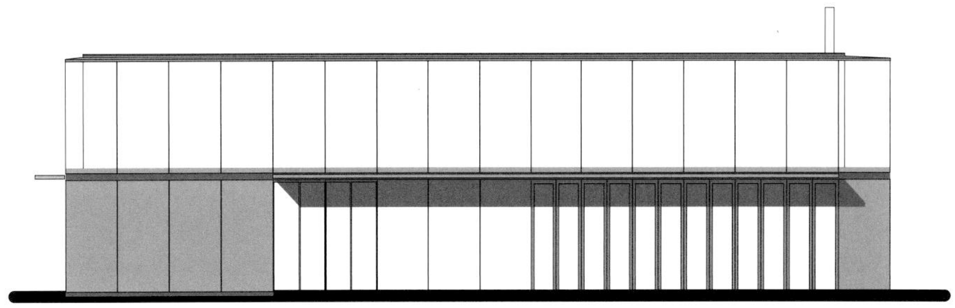

EAST ELEVATION

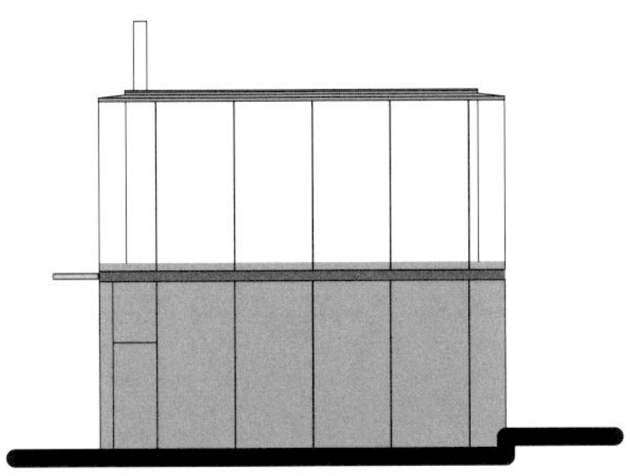

NORTH ELEVATION

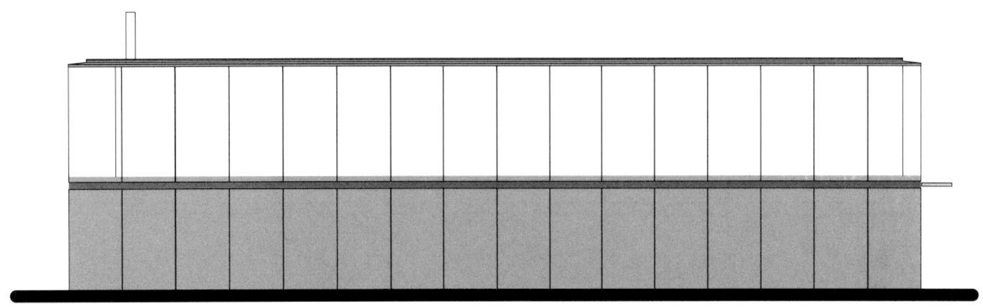

WEST ELEVATION

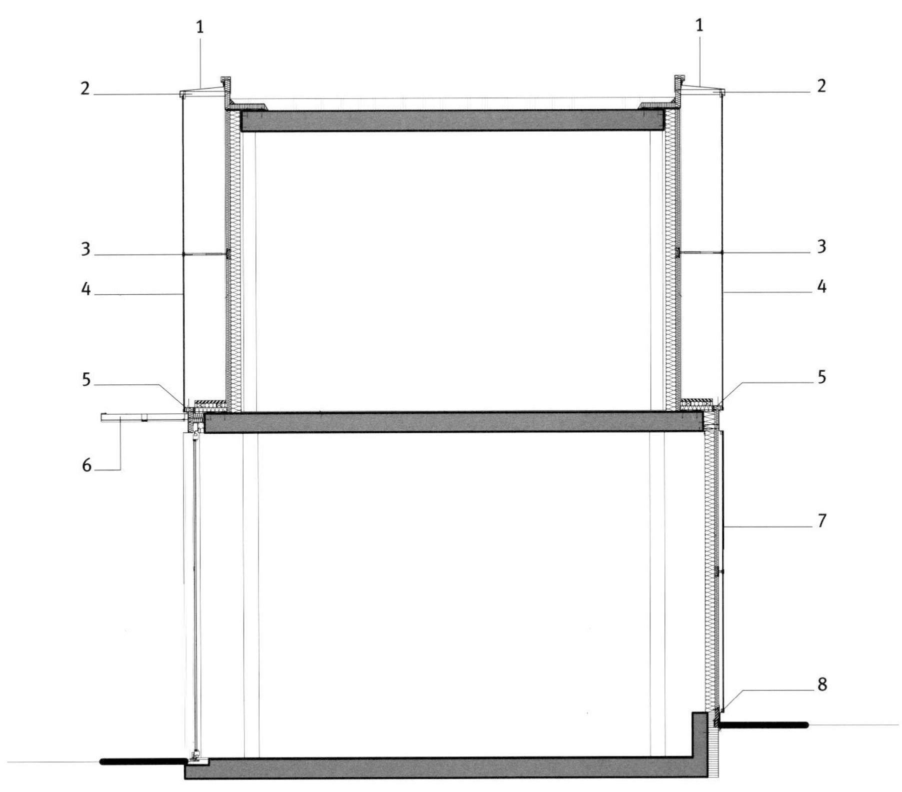

1. GALVANIZED STEEL SHEET
2. GALVANIZED STEEL TUBE
3. STEEL TUBE TO SUPPORT GLASS
4. 1/2 IN. (10 MM) SAFETY GLASS, JOINTS SEALED
5. U-SHAPE STEEL OUTLINE
6. GALVANIZED STEEL CANOPY
7. 1/2 IN. (10 MM) SAFETY GLASS, JOINTS OPEN
8. GALVANIZED STEEL BASEBOARD

TYPICAL SECTION

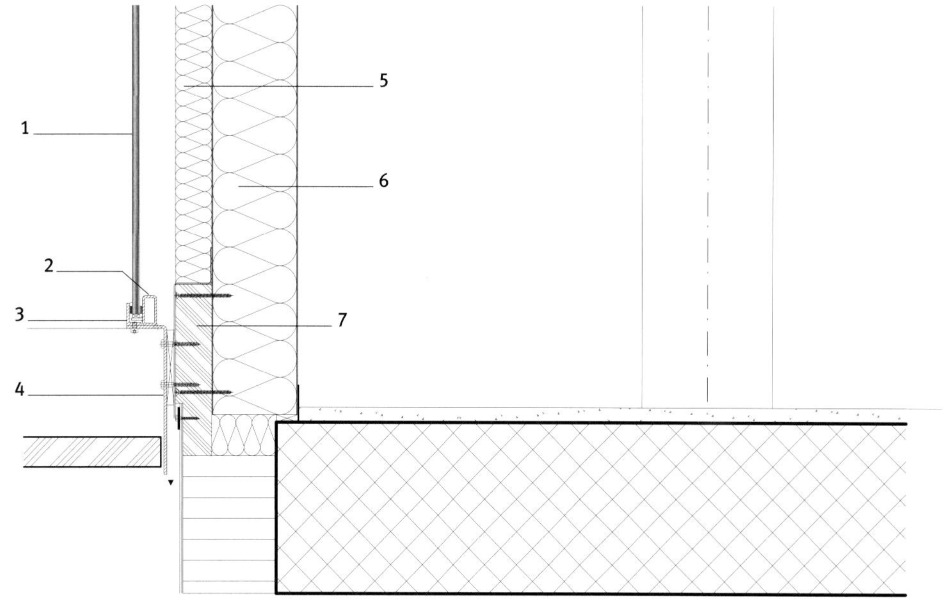

CONSTRUCTION DETAIL OF THE GROUND FLOOR

1. GLASS WITH OPEN JOINTS
2. STEEL TUBE
3. STEEL BRACING
4. 1/8 IN. (4 MM) STEEL STRIP
5. 2 IN. (50 MM) INSULATION
6. 5 IN. (120 MM) WALL
7. LAMINATED WOOD

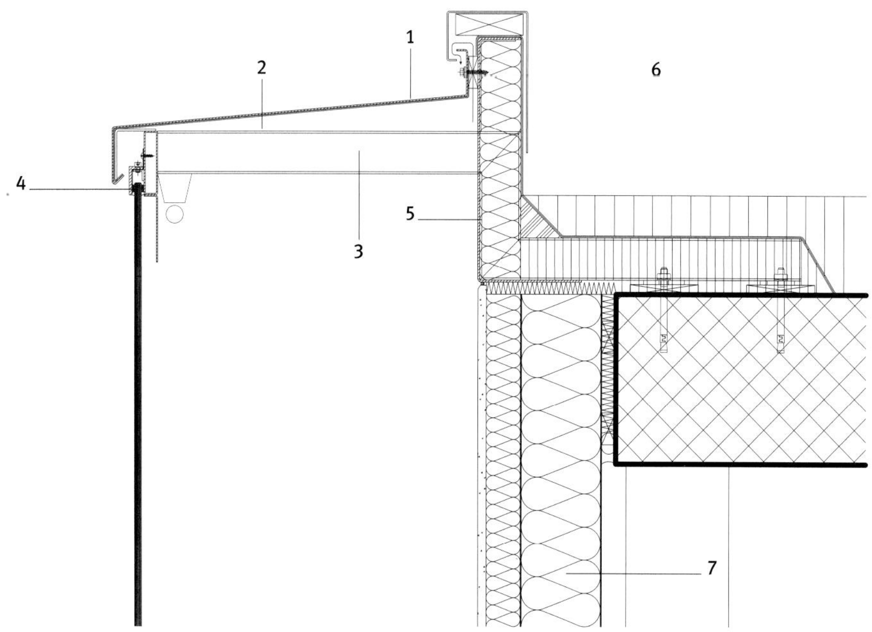

CONSTRUCTION DETAIL OF THE ROOF

1. STEEL SHEET / HOT-DIPPED GALVANIZED
2. ALUMINUM SHEET
3. STEEL TUBE
4. STEEL BRACING
5. STEEL SHEET / HOT-DIPPED GALVANIZED
6. INSULATION 1/5 IN. (5 MM)
7. WALL PANELING 5 IN. (120 MM)

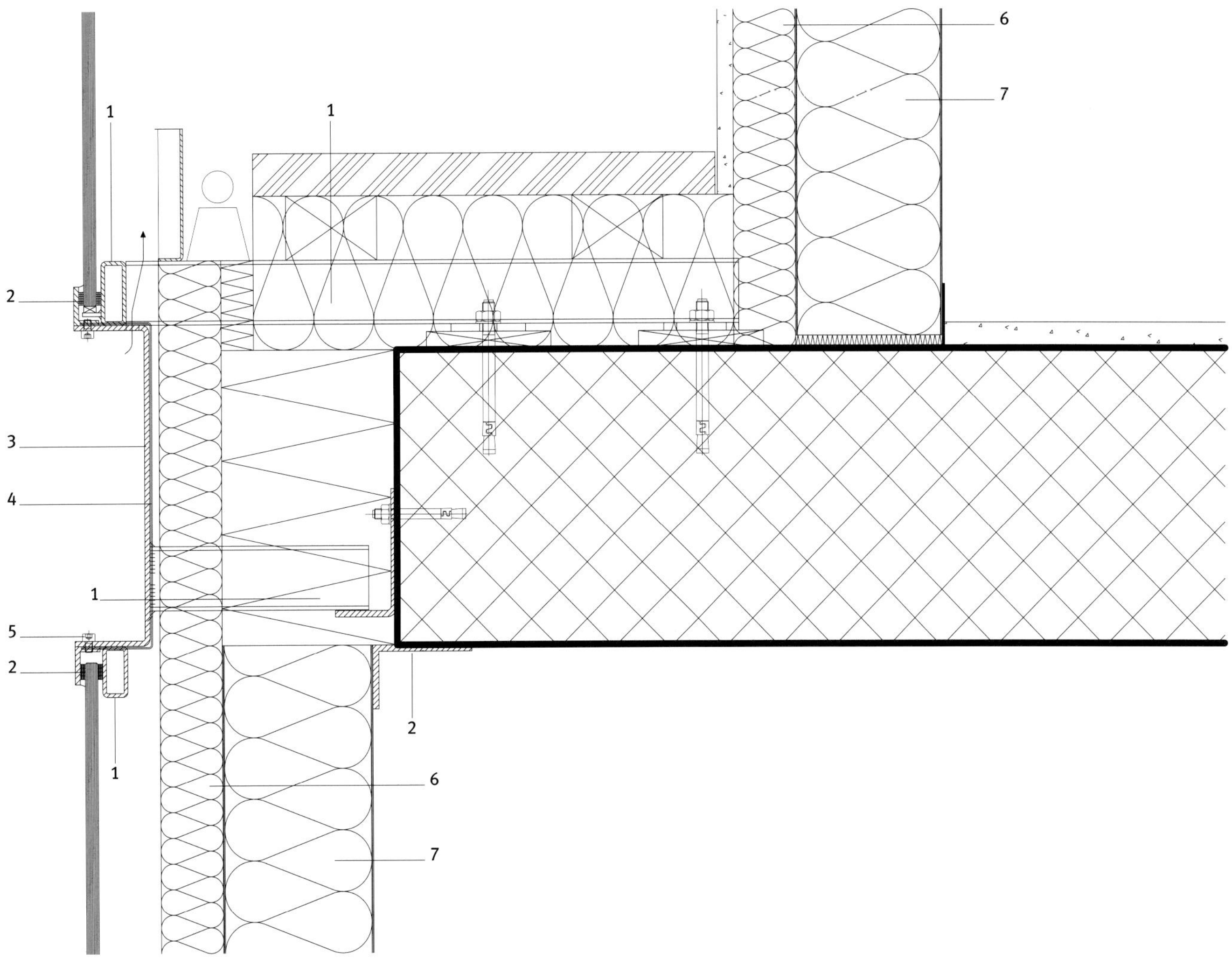

CONSTRUCTION DETAIL—SECOND FLOOR

1. STEEL TUBE
2. STEEL BRACING
3. STEEL TUBE
4. STEEL SHEET $^1/_8$ IN. (4 MM)
5. BOLT
6. INSULATION $^1/_5$ IN. (5 MM)
7. WALL PANELING 5 IN. (120 MM)

Watercube

PTW ARCHITECTS | BEIJING, CHINA 2008

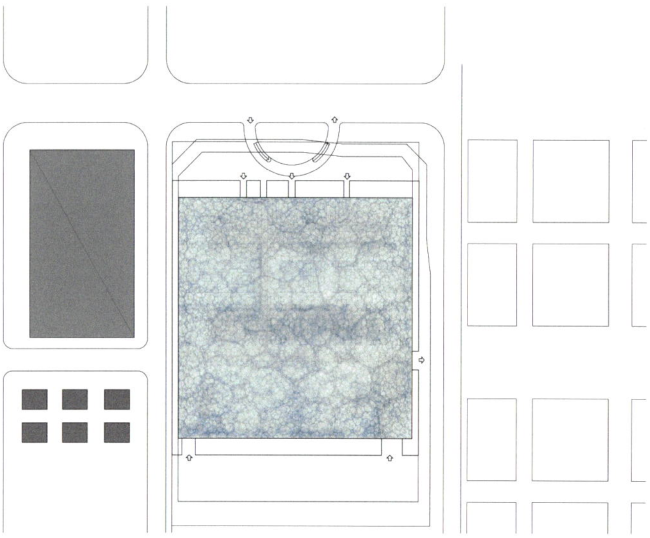

SITE PLAN

The National Aquatic Center, or Watercube, was built for the 2008 Olympic Games in Beijing. The building links water with the essential symbolic form of the square in traditional Chinese culture, resulting in a light construction inspired by the shape of soap bubbles—transposing a natural organic form into a tangible cultural one.

The building is situated opposite the National Stadium in the Olympic Park, at the northern end of Beijing. The park was intended as a hub for the city's sporting, cultural, and recreational activities, both before and after the Olympic Games. The Watercube was designed for Olympic water sports events, as well as for a variety of health and leisure activities before and after the Games.

Arup and PTW designed a shell made up of 22,000 streamlined beams to minimize the load of the building. Furthermore, this shell was made in compact sections that were flexible enough to resist any possible earth tremors. The Watercube's shape was inspired by the Weaire-Phelan plan developed by two Irish physics professors: a complex, three-dimensional structure in which uniform cells are joined together by the smallest possible contact area.

TYPE OF PROJECT **Sports facility**

TEAM **CSCEC, Arup**

TOTAL SURFACE AREA **750,000 sq. ft. (70,000 m²)**

PHOTOS © **Ben McMillan, Blain Crellin, John Pauline, PTW Architects**

The engineers from Arup developed a program that allowed them to analyze each of the 22,000 beams in the structure, in order to find the ideal size both to satisfy all the design requirements and to reduce the overall weight of the building as much as possible. They came up with 57 million different design restrictions and 190 different loads before deciding on a definitive version of the construction.

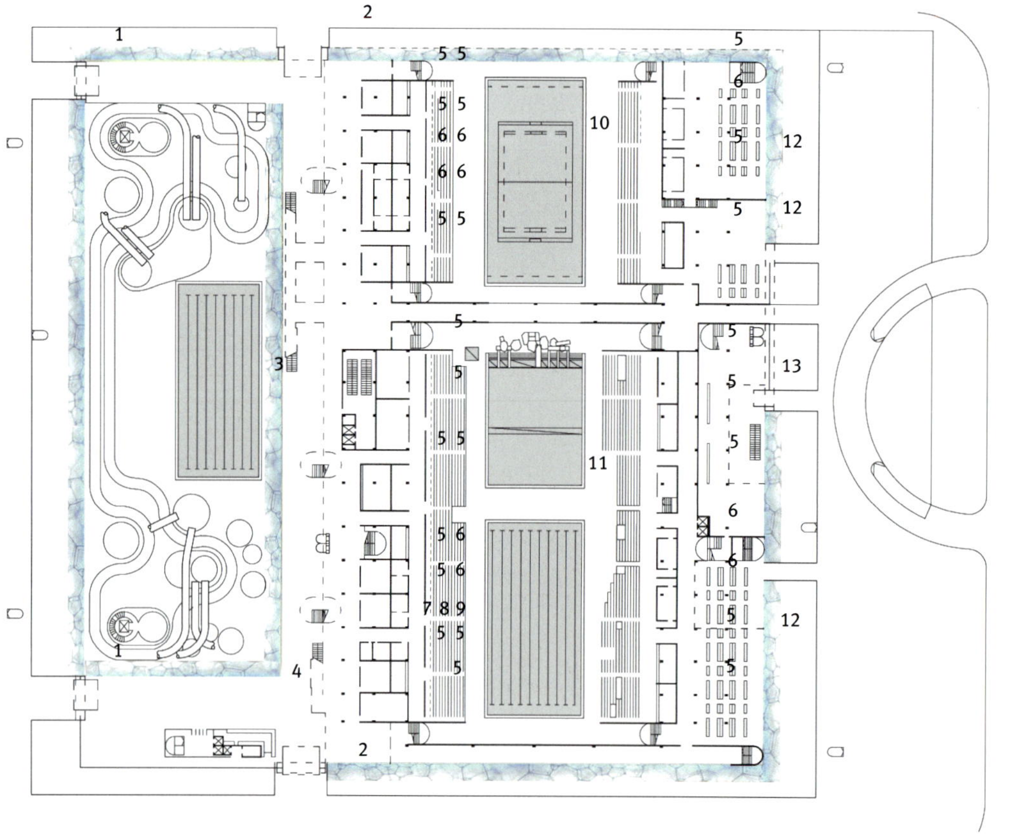

GROUND FLOOR

1. ENTRANCES
2. EXITS
3. RECREATIONAL POOL
4. COUNTER
5. COMMERCIAL PREMISES
6. PUBLIC SERVICES
7. FIRST AID
8. MEDICAL STATION
9. LOST AND FOUND
10. WATER POLO
11. OLYMPIC POOLS
12. PRESS HALL
13. VIP RECEPTION

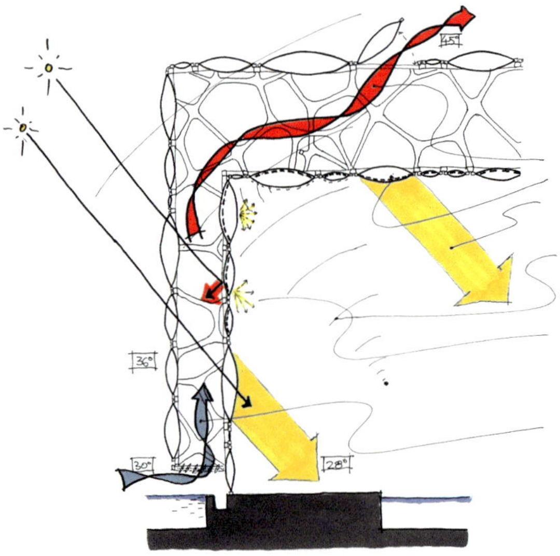

SUMMER DIAGRAM

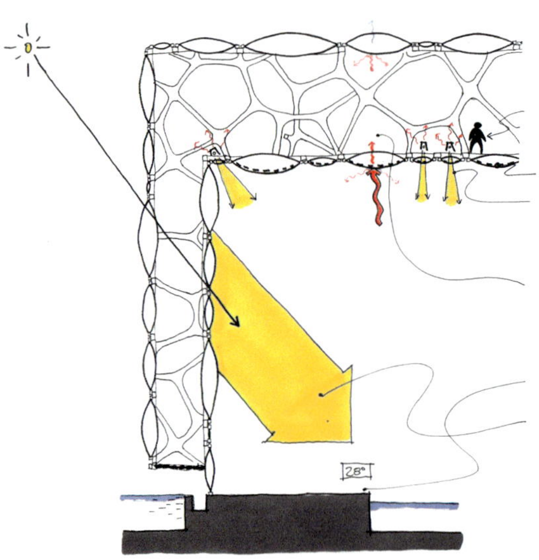

WINTER DIAGRAM

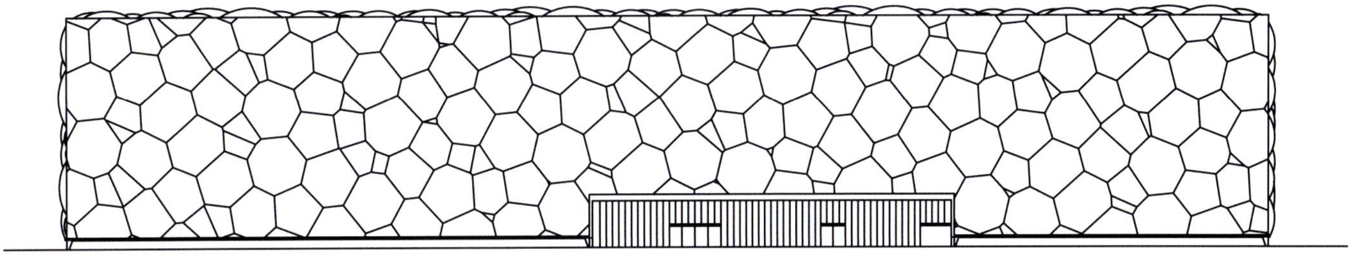

NORTH ELEVATION

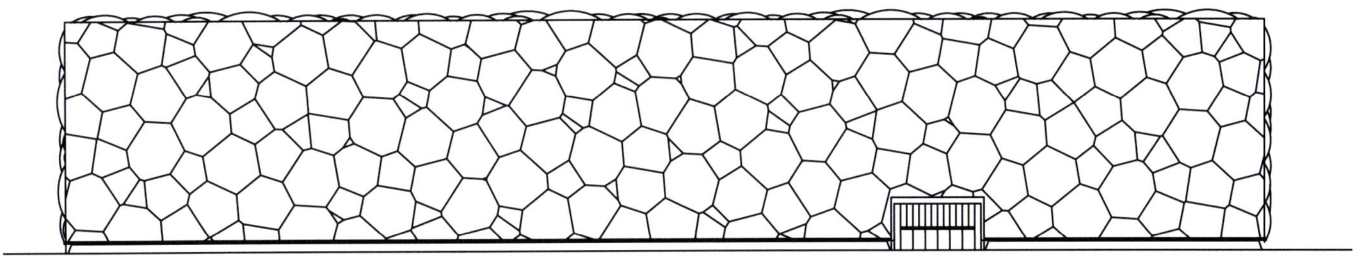

WEST ELEVATION

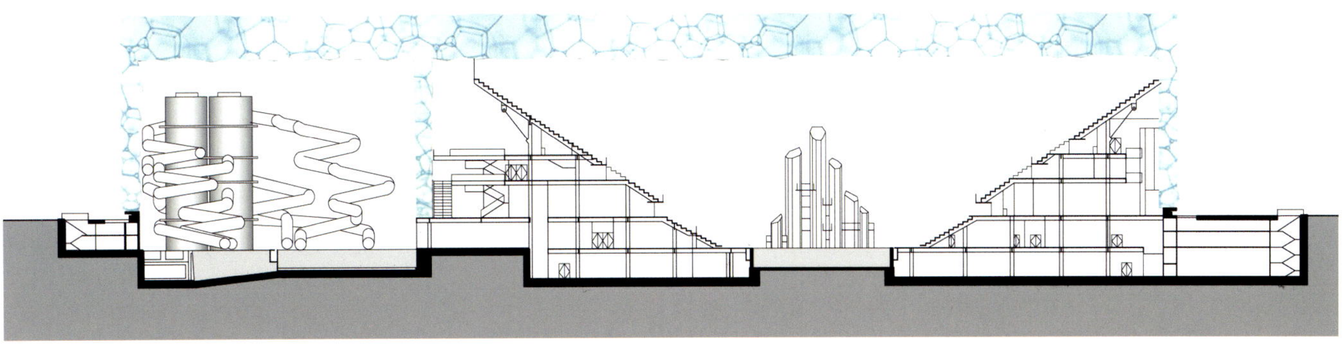

LONGITUDINAL SECTION

The building's infrastructure was based on the three-dimensional subdivision of space into uniform cells, similar to the organic constitution of soap bubbles. The steel skeleton was covered with cushions made of ETFE (ethylene tetrafluorethylene), which has insulating properties that establish a greenhouse effect inside. These cushions form the skin of the building, allowing natural light into the interior while regulating the artificial light emanating to the exterior and thus reducing energy consumption by up to 55 percent. Other energy-saving devices have been introduced, such as conservation of the heat produced by pipes from the heating system.

The architects also sought to control water consumption by creating a system that maximizes recycing up to 80 percent, by trapping water from the roof, gutters, and pool-washing system. Moreover, the ETFE cushions allow 90 percent of the solar energy to be trapped inside the building, so that spaces and pools can be maintained at a comfortable temperature.

Spots

REALITIES:UNITED | BERLIN, GERMANY 2007

SITE PLAN

Spots was a temporary installation mounted in an office building at Potsdamer Platz 10, in Berlin. From November 2005 to March 2007, the glass facade became a show case for media art that lit up the city center.

The team, headed by the architects Jan and Tim Edler, aimed to produce communication methods that articulated spaces and images, creating a continuation of architecture by exploring its relationship with graphic design, art, and marketing. In the case of Spots, the images on show had to be specially created to fit in with the visual features of the display designed by the architects.

A matrix of 1,800 fluorescent lamps was incorporated into the facade. A central computer turned them on and off individually while also adjusting their brightness, thereby generating luminous moving images on the facade. Various types of lamps were gathered together in enormous hexagonal structures, which then were covered by a translucent colored film that acted as a filter, rendering the facade a graphic extension of the building's interior during the day.

For over a year, this facade was turned into a communicative membrane for displaying artworks. The images on show matched the surrounding buildings and the square itself in terms of scale and visual impact.

TYPE OF PROJECT **Temporary installation**

INVITED ARTISTS **Jim Campbell, Nina Fischer and Maroan El Sani, Terry Gilliam, Rafael Lozano-Hemmer, Jonathan Monk, Frieder Nake and Hendrik Poppe, Carsten Nicolai, Timm Ringewaldt, Ruth Schnell, realities:united with John Dekron, and others**

TOTAL SURFACE AREA **14,500 sq. ft. (1,350 m²)**

PHOTOS **© Bernd Hiepe**

Potsdamer Platz 10
BALZAC COFFEE
BUS
BUS

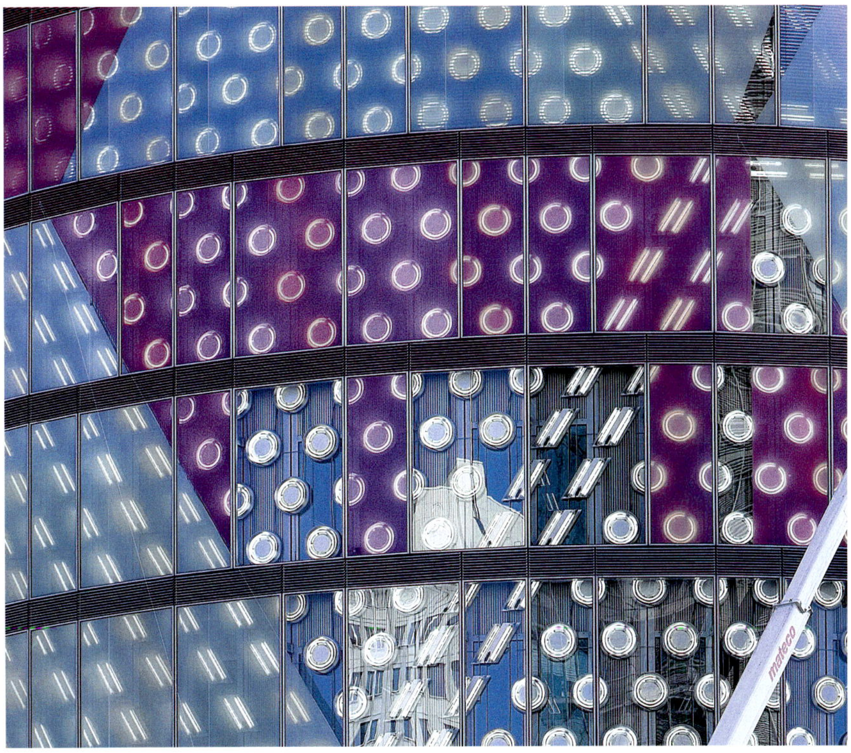

The architects from realities:united used a well-known technological resource—fluorescent lamps—to allow the building to communicate with its surroundings, making the glass facade a dynamic surface and thus a means of communication. The skin of the building on Potsdamer Platz is completely integrated into the architecture and acts as an intermediary between the interior and exterior space.

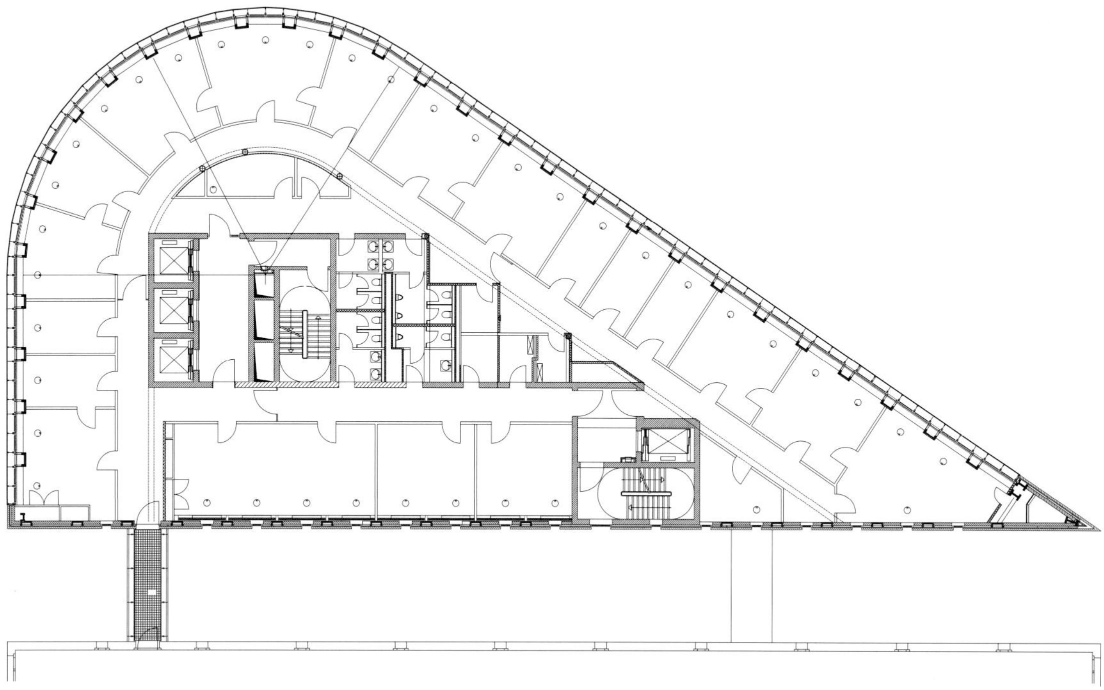

GROUND FLOOR

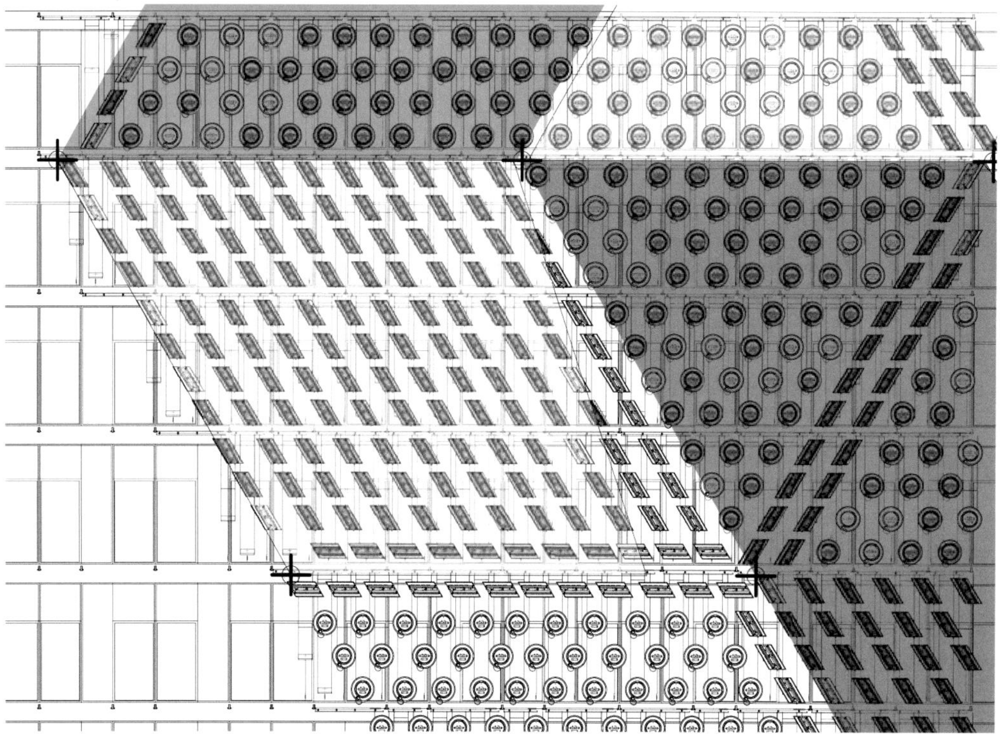

DETAIL OF THE FACADE

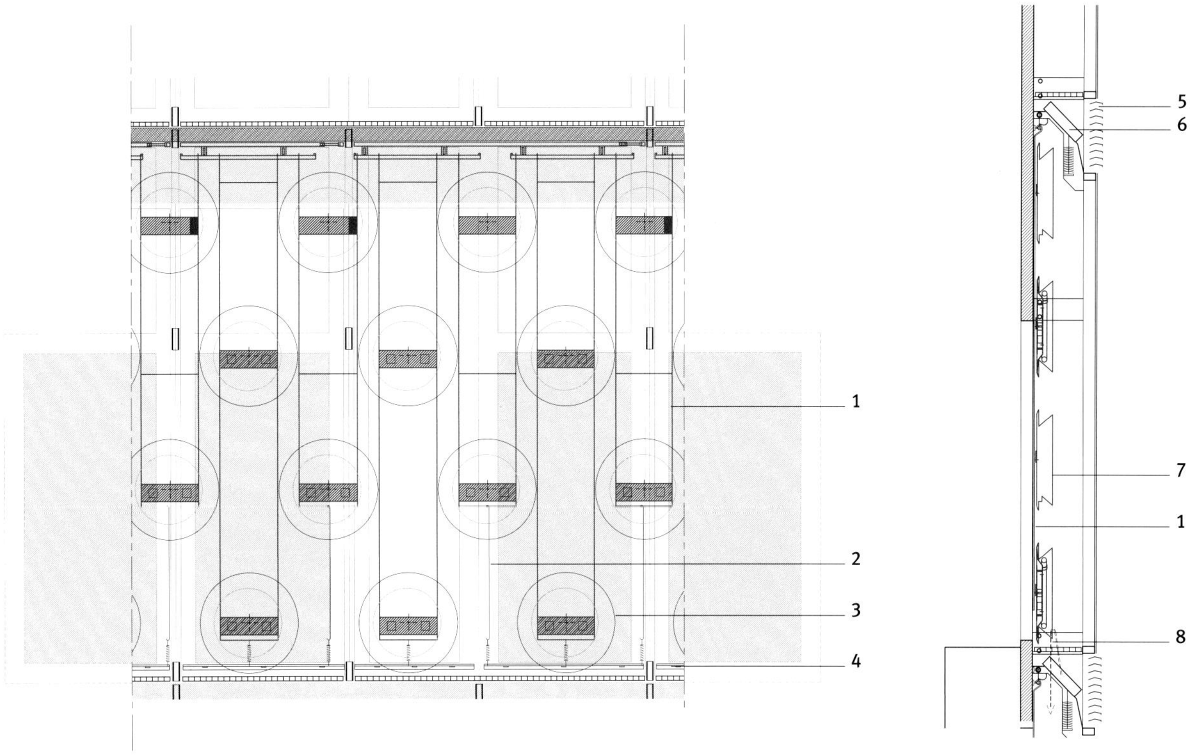

DETAIL OF MOUNTING

1. FIXED STAIRCASE
2. CONNECTING WIRE
3. LIGHTING BASE
4. ANCHORING PROFILE
5. GRID FOR INTAKE AND EXHAUST OF AIR
6. VOLTAGE REGULATOR
7. ANCHORED LIGHTING
8. CONNECTION VIA THE INTERIOR WINDOW
9. METAL TUBE
10. STEEL SPRING

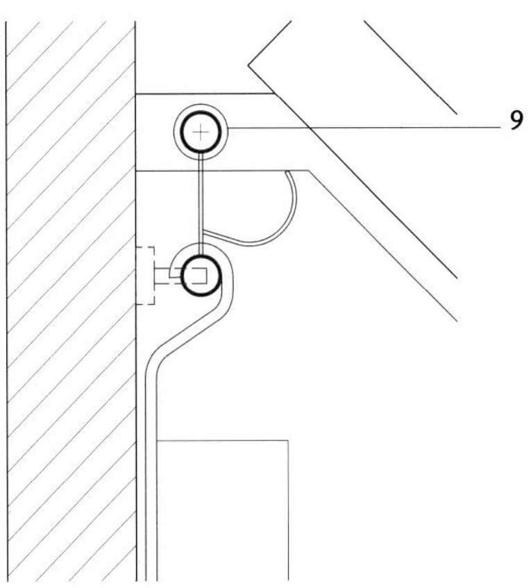

UPPER ASSEMBLY

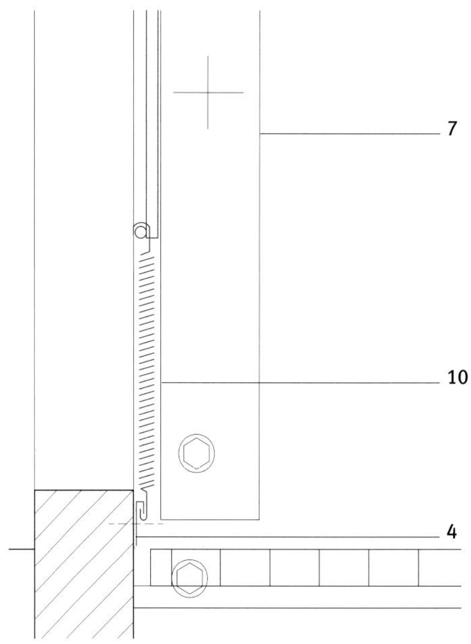

LOWER ASSEMBLY

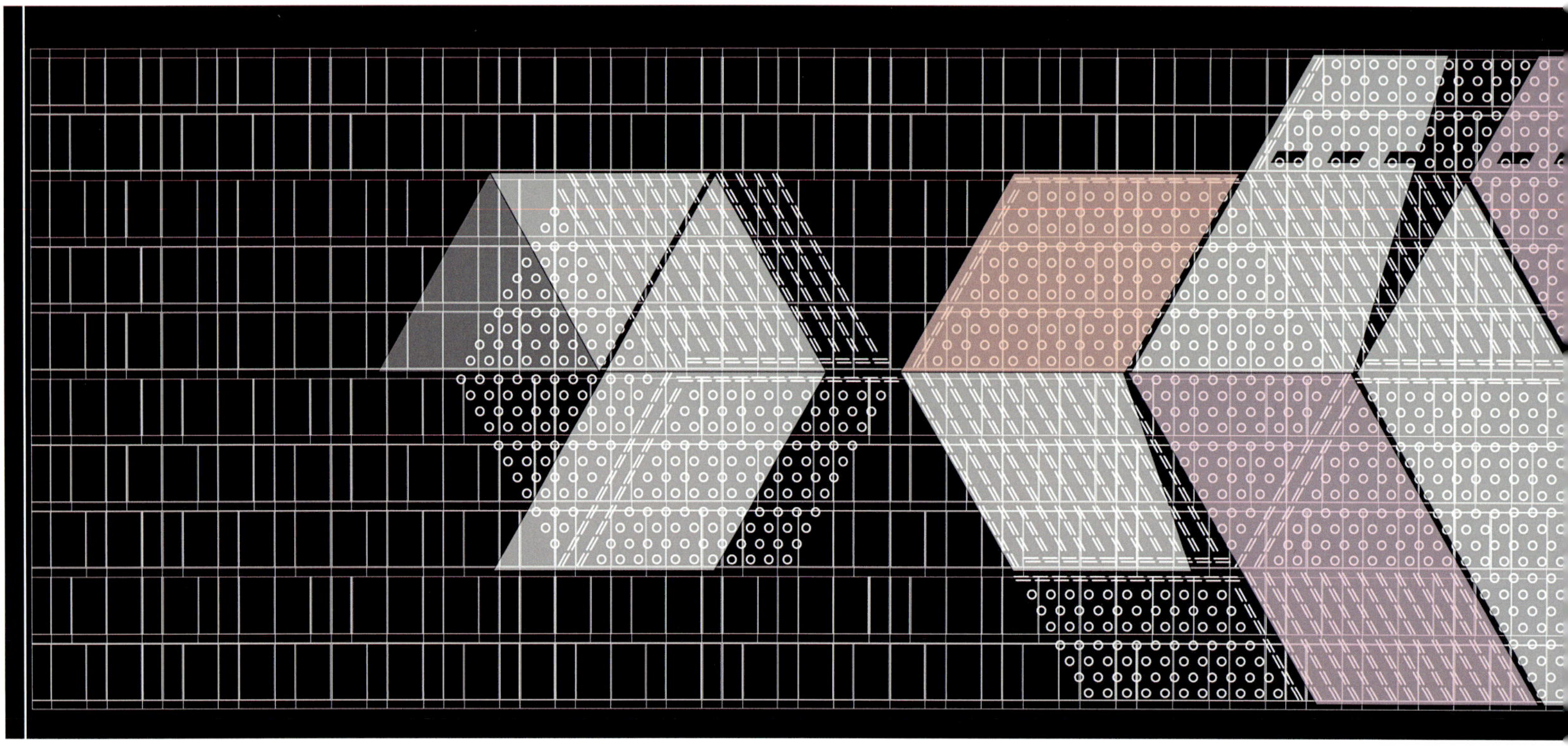

The starting point for Spots was the building's distinctive and diverse architecture. Different types of lamps were assembled into a single graphic template. The transparency of the color film can be adapted to the requirements of any display. The lamps were set in an irregular formation and divided into two separate screens, and finally the pixels were set on a horizontal gradient of 30 degrees.

Kubik

MODULORBEAT | BARCELONA, SPAIN 2007

SITE PLAN

Kubik is an installation that combines architecture with light and music. It is a temporary open-air construction that is used as a nightclub in the summer. The first Kubik opened in Berlin, on the banks of the Spree River, and it stayed open for two months in the summer of 2006. Two further Kubik structures were put up the following summer: one in Lisbon, on the banks of the Tajo, the other in Barcelona, in Forum Park (seen here). A third Kubik structure was built for a show mounted by Diesel clothing in the Palazzo del Ghiaccio during Milan Design Week in 2008.

The walls and pillars that create the spaces in this nightclub are made of stackable plastic tanks, normally used in the chemical industry. Each tank is stabilized with a framework of metal bars, while its interior is fitted with a standard 150-watt reflector, colored filters, and digital voltage regulators. The lights are synchronized by a computer program with the music played by the disk jockeys, so the club's geometry changes constantly in time with the rhythm.

The Barcelona Kubik was equipped with 275 stacked tanks lit up to create two different spaces: a bar swathed in magenta and a green dance floor. It was decided to set the Kubik in the Forum, in order to reclaim this area as a genuine public space appreciated by Barcelona's inhabitants.

TYPE OF PROJECT **temporary installation**

LIGHTING **Lightlife**

TOTAL SURFACE AREA **Green structure 1,884 sq. ft. (175m2)**

Magenta structure 700 sq. ft. (65 m2)

PHOTOS **© Thorsten Arendt**

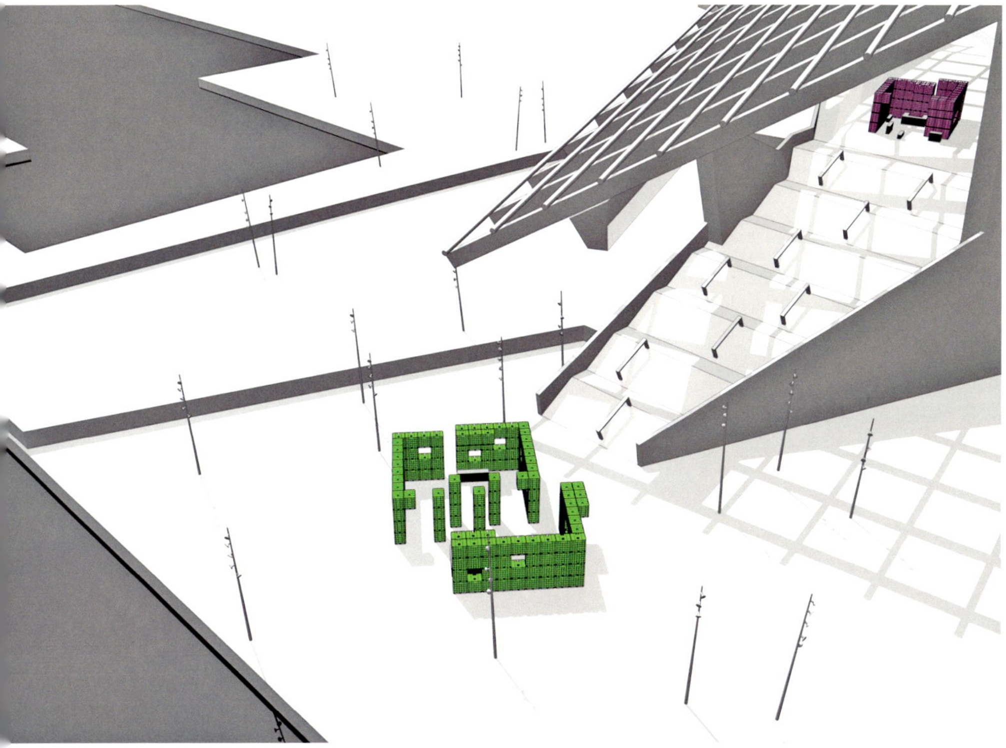

This project involved low-consumption bulbs that were regulated by means of standard dimmer switches. Even when all 275 tanks were switched on at the same time, they only consumed a maximum of 40 kilowatts. It was unusual, of course, for all of them to be switched on simultaneously at full power, so in practice the mean energy consumption for the entire Kubik club was less than 18 kilowatts.

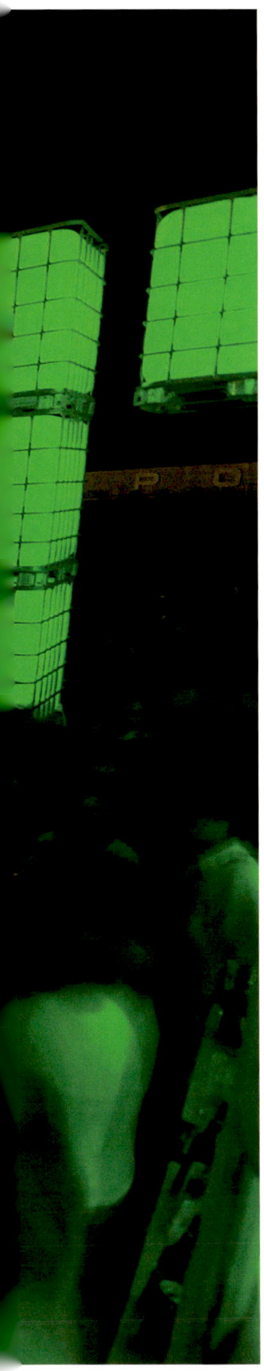

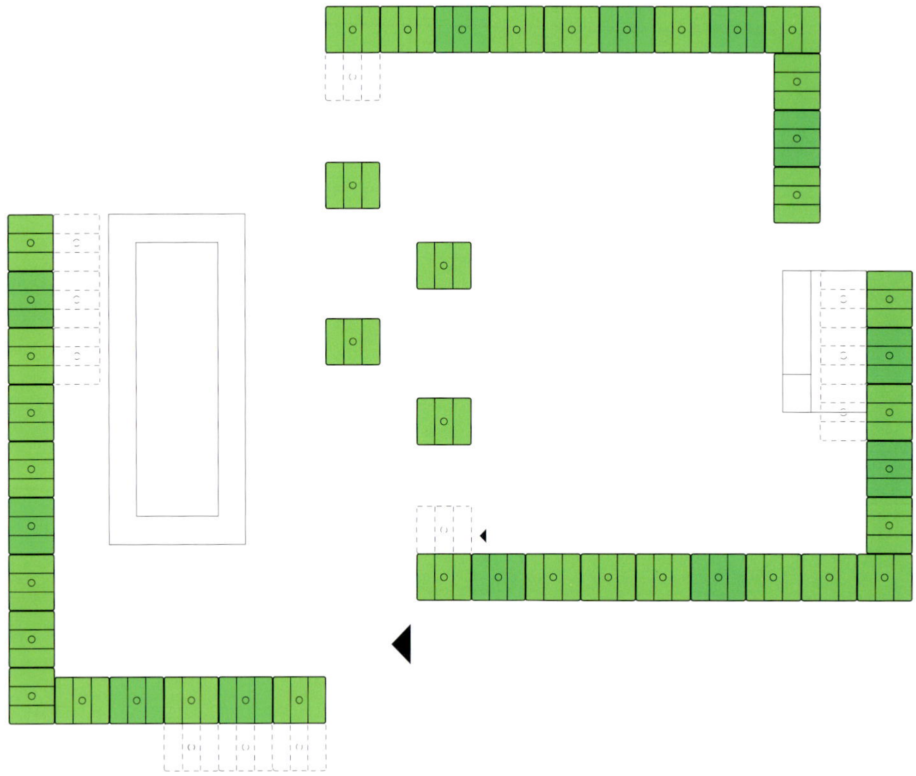

PLAN OF DANCE FLOOR

1. DANCE FLOOR
2. DJ CABIN
3. BAR

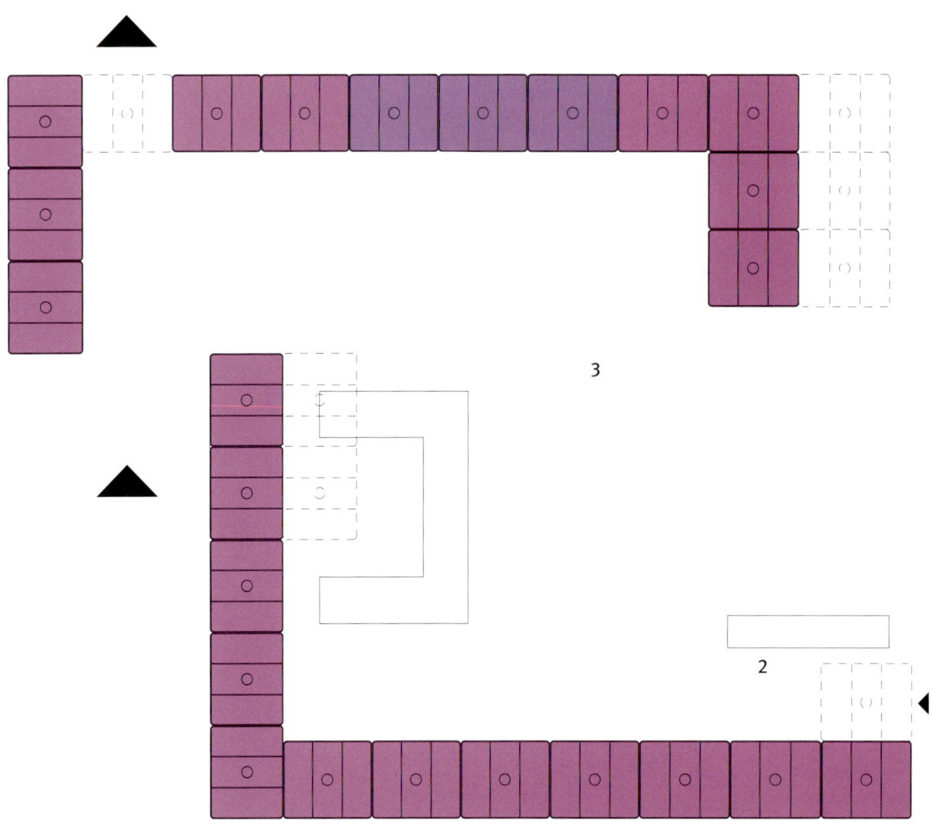

PLAN OF BAR

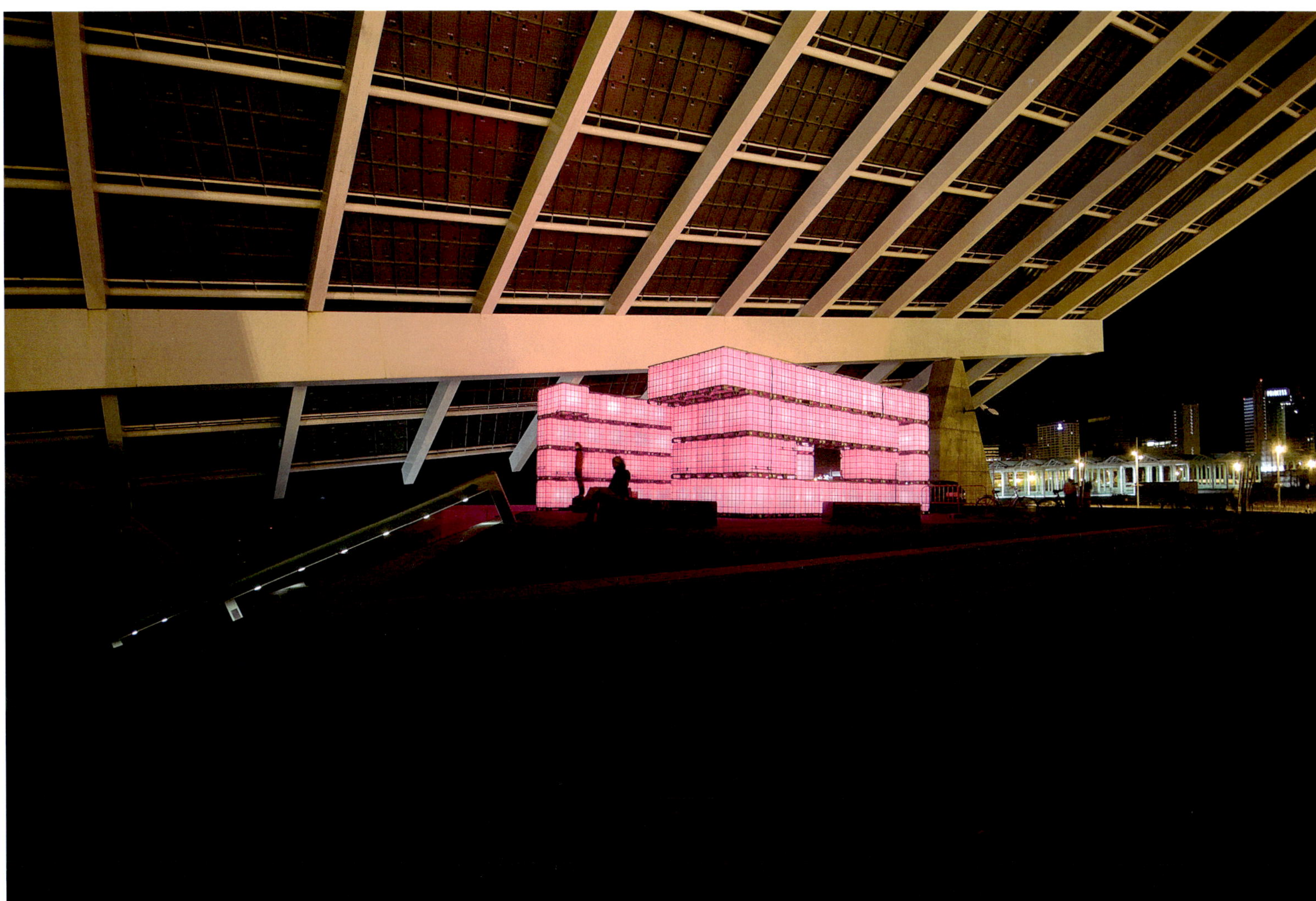

RNATIONAL RECRUITMEN CONSULTANTS
TEL 490 2000
FAX 490 2001

Urban Oasis

Chetwoods Associates | Various European Cities 2006 (Most recent installation)

The urban sculpture designed by Chetwoods Associates was created to fit in with a range of different places. It has been set up in various squares in the United Kingdom—in Clerkenwell, London; in Manchester; in Brindley Place, Birmingham; and even at the Chelsea Flower Show in London—as well as in Cannes, France. The work reproduces the form and elements of a tree: the branches, clad with photovoltaic cells, fold up and open out in reaction to the sun; the trunk is a thermal chimney that cools the structure's base. The movement of the branches is complemented by batteries running on hydrogen and a wind turbine that turns the urban oasis into a self-sufficient unit. Similarly, the branches collect rainwater that is stored in a tank and used to contribute to the system's refrigeration and the watering of the surrounding vegetation.

The base of the trunk is fitted with five individual compartments that serve as relaxation spaces for passersby. They are endowed with filtered air and the environmental noise is cut out by soundproofing foam set at head height. The colored lights, sounds, and images inside these spaces change as soon as they are occupied.

At night, the structure turns into a light sculpture, with 350 fiber-optic cables with lateral emission used to create rays of light that emphasize the connections between air, water, and energy. A matrix of 40 LEDs rises in a spiral through the trunk and generates bursts of light that interact with pedestrians.

TYPE OF PROJECT **Temporary installation**

LIGHTING **Arup Lighting and Microclimate Design**

TOTAL SURFACE AREA **10,700 sq. ft. (1,000 m²)**

PHOTOS **© David Churchill, Edmund Sumner, Chetwoods Associates**

122

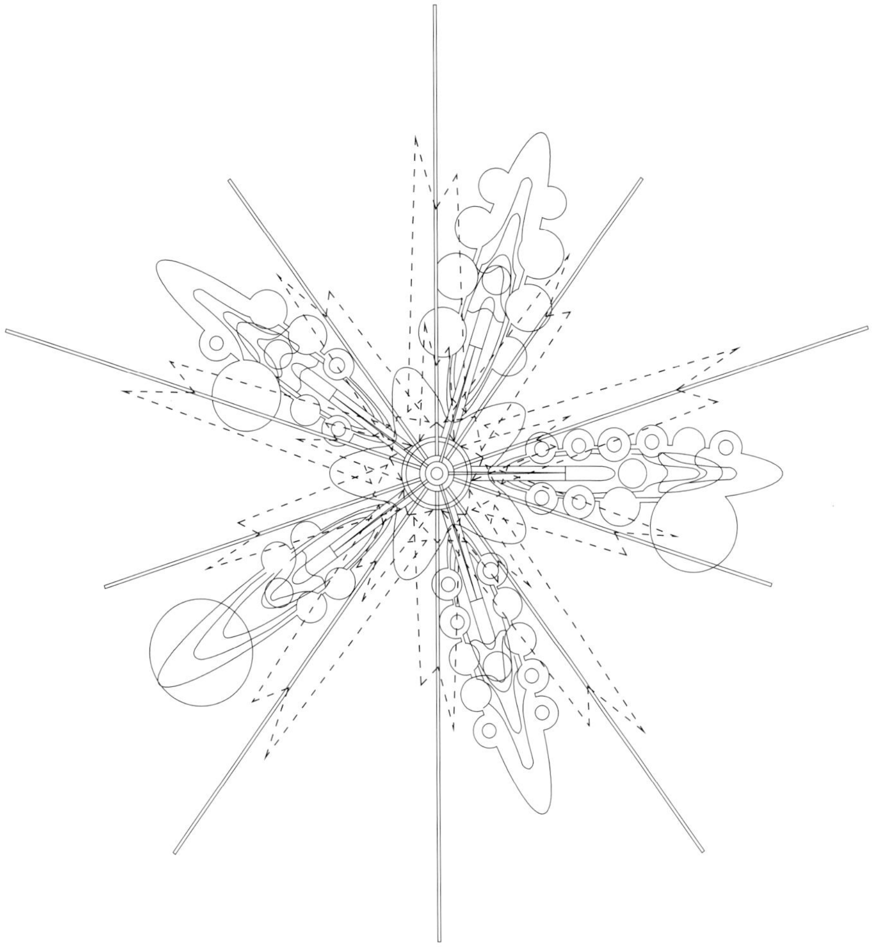

PLAN

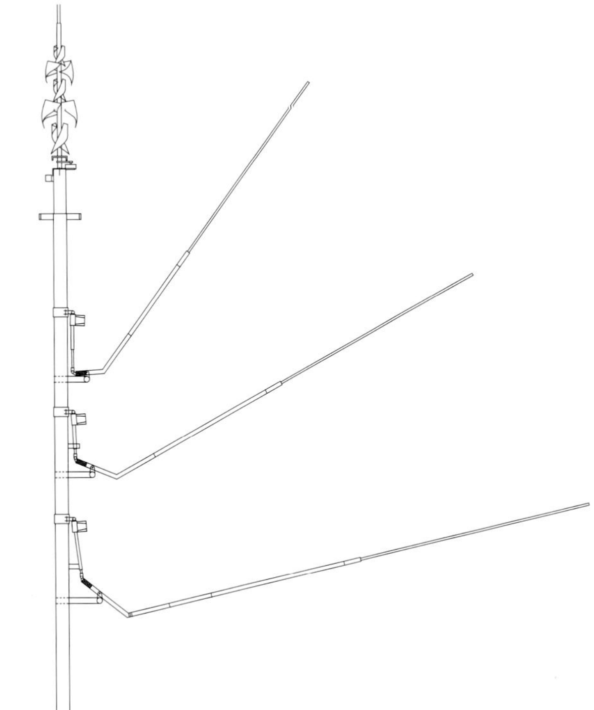

SECTION—OPEN BRANCHES

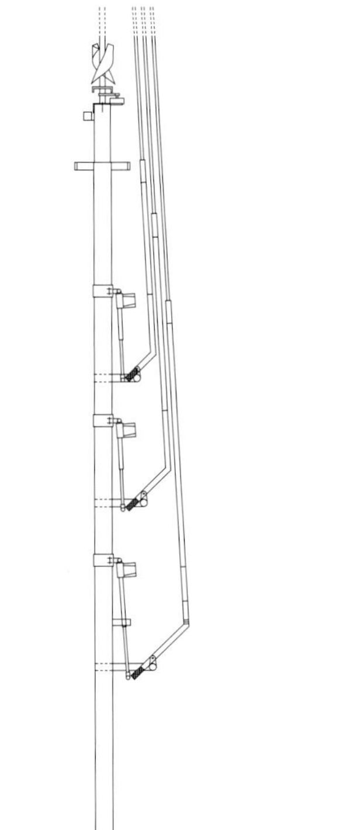

SECTION—CLOSED BRANCHES

GENERAL PERSPECTIVE

DRURY
crescent

Approximately 930 low-voltage LED lamps illuminate the individual compartments, the air turbine, and the platform around the structure. Apart from this lighting, the solar panels, the wind turbines, the thermal chimney, the rainwater tanks, and the recyclable batteries combine to form a prototype that allowed the architects to assess and optimize energy consumption. This was the first step toward a space focusing on innovation that would provide an oasis for the inhabitants of a city.

Center for Contemporary Artistic Creation

NIETO SOBEJANO ARQUITECTOS AND REALITIES:UNITED | CÓRDOBA, SPAIN 2011

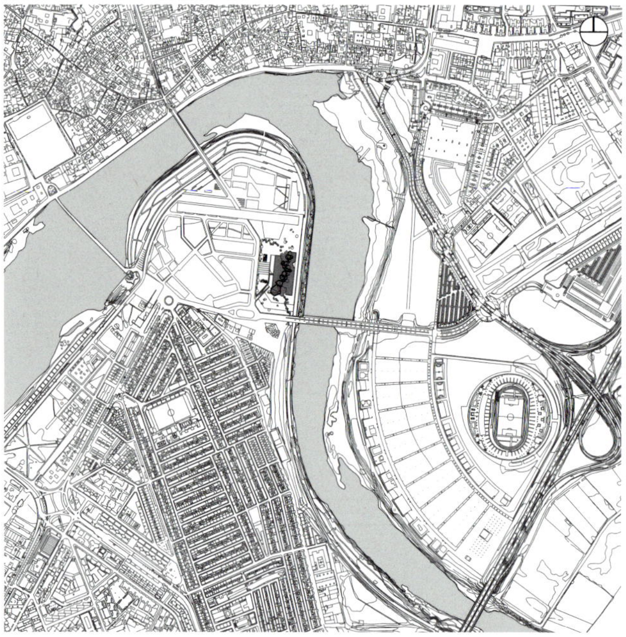

SITE PLAN

The Center for Contemporary Artistic Creation, designed by the architectural studio of Fuensanta Nieto and Enrique Sobejano, is situated in Miraflores Park in Córdoba, on the south bank of the Guadalquivir River. The cultural space, which is currently under construction, is a building inspired by Hispano-Muslim spaces and structures in the famous Spanish city, so simple geometry, interior patios, and links with the surroundings all were determining features in developing this project.

The center is a building made up of individually configured interior spaces that change and expand in accordance with what the architects describe as an "autosimilar geometric pattern." The starting point is a hexagon that contains three galleries of different dimensions—646, 969, and 1,614 square feet (60, 90, and 150 m^2)—which interact to create either a series of spaces or one large exhibition hall.

The building was conceived as a meeting point for citizens and artists that brings together the phases of research, creation, debate, and display of finished work; and the facades, in turn, were designed as elements that bring together what is going on inside and in the immediate surroundings. The dominant feature in this respect is the east facade, which overlooks the river: it was designed by the architects from realities:united as a three-dimensional screen that reflects the building's interior structure through its array of polygonal holes. These holes are fitted with lamps of various sizes and densities that are controlled by a computer program to generate images, texts, and colors. This large screen will have a resolution similar to that of the retina of the human eye and will be able to show images in movement at a rate of 20 frames per second. Natural light will pass through these perforations during the day.

TYPE OF PROJECT **Cultural facility**

COMMUNICATIVE FACADE LIGHTING **realities:united**

TOTAL SURFACE AREA **108,000 sq. ft. (10,000 m²)**

DRAWINGS **Nieto Sobejano Arquitectos, realities:united**

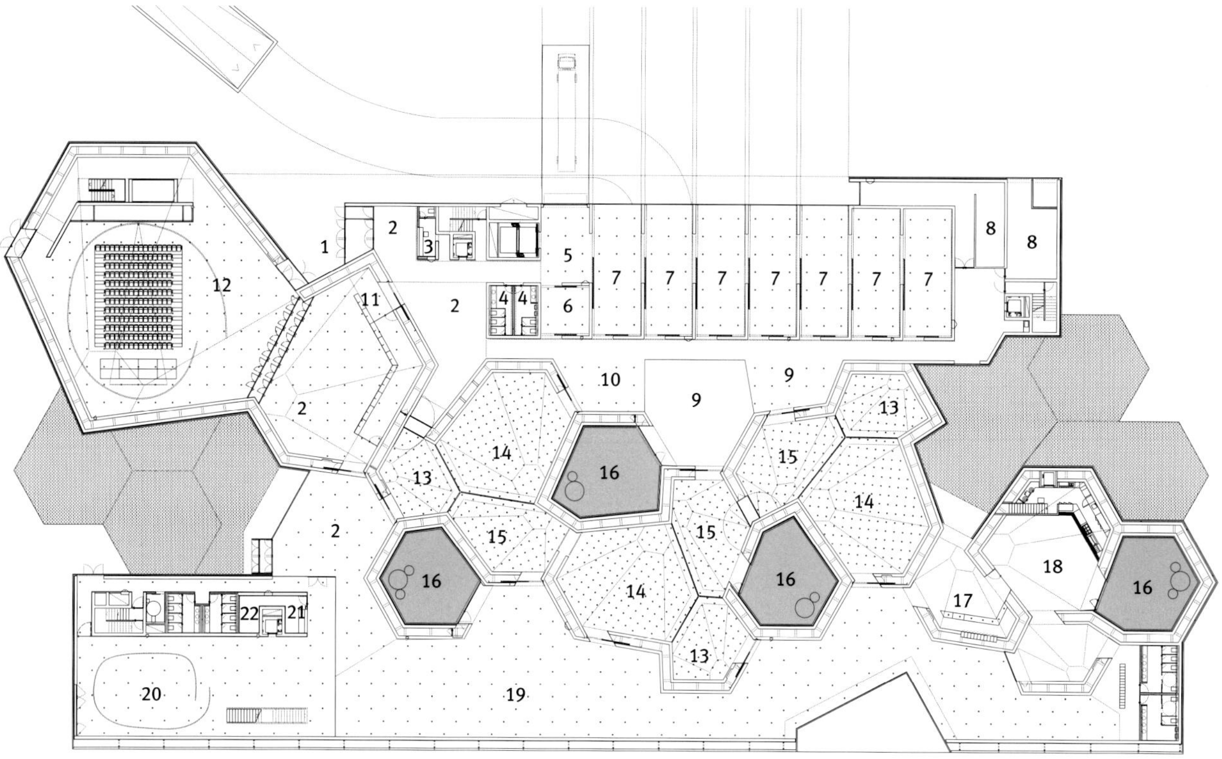

GROUND FLOOR

1. ENTRANCES
2. FOYERS
3. JANITOR'S AREA
4. RESTROOMS
5. LOADING AND UNLOADING AREA
6. TRANSIT STORAGE AREA
7. STUDIOS
8. INSTALLATIONS
9. EXTENSION TO THE STUDIOS
10. SOCIAL AREA
11. BOOKSHOP AND STORE
12. CONFERENCE ROOM
13. SMALL GALLERY
14. LARGE GALLERY
15. MEDIUM-SIZE GALLERY
16. PATIOS
17. BOX OFFICES
18. CAFETERIA
19. STREET FOR EXHIBITIONS
20. MULTIMEDIA AREA
21. INFORMATION POINT
22. OFFICE

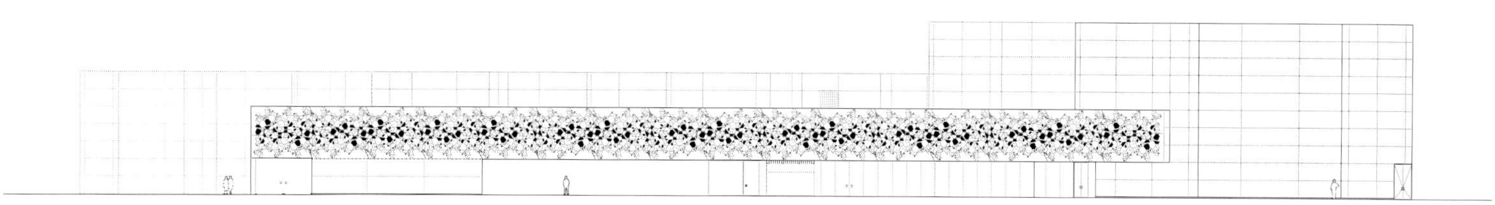

WEST ELEVATION

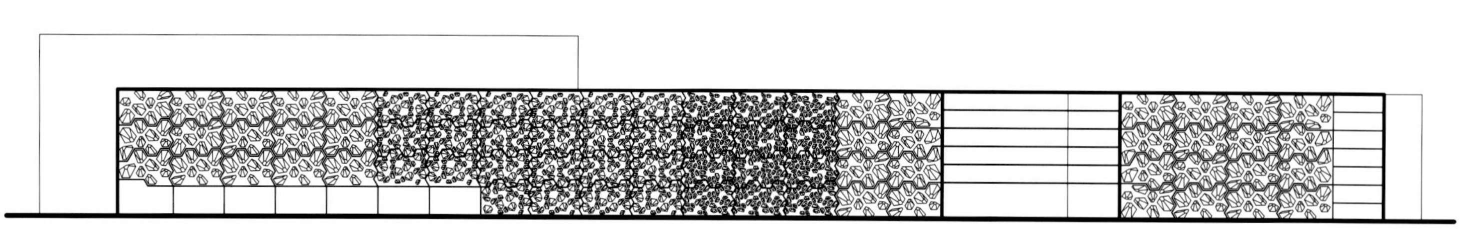

EAST ELEVATION

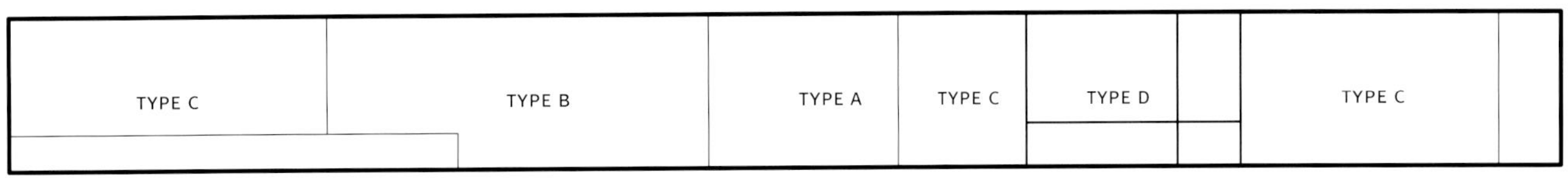

LAYOUT OF THE PANELS

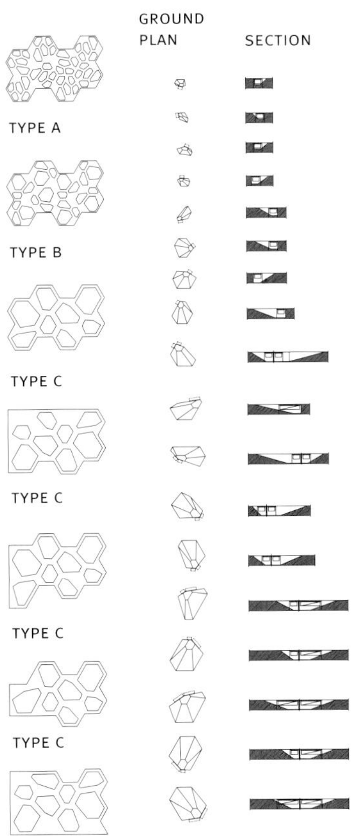

TYPES OF LAMP

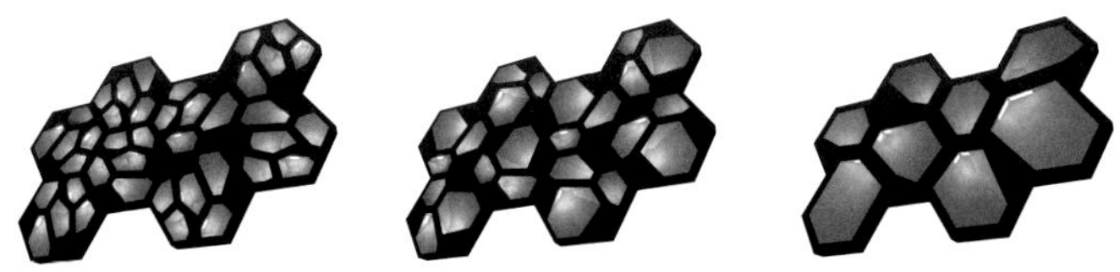

PANEL TYPE A   PANEL TYPE B   PANEL TYPE C

1. 36-WATT LAMP
2. OPENING
3. REFLECTOR
4. LIMIT OF THE DIRECTION OF THE LIGHTING
5. 10-, 13-, 18-, AND 26-WATT LAMPS

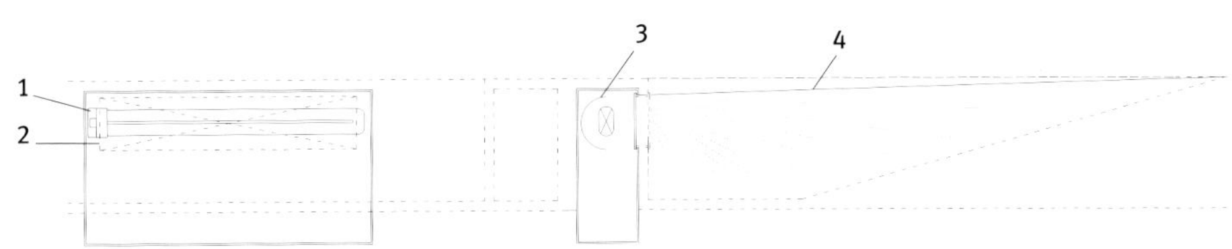

SECTION—LARGE-SCALE LIGHTING

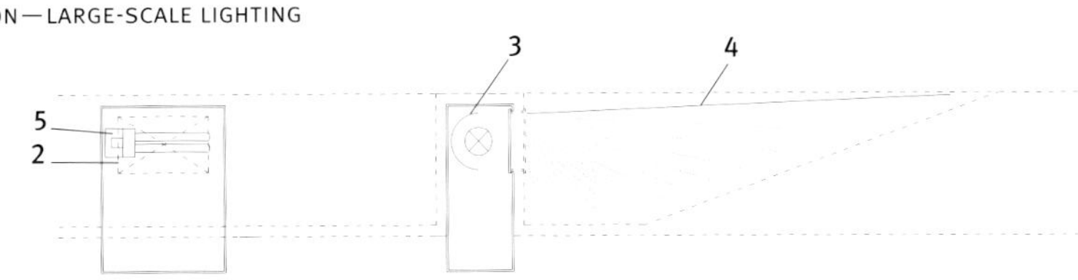

SECTION—SMALL-SCALE LIGHTING

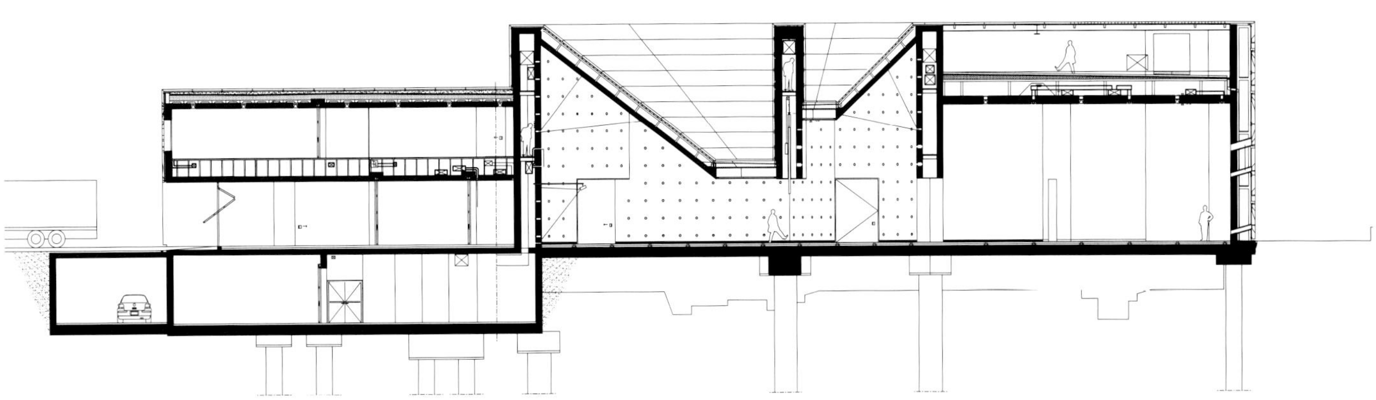

CROSS SECTION

The selection of materials ties in with the concept of an industrialized system, as the architects were aiming at spaces that evoked the idea of an "art factory." The interior tiles and walls will be made of concrete, and will thus be easy to build, maintain, and modify. The exterior (facades and roofs) will be clad with prefabricated GRC panels, while the arrangement of electrical, digital, audio, and lighting installations will facilitate connections throughout the building.

WHOSE SHAPE WAS
QUARRELED OVER
FOR MONTHS:
SHOULD WE ARBITRATE
LIFE AND DEATH
AROUND TABLE OR
SQUARE ONES?
Cybernet Network Limited

CARTER HOTEL
CARTER HOTEL
42
DUK
For Leasing Information Contact
Frank Gallo 212-399-3632
American Airlines Theatre

New 42nd Street Studios

PLATT BYARD DOVELL WHITE ARCHITECTS | NEW YORK, NY, 2000

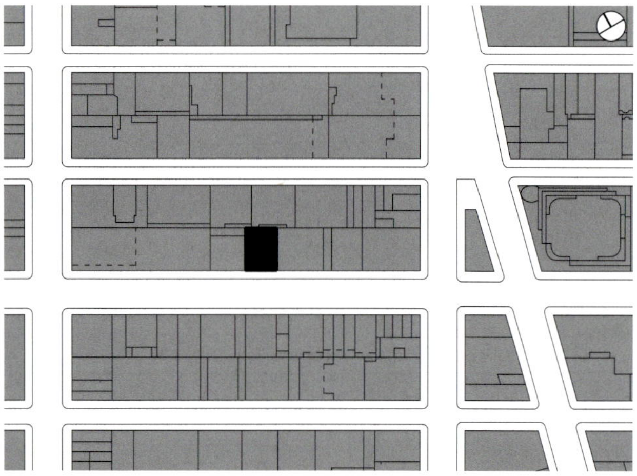

SITE PLAN

The building for the studios of the theater production company New 42nd Street Inc. is set on 42nd Street, between Times Square and Eighth Avenue. The architects from PBDW departed from the traditional commercial look of nearby architecture to create a project in keeping with the groundbreaking work of the artists rehearsing inside the building. Similarly, the design sought a different way to display the neon signs so typical of Times Square, while still fitting in with the character of the area.

Instead of using conventional signs, the Studios' facade is a collage of metal and glass, conceived as a large "light structure." Its base is fitted with dichroic panes of glass, set on top of a row of metal strips, while the west side is marked by a vertical tube of light 174 feet (53 m) high. At night, the building becomes a wash of light and motion, as the movements of the performers and the colorful spots of light on the facade merge through metal strips and transparent panes of glass.

The interior consists of five floors with twelve rehearsal rooms boasting high ceilings, superb acoustics, and a total absence of columns, plus another three floors containing offices used by various theater companies. There is also a black-box theater—an experimental auditorium with a seating capacity for 199 spectators—while the ground floor plays host to various commercial enterprises and leads to the foyer of the American Airlines Theater, which houses the Roundabout Theatre Company.

TYPE OF PROJECT **Educational facility**

LIGHTING **Anne Militello**

TOTAL SURFACE AREA **84,000 sq. ft. (7,804 m²)**

PHOTOS **© Elliot Kaufman, Charles A. Platt**

CARTER
HOTEL
CARTER
HOTEL
42
DUK
AmericanAirlinesTheatre

The facade of the dance studios was designed as a large expanse of light. During the day, the building merges into its context, but at night it stands out by the very austerity of its lighting, in contrast to the gaudiness of Times Square.

The light show begins at dusk and ends at 2 AM. A computer controls the images, which are introduced every day by means of pixel-mapping technology.

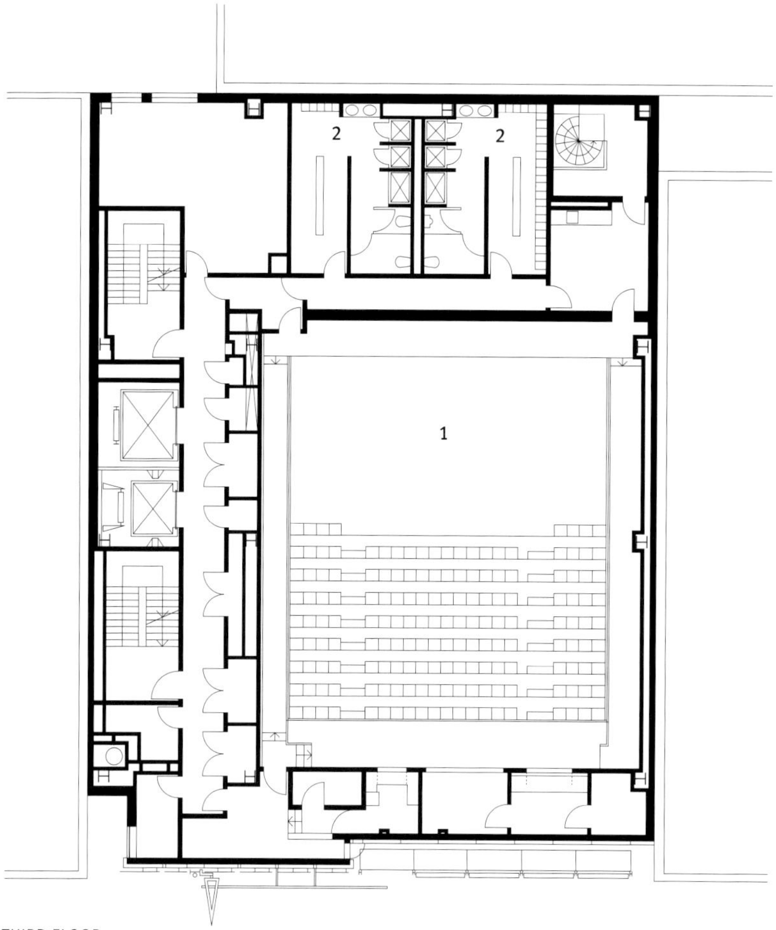

THIRD FLOOR

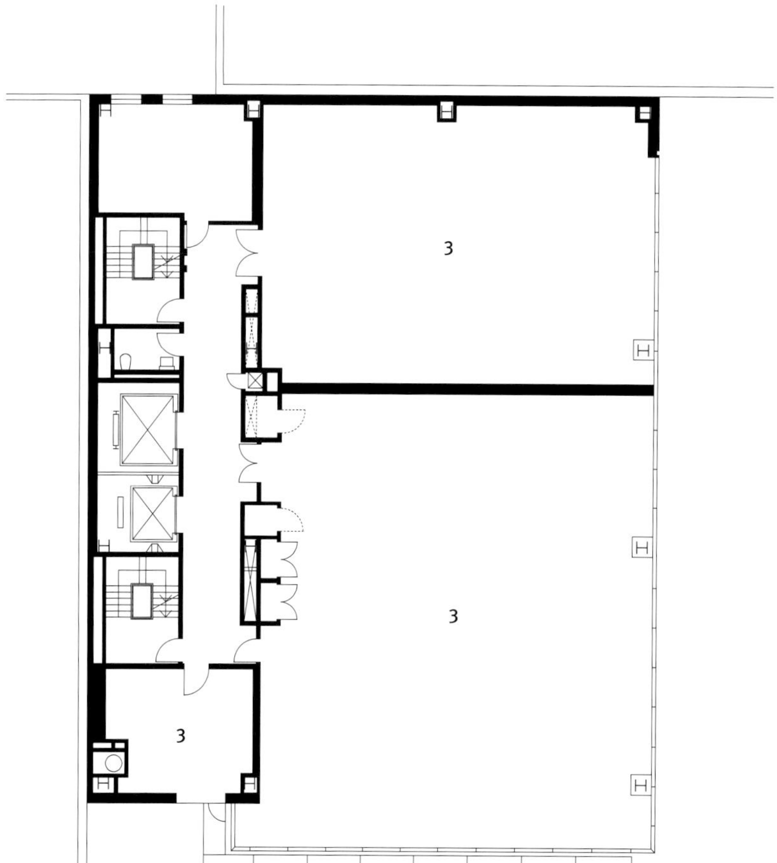

SEVENTH FLOOR

1. BLACK BOX THEATRE
2. RESTROOMS
3. REHERSAL STUDIOS

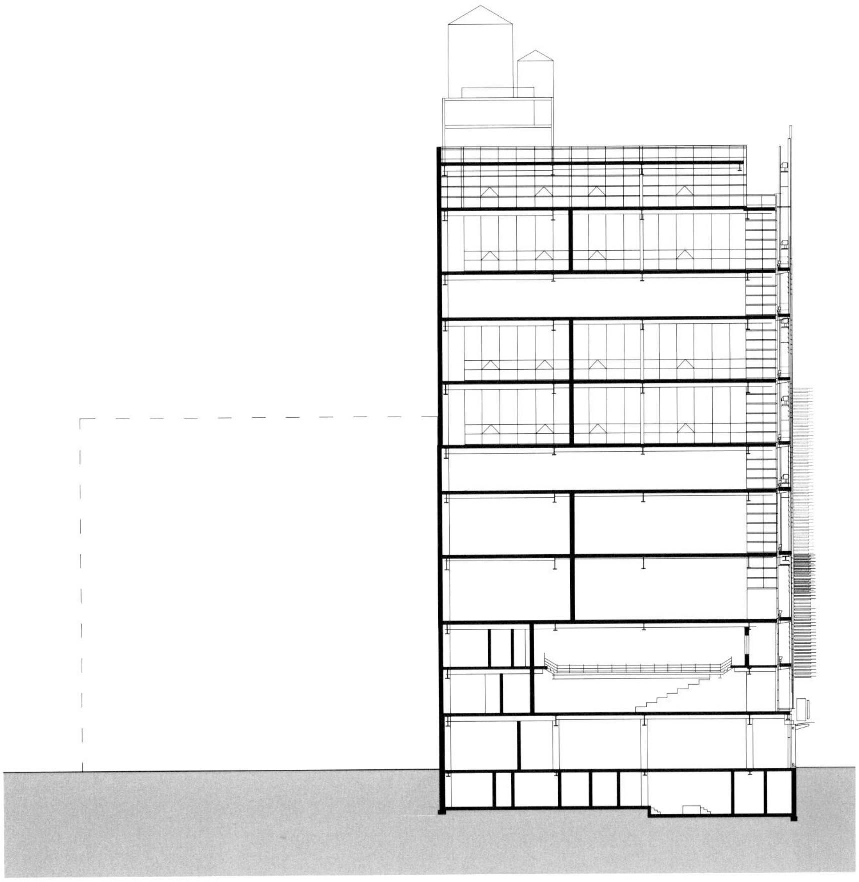

LONGITUDINAL SECTION

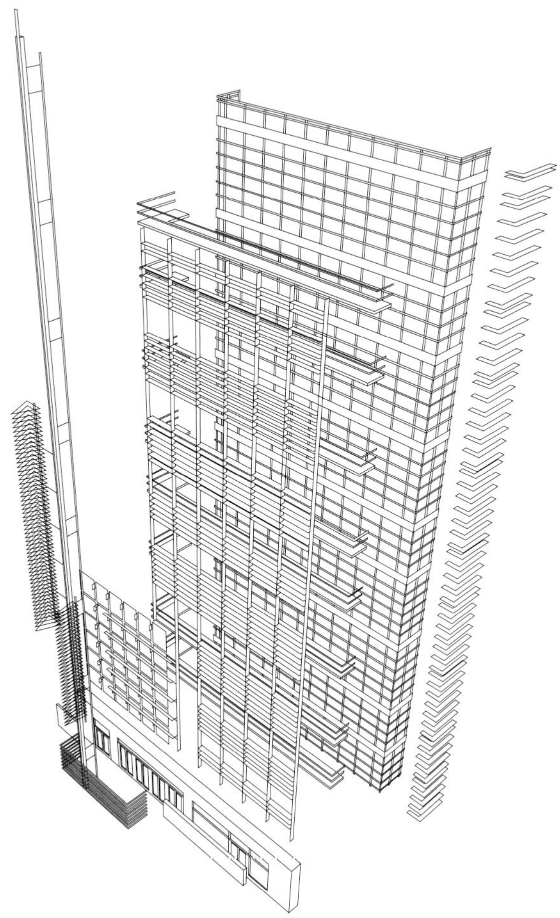

EXPLODED FACADE

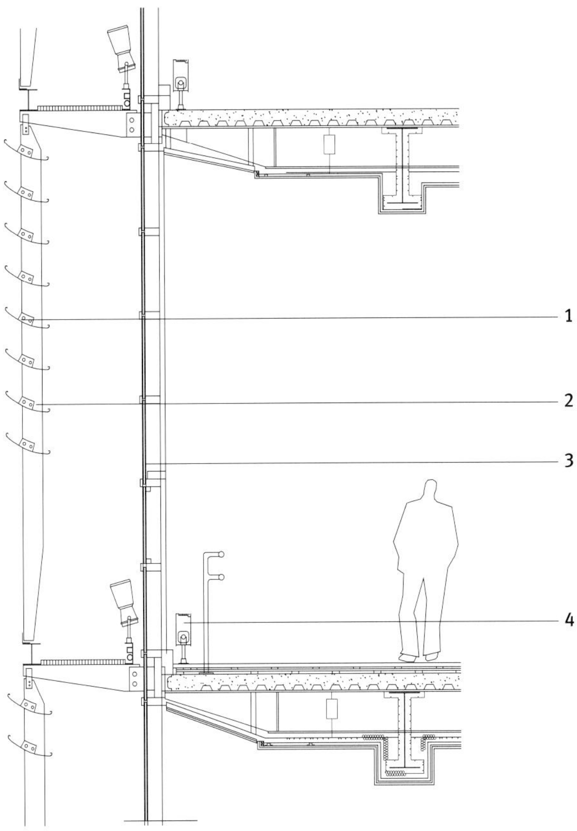

CONSTRUCTION DETAIL

1. VERTICAL STEEL SUPPORT
2. PERFORATED STAINLESS-STEEL WINGS
3. LIGHT SCREEN DIFFUSING
4. TUBE RADIATOR AND WINGS

The layout, materials, and colors in the interior spaces continue the idea of the collage underlying the main facade. The design also focuses on the problems common to dance studios, the main one being soundproofing that enables each room to be completely independent.

GreenPix

SIMONE GIOSTRA & PARTNERS ARCHITECTS | BEIJING, CHINA 2008

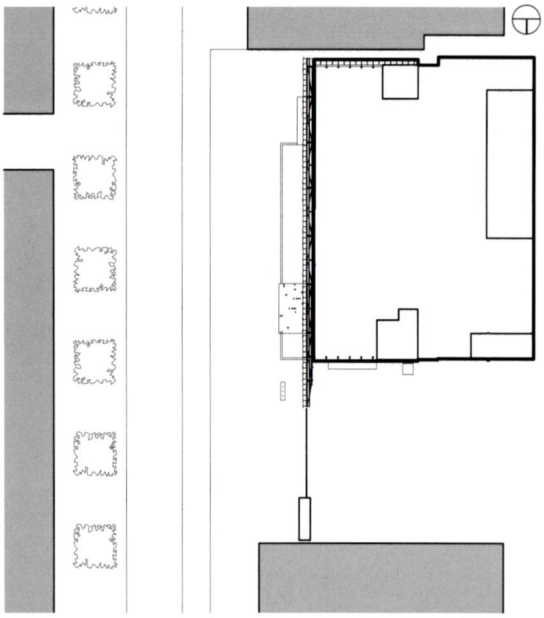

SITE PLAN

Simone Giostra and Arup designed a new facade for the Xicui Building, which is situated near the basketball and baseball venues for the 2008 Olympic Games in Beijing, China. The building is an opaque box containing a movie theater and an upmarket restaurant. One facade interacts with its surroundings by means of state-of-the-art digital technology. This facade, known as GreenPix, is a gigantic curtain wall consisting of 2,292 colored LEDs that comprise a low-resolution screen—an intelligent, self-sufficient skin that captures solar energy during the day, stores it in batteries, and uses it to generate light that same night.

The building faces one of Beijing's main avenues, and the huge poster effect created by GreenPix can be seen from a great distance. It displays abstract projections that are constantly changing: digital artworks, videos, animation, colored games, and even contents generated by users of the Xicui Building. This installation has attracted architects, engineers, computer programmers, and artists, and since it was unveiled in 2008 it has sought to promote emerging artists from Beijing and beyond. Its programming has involved independent curators, art institutions, media schools, galleries and corporations, collectors and art patrons.

TYPE OF PROJECT **Digital mural**

LIGHTING **Arup Lighting**

SURFACE AREA OF THE FACADE **20,000 sq. ft. (1,858 m²)**

PHOTOS **© Simone Giostra**

GreenPix represents the total integration of technology and architecture. This large screen has become a means for communicating new artistic concepts in a city that is itself a hub of urban experimentation.

During the day, the photovoltaic cells store the solar energy that is left over from activities undertaken inside the building; these panels also serve to shelter the interior from sunlight.

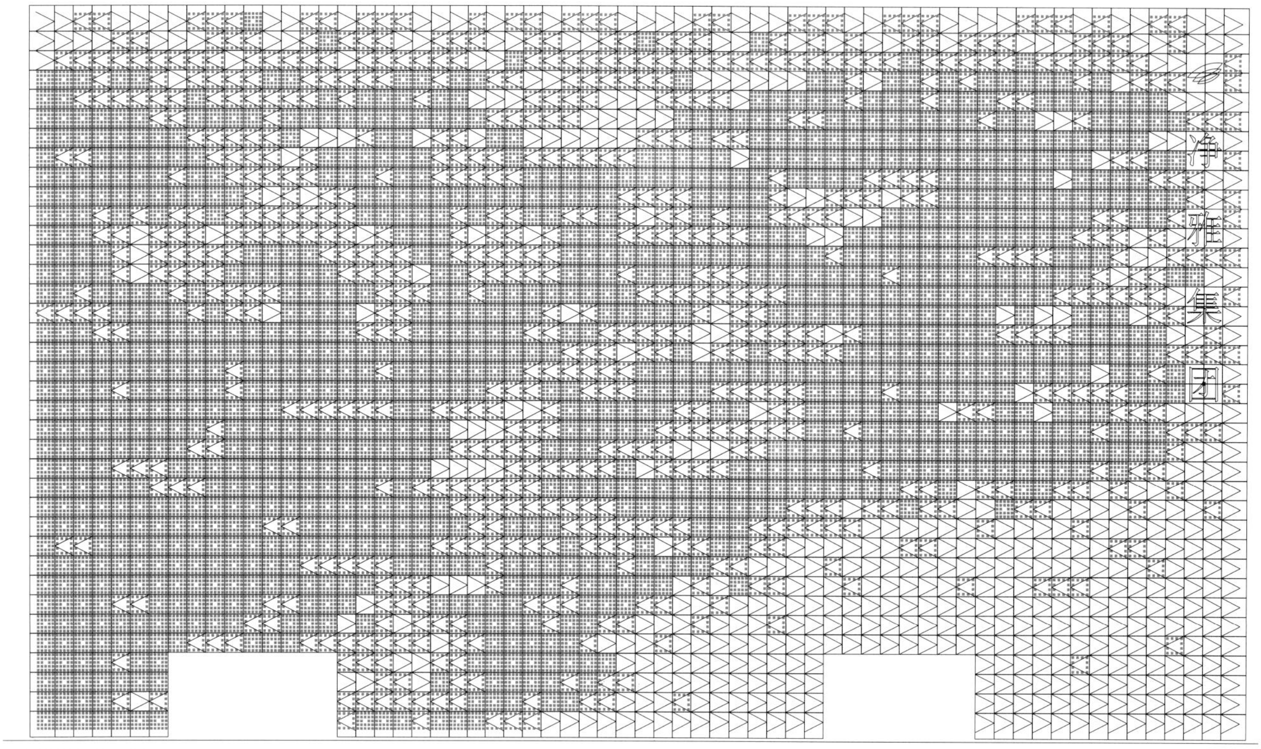

EAST ELEVATION

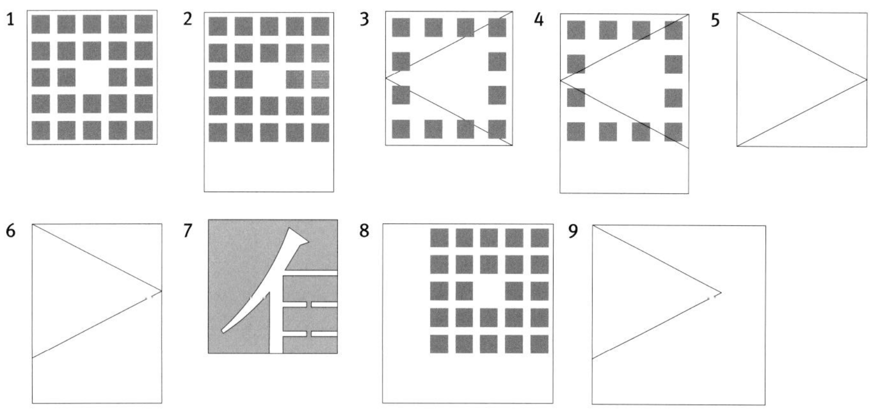

PANEL CHARACTERISTICS

1. LOW TRANSPARENCY
   24 PHOTOVOLTAIC CELLS
   1,027 PANELS WITH NO GRADIENT
2. LOW TRANSPARENCY
   24 PHOTOVOLTAIC CELLS
   45 PANELS WITH NO GRADIENT
3. MEDIUM TRANSPARENCY
   12 PHOTOVOLTAIC CELLS
   660 PANELS
   5° GRADIENT
4. MEDIUM TRANSPARENCY
   12 PHOTOVOLTAIC CELLS
   46 PANELS
   5° GRADIENT
5. HIGH TRANSPARENCY
   0 PHOTOVOLTAIC CELLS
   414 PANELS
   5° GRADIENT
6. HIGH TRANSPARENCY
   0 PHOTOVOLTAIC CELLS
   86 PANELS
   5° GRADIENT
7. SIGNALS
   0 PHOTOVOLTAIC CELLS
   20 PANELS WITH NO GRADIENT
8. HIGH TRANSPARENCY
   24 PHOTOVOLTAIC CELLS
   1 PANEL WITH NO GRADIENT
   5° GRADIENT
9. HIGH TRANSPARENCY
   0 PHOTOVOLTAIC CELLS
   3 PANELS
   5° GRADIENT

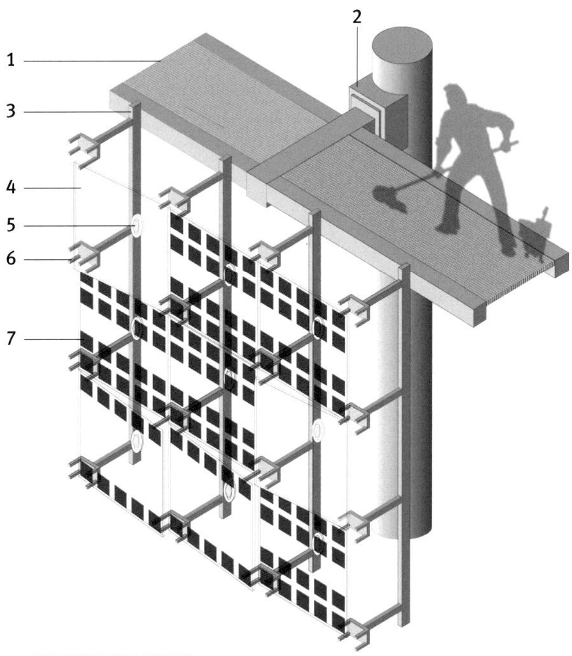

AXONOMETRIC DETAIL

1. MAINTENANCE WALKWAY
2. STRUCTURE FIXED TO THE PREEXISTING COLUMNS
3. VERTICAL BRACING
4. 3 x 35 IN. (89 x 890 MM) GLASS PANEL
5. LED LAMP
6. SPIDER BRACE
7. PHOTOVOLTAIC CELL

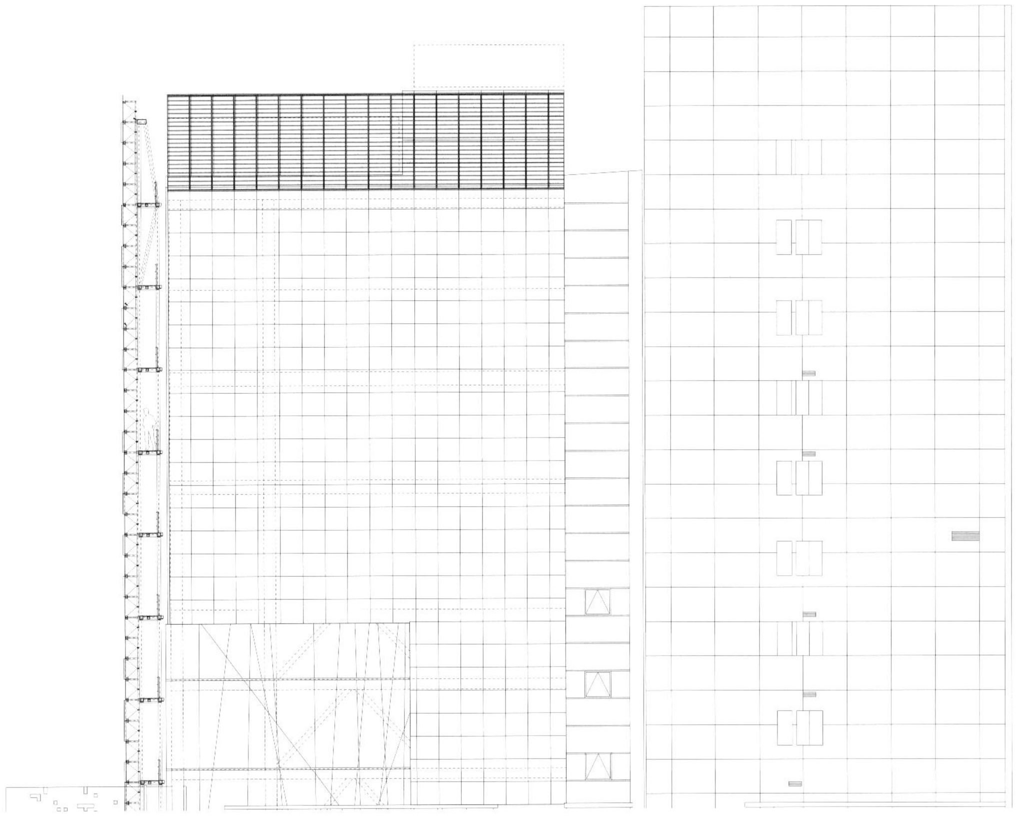

NORTH ELEVATION

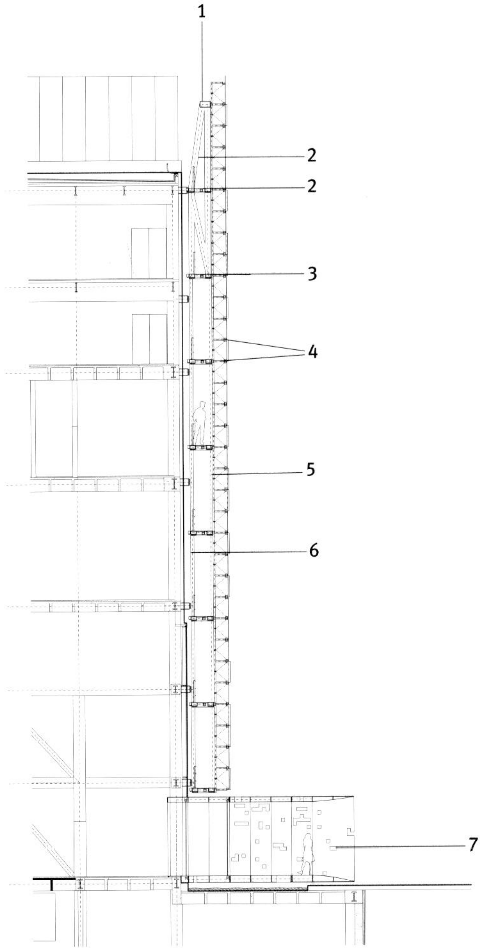

1. HOLLOW ENTRANCE 16 X 8 IN. (400 X 200 MM)
2. HOLLOW STEEL FRAME 6 X 6 IN. (150 X 150 MM)
3. MAINTENANCE WALKWAY
4. SUPPORT OF VARIOUS LENGTHS FOR GLASS PANES
5. VERTICAL BRACING
6. VERTICAL STEEL REINFORCEMENT 10 X 6 IN. (250 X 150 MM)
7. ENTRANCE TO THE BUILDING

SECTION OF THE FACADE

A Chinese firm, assisted by two experienced German manufacturers, developed a new technology to create the photovoltaic panels that make up the facade. This involved laminated polycrystal cells placed between the glass panes of the wall. The surface density was varied by combining three textures of differing degrees of roughness, resulting in glass of a low, medium, or high transparency. This change in density allows natural light to filter through according to the requirements of the lighting program, thereby reducing the accumulation of heat and transforming excess solar radiation into energy for the screen. Translucent diffusors were installed behind the photovoltaic panels to blur the light sources and increase the illuminated area on all the panels.

In short, a complex system was created to make the facade behave like an organic ecosystem that reproduced the climatic cycle running from day to night. Similarly, Simone Giostra drew on the characteristics of a coastal landscape to design the large screen, and he set some of the panels that make up the facade at an angle of 5 degrees in order to duplicate the constant flickering of lights reflected in the sea. He also added a maintenance area that combines with the curtain wall of the screen, giving the project a depth of over 6.6 feet (2 m).

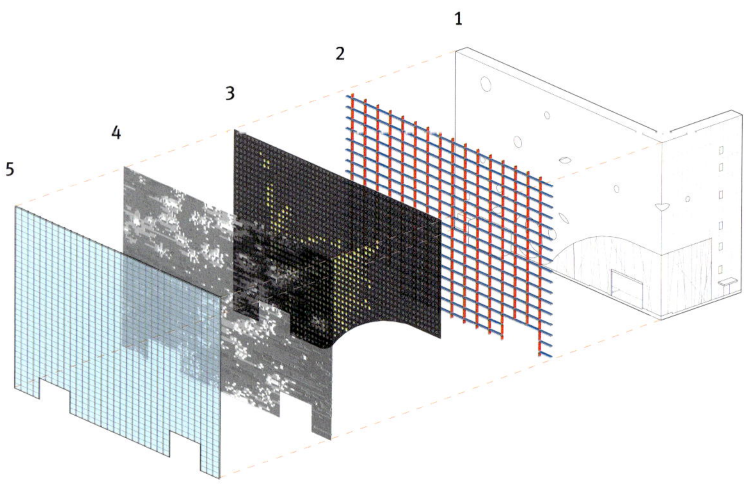

DIAGRAM OF THE LAYERS OF THE FACADE

1. PRINTS ON THE FACADE
2. REINFORCEMENTS AND CLAMPS
3. LED LAMPS
4. PHOTOVOLTAIC CELLS
5. GLASS

1. LED LAMP
2. STAINLESS-STEEL SAFETY CABLES
3. LED CONTROL BOXES
4. ALUMINUM GRILLE
5. HORIZONTAL SUPPORT FOR LEDS
6. VERTICAL STEEL BRACING 3 X 2 IN. (80 X 40 MM)
7. SPIDER BRACE

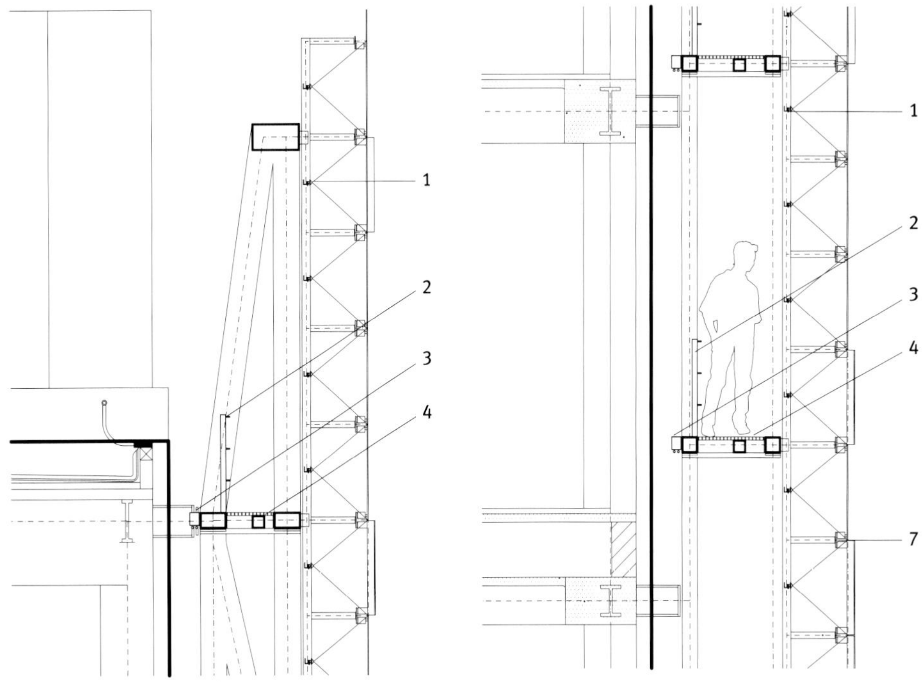

CONSTRUCTION DETAILS

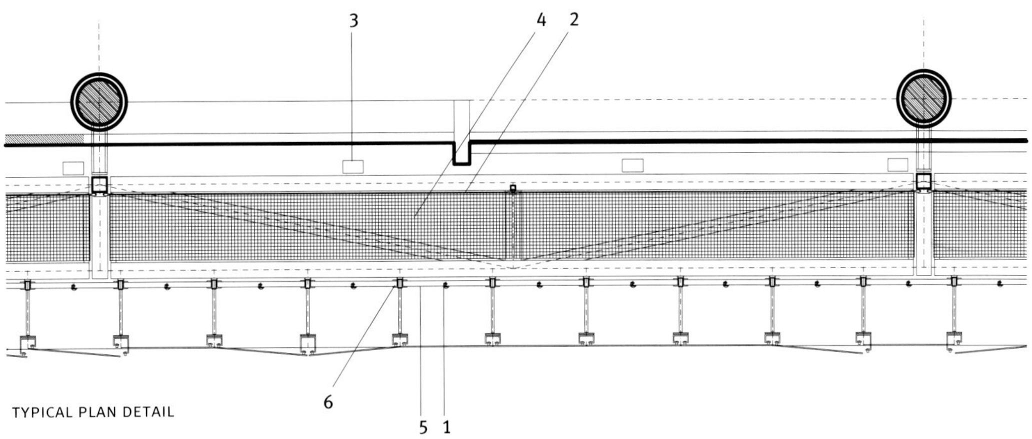

TYPICAL PLAN DETAIL

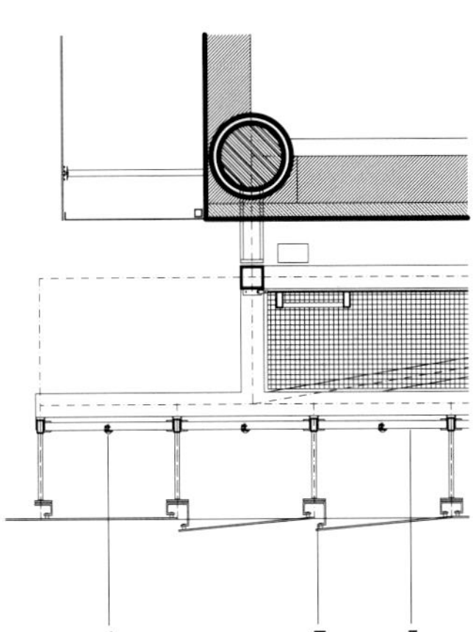

PLAN DETAIL SOUTH END

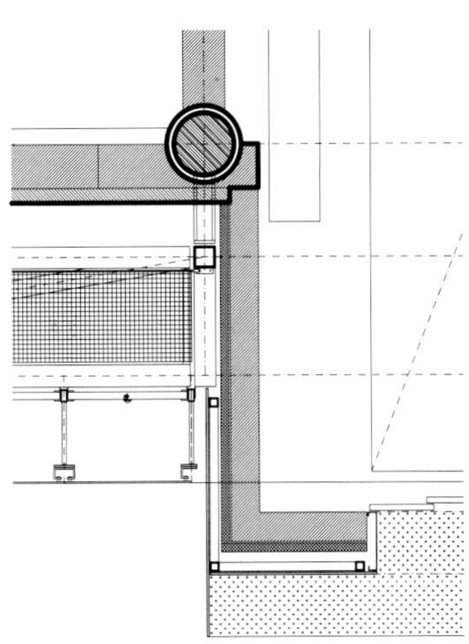
PLAN DETAIL ELEVATOR

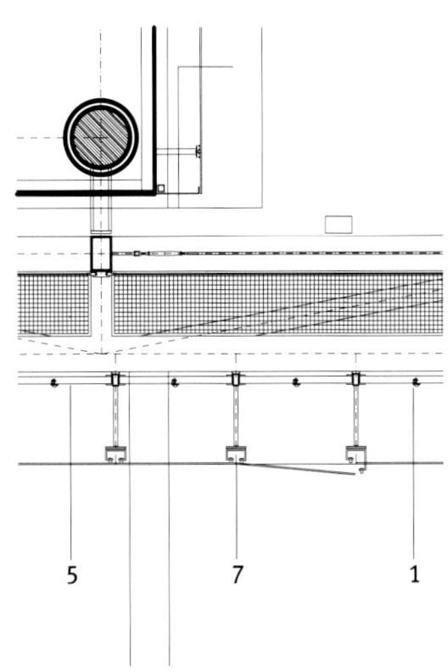

PLAN DETAIL NORTH END

During the day the facade produces energy, which goes on to be consumed at night. The screen then becomes a huge beacon and the building evolves into a new experience in Beijing's nighttime landscape.

With this project, Giostra sought to emphasize the fusion of digital technology and environmental reaction as a new way of creating architecture.

Club Nox

METRO ARQUITETURA AND JULIANO DUBEUX | RECIFE, BRAZIL 2006

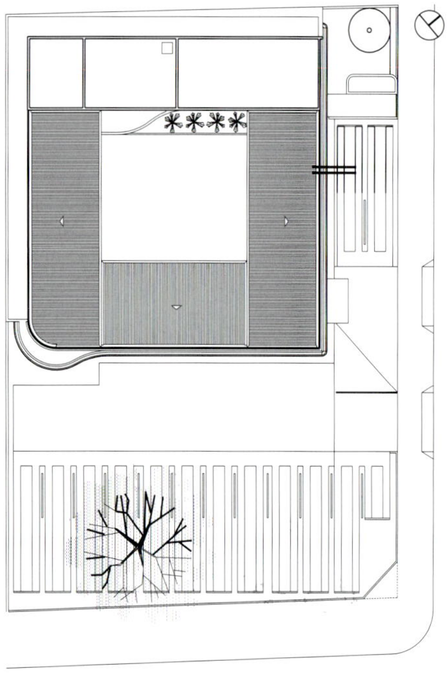

SITE PLAN

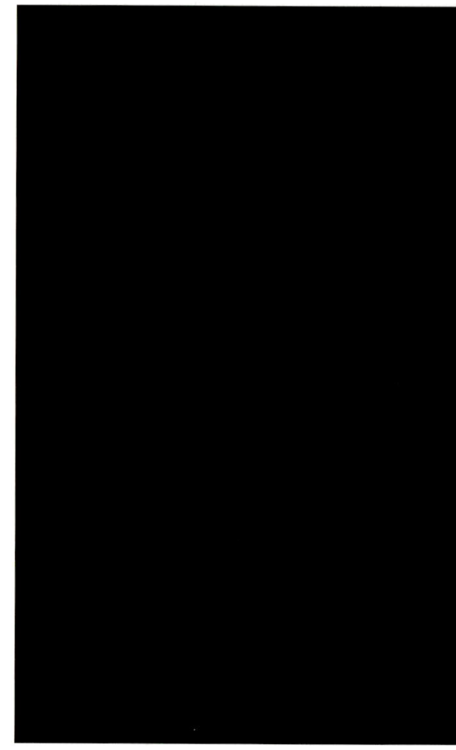

Club Nox has become a reference point in Recife, both for its location at a corner on one of the city's main avenues and for its original approach to discotheque design. The building was conceived as two complementary but contrasting parts: a dance floor on the ground floor, marked by a large box made of weathering steel; and a bar on the upper floor with an expansive terrace endowed with panoramic views. The steel box surrounds a protruding glass volume that contains the bar. The lighting in this volume is constantly changing color and so creates a host of different configurations in its interior.

The high ceiling and inner walls of the dance floor are covered by a translucent skin that appears to peel off and move to the rhythm of the music. This membrane is made of glass-fiber strips that are interwoven to form a large mesh which allows light to pass through while also reflecting the vibrations of sound. This mesh is lit by a complex system of 256 groups of lamps fitted with LED diodes, which are controlled in their turn by a DMX (Digital MultipleX) system that makes it possible to combine more than 16 million colors to create varied color schemes and movements.

TYPE OF PROJECT **Discotheque**

LIGHTING **Metro Arquitetura with Lonardi Dona and Edite Araújo**

TOTAL SURFACE AREA **12,000 sq. ft. (1,100 m²)**

PHOTOS **© Leonardo Finotti**

The glass volume protruding from the large steel box reflects the concept of continual transformation underlying this project. The soft, shifting light patterns reflected through this prism transform the building into an enormous lamp that has become an urban landmark.

nox

nox

nox

162

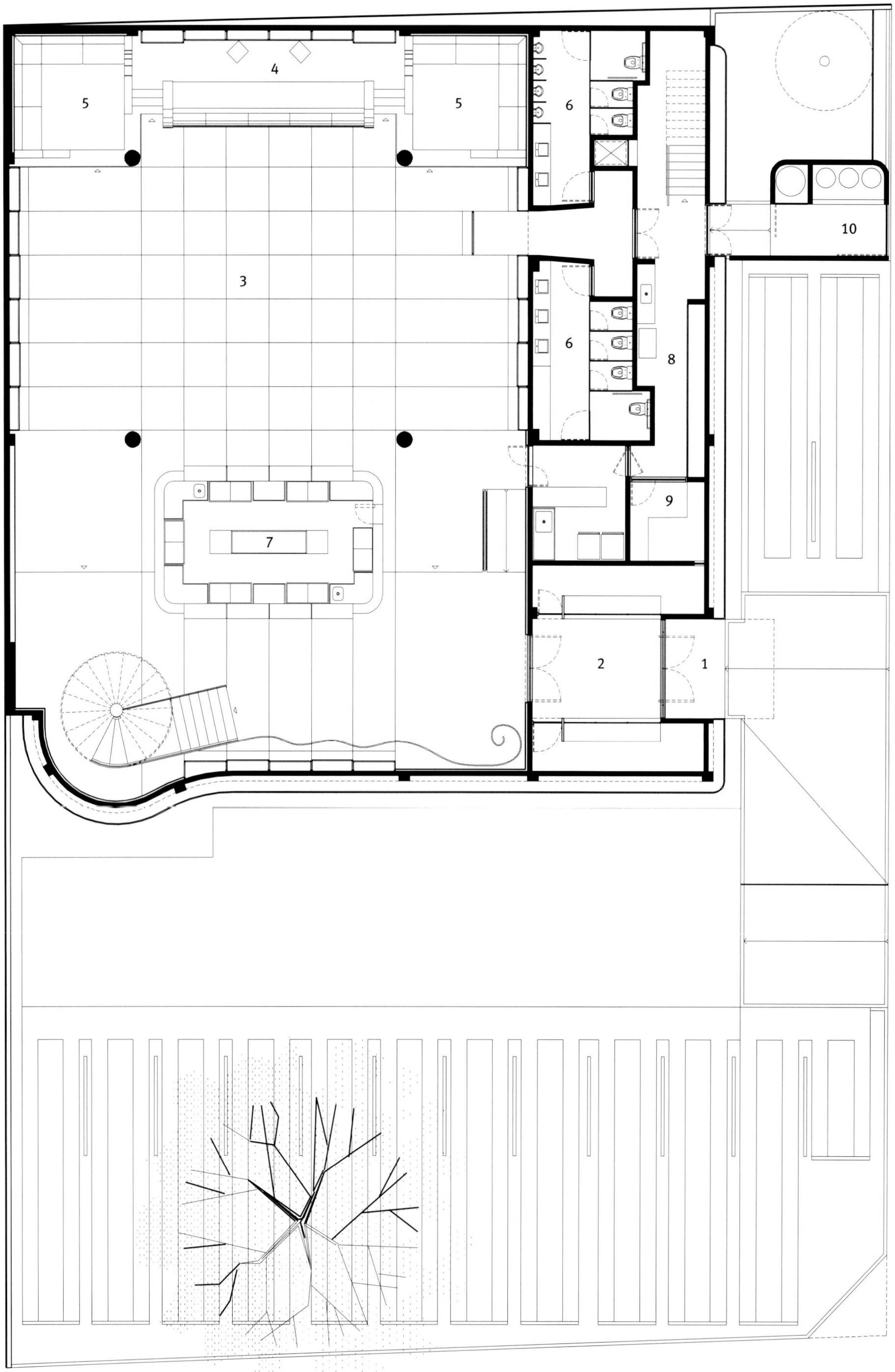

GROUND FLOOR

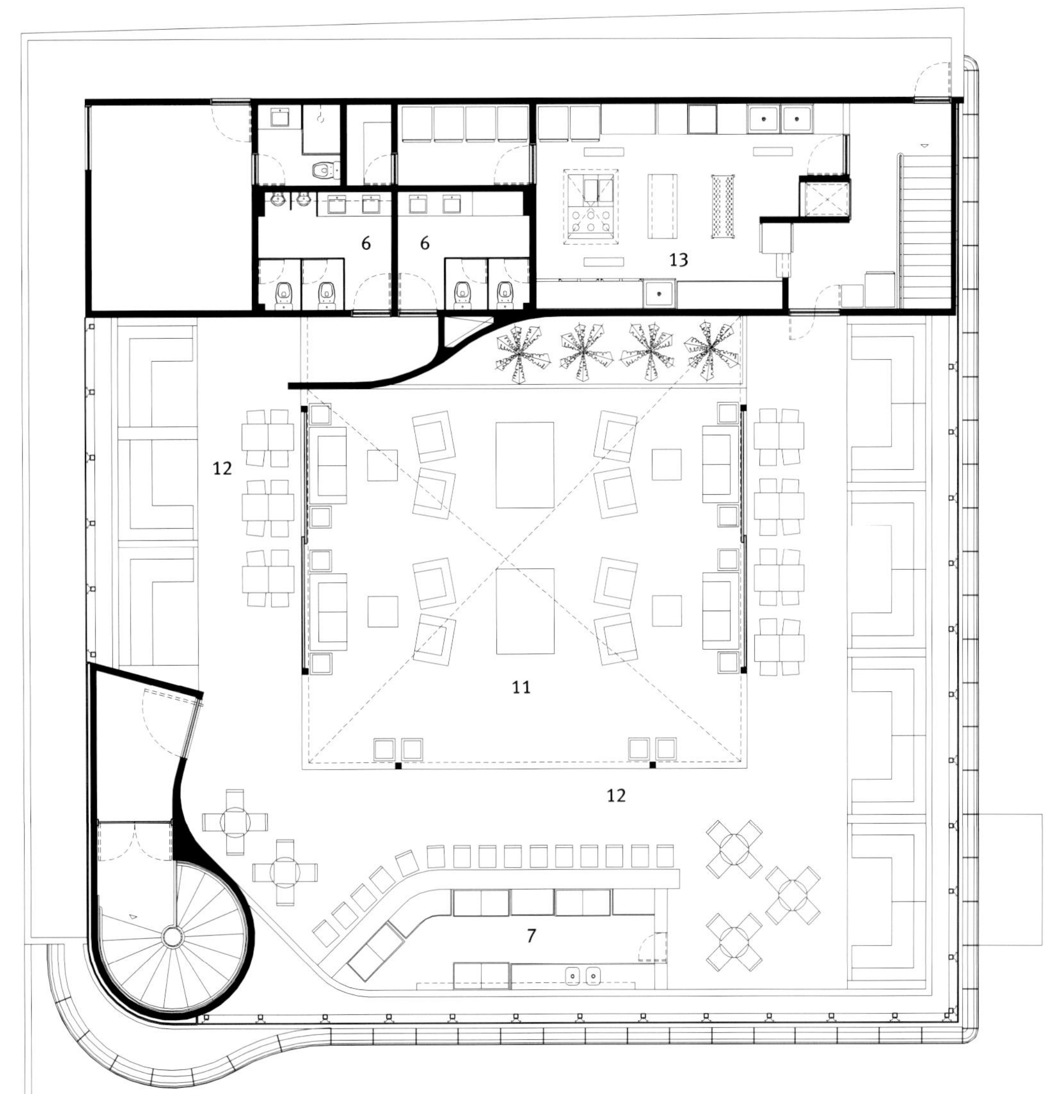

SECOND FLOOR

1. ENTRANCE
2. RECEPTION
3. DANCE FLOOR
4. DJ CABIN
5. VIP AREAS
6. RESTROOMS
7. BAR
8. STORE
9. OFFICE
10. SERVICE ENTRANCE
11. OPEN-AIR LOUNGE
12. ROOFED LOUNGE
13. KITCHEN

The project was commissioned by three young businessmen, two of whom are professional DJs. The DJ's booth is set to one side of the dance floor and is large enough to hold bands and their equipment, if necessary. The organization of the spaces and the sound system was of primary importance in designing Club Nox. A line-array configuration was used for the sound, meaning that the speakers were stacked vertically to control the direction of the sound more effectively and achieve uniform coverage. Moreover, the dance floor area is reinvented every time there is a variation in the lighting—in itself a result of changes in the music. This constant transformation is also evident outside through the glass volume on the top floor.

The upper bar area is totally white, fitted out with couches, tatamis, and an array of plants. It is a quiet place for dining and chatting—in contrast to the high energy of the dance floor—and the views allow the city itself to become an integral part of the design.

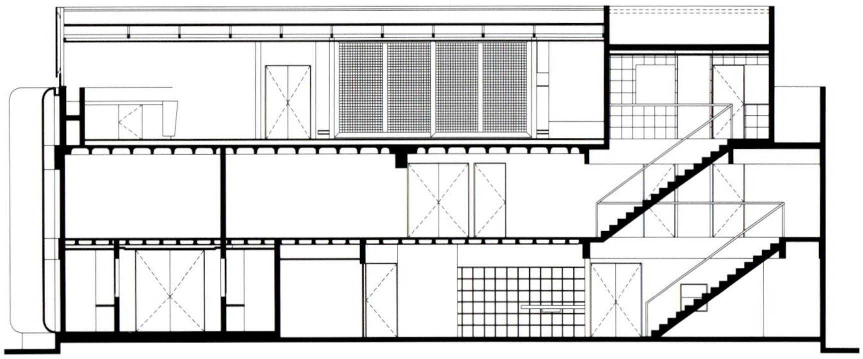

CROSS SECTION—ENTRANCE

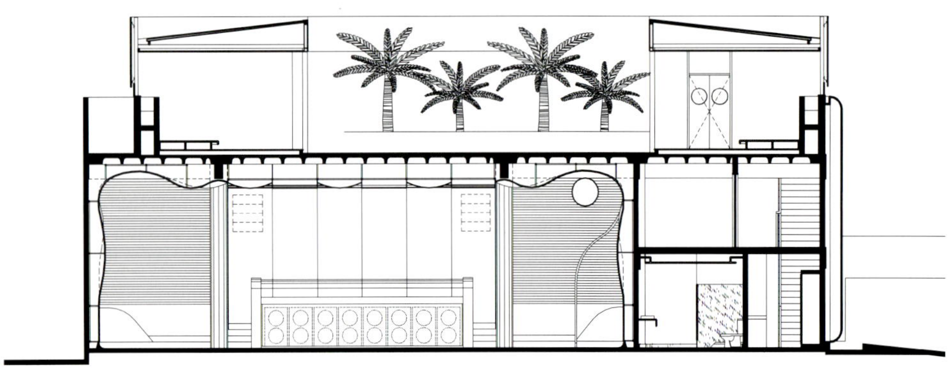

LONGITUDINAL SECTION—TOWARD DJ CABIN

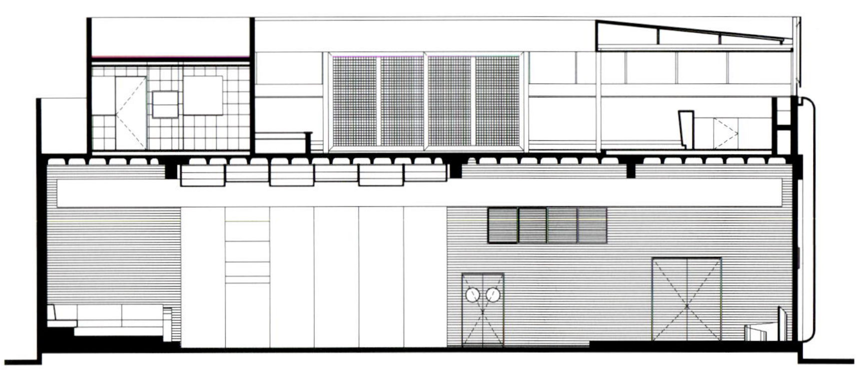

CROSS SECTION—DANCE FLOOR

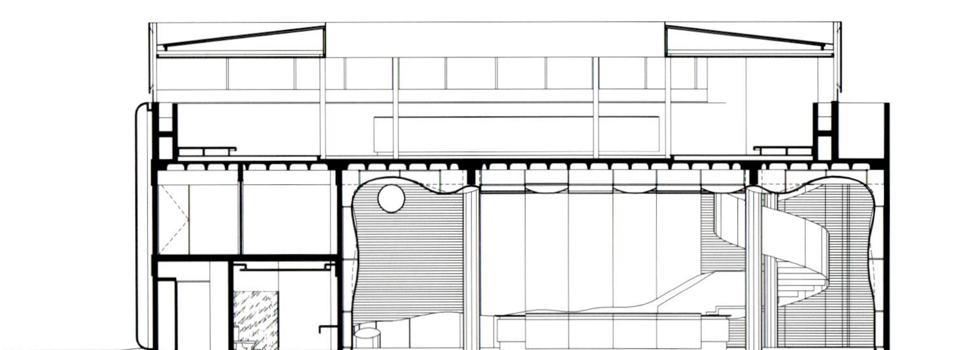

LONGITUDINAL SECTION—TOWARD GROUND-FLOOR BAR

Movement and colors are the elements that bestow individuality on the different floors, and on the architectural composition in general. The choice of materials and colors was determined by the activities that take place within each particular space.

The relaxing music on the top floor is complemented by light that circulates through the setting before shining outside via the glass prism.

Luxembourg Philharmonic

CHRISTIAN DE PORTZAMPARC | LUXEMBOURG, LUXEMBOURG 2005

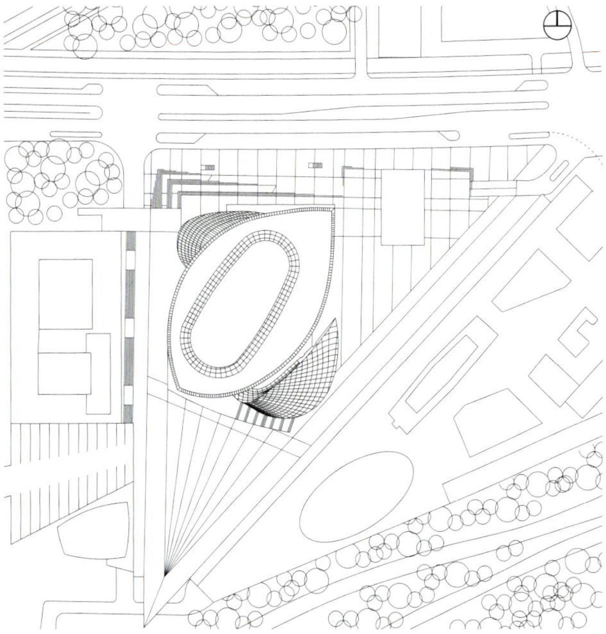

SITE PLAN

Christian de Portzamparc's building for the Luxembourg Philharmonic emerged from an international competition organized in 1997. It is situated in Kirchberg, a neighborhood northeast of the city center given over to offices and European Union institutions. The Philharmonic is set in the middle of the Place de l'Europe, a triangular square with one side overlooking the old city, the second facing the area's main thoroughfare, and the final one giving onto a road that was under construction. The elliptical shape and the large peristyle with 827 steel columns leading to the main foyer contrast with the form of the square and the surrounding buildings. The program is divided into three spaces: a 1,500-seat concert hall; another 300-seat hall for chamber music; and an open space for contemporary music, with seating capacity for 120 people.

The peristyle, with its thin 56-foot (17-m) high steel columns, frames the entrance to the building. This design allows light from the interior to filter outside, transforming the building into a huge lantern. Inside, the walls around the main auditorium fold to form niches that change color over the course of the night in accordance with a sequential scale.

A large bridge in the interior provides links with the three halls and the administrative offices. The concert hall is distinguished by eight levels of balconies arranged around the orchestra pit. The 300-seat hall is an external volume that seems to grow out of the larger hall, while the open space, spread over 2,300 square feet (211 m^2), is set between the ground floor and the basement.

The glass volume, which juts out of the large steel box containing the project, highlights the architect's concept of constant transformation. The changes in soft lighting reflected through this prism turn the building into an enormous urban lamp, and thus a reference point for the city.

TYPE OF PROJECT **Cultural facility**

LIGHTING **Christian de Portzamparc**

TOTAL SERVICE AREA **215,000 sq. ft. (20,000 m²)**

PHOTOS **© Christian Richters**

The colored lights that change on the wall of the vestibule gallery are a special characteristic of this building and the culmination of an investigation that began twenty years ago. Christian de Portzamparc began thinking of this in 1986 in the design of the auditorium at La Villette in Paris; the colored light reflects differently according to the angles of inclination of the planes that form the niches.

174

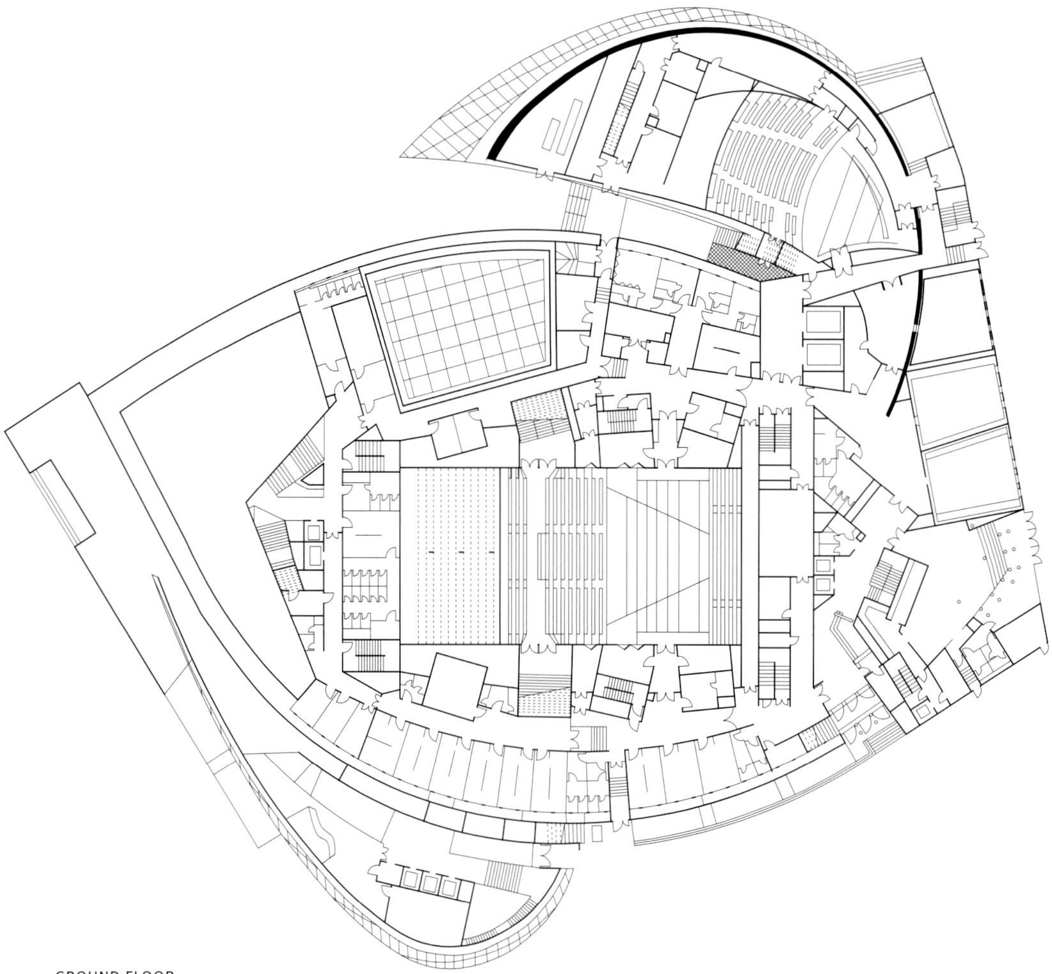

GROUND FLOOR

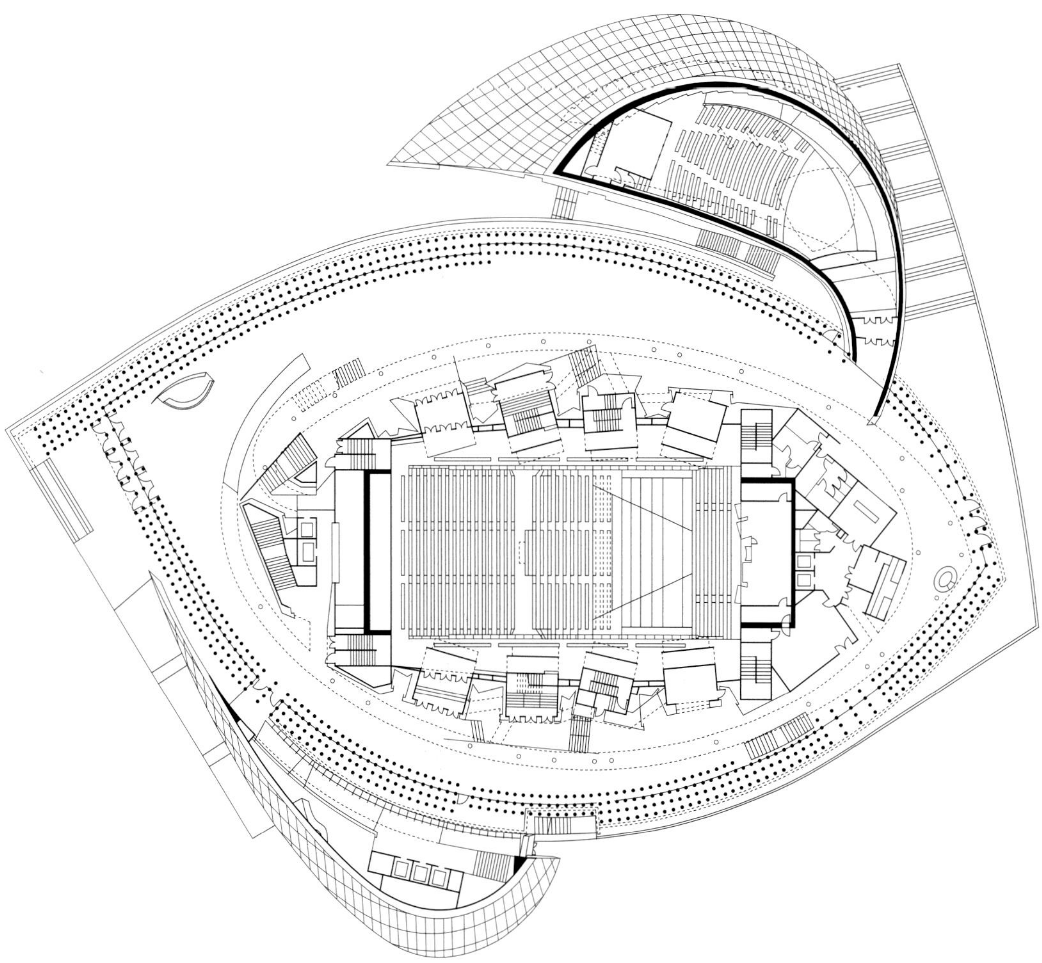

SECOND FLOOR

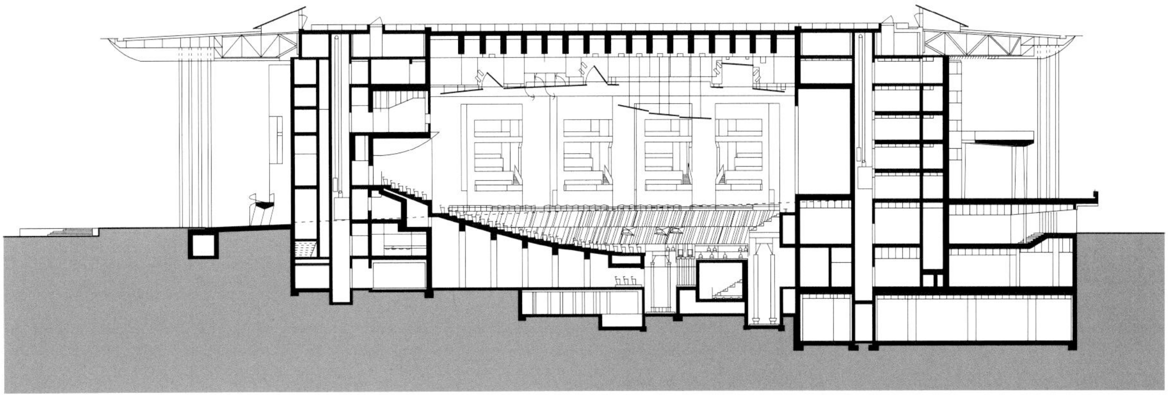

LONGITUDINAL SECTION

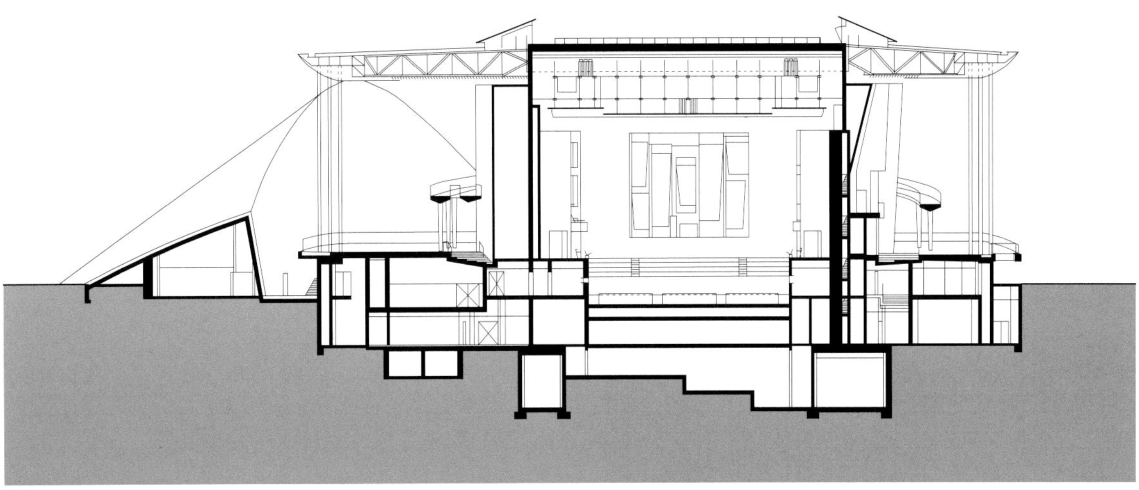

CROSS SECTION

color

180
Didden Village | Rotterdam, Netherlands
MVRDV

190
Atrium—University of Jussieu | Paris, France
Périphériques architectes

202
Fire station | Houten, Netherlands
Philippe Samyn and Partners

214
Montreal Congress Palace | Montreal, Canada
Tétrault, Dubuc, Saia et associés, and Hal Ingberg

222
Els Colors Kindergarten | Manlleu, Spain
RCR Arquitectes

234
The Reece School | New York, NY
Platt Byard Dovell White Architects

242
Parque Explora | Medellín, Colombia
Alejandro Echeverri Restrepo

254
Netherlands Institute of Sound and Vision | Hilversum, Netherlands
Neutelings Riedijk Architecten

266
Agora Theater | Lelystad, Netherlands
UNStudio

Didden Village

MVRDV | ROTTERDAM, NETHERLANDS 2007

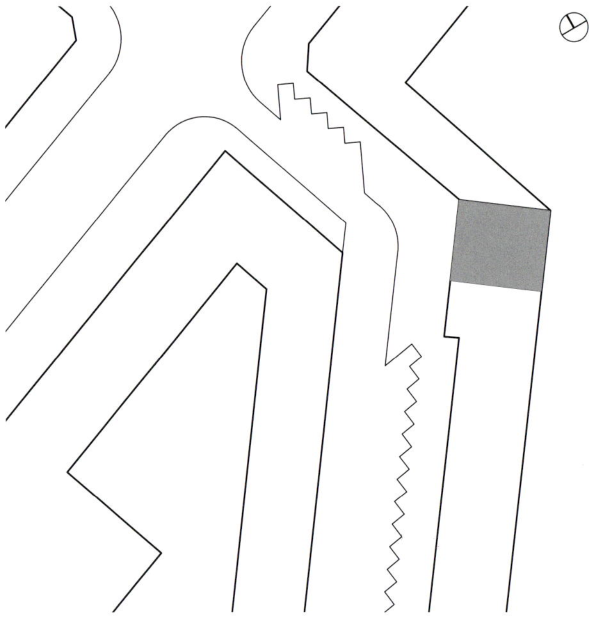

SITE PLAN

The Didden family asked the studio of Winy Maas, Jacob van Rijs, and Nathalie de Vries to enlarge their home, which was at the top of a three-story building in an old residential area in Rotterdam. The architects treated the bedrooms as separate homes, in order to optimize the privacy of each family member. These "houses" form a small town, complete with squares and streets, which stands out in the city like the top of a major monument.

In the opinion of the architects, the concept of Didden Village can become a model for handling density in old areas in a city. In this respect, the project has served to breathe new life into roof terraces, turning them into a distinctive feature of a neighborhood. Furthermore, this approach made it possible to ascertain the cost of putting a new structure on top of a preexisting one and providing this extension with the services it requires. In fact, these costs proved considerably lower than those usually found at ground level.

Didden Village is surrounded by high walls, with long windows that frame the project on the roof terrace. Life in this small "village" is enhanced by tables, open-air showers, benches, and trees distributed around the volumes. A layer of blue polyurethane alters the Rotterdam panorama by seemingly adding a new patch of sky.

TYPE OF PROJECT **Housing**

COLOR **Kunststof Coatings Nederland B.V. Zevenhuizen NL**

TOTAL SURFACE AREA **Extension of 484 sq. ft. (45 m²)**
and roof terrace of 1,300 sq. ft. (120 m²)

PHOTOS **© Rob 't Hart**

ELEVATIONS

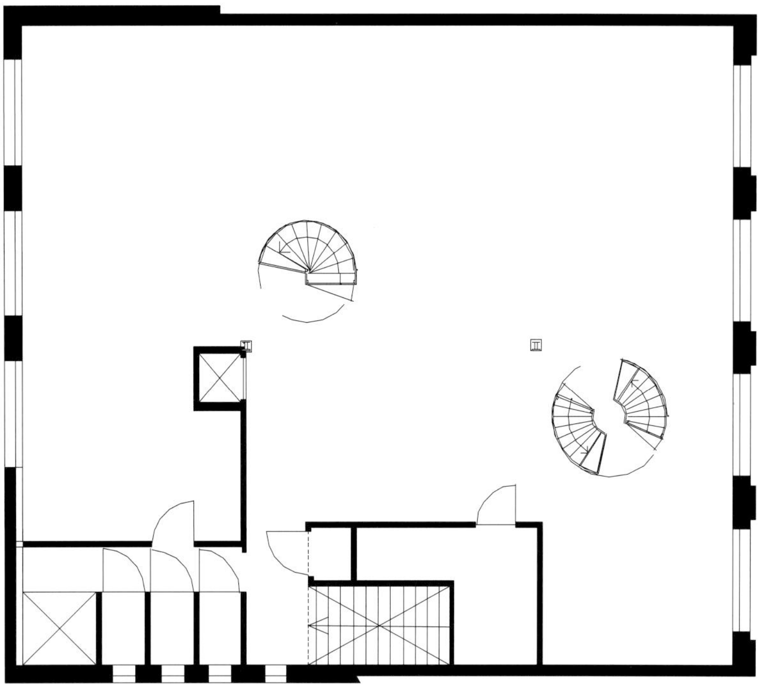

PLAN OF EXISTING FLOOR

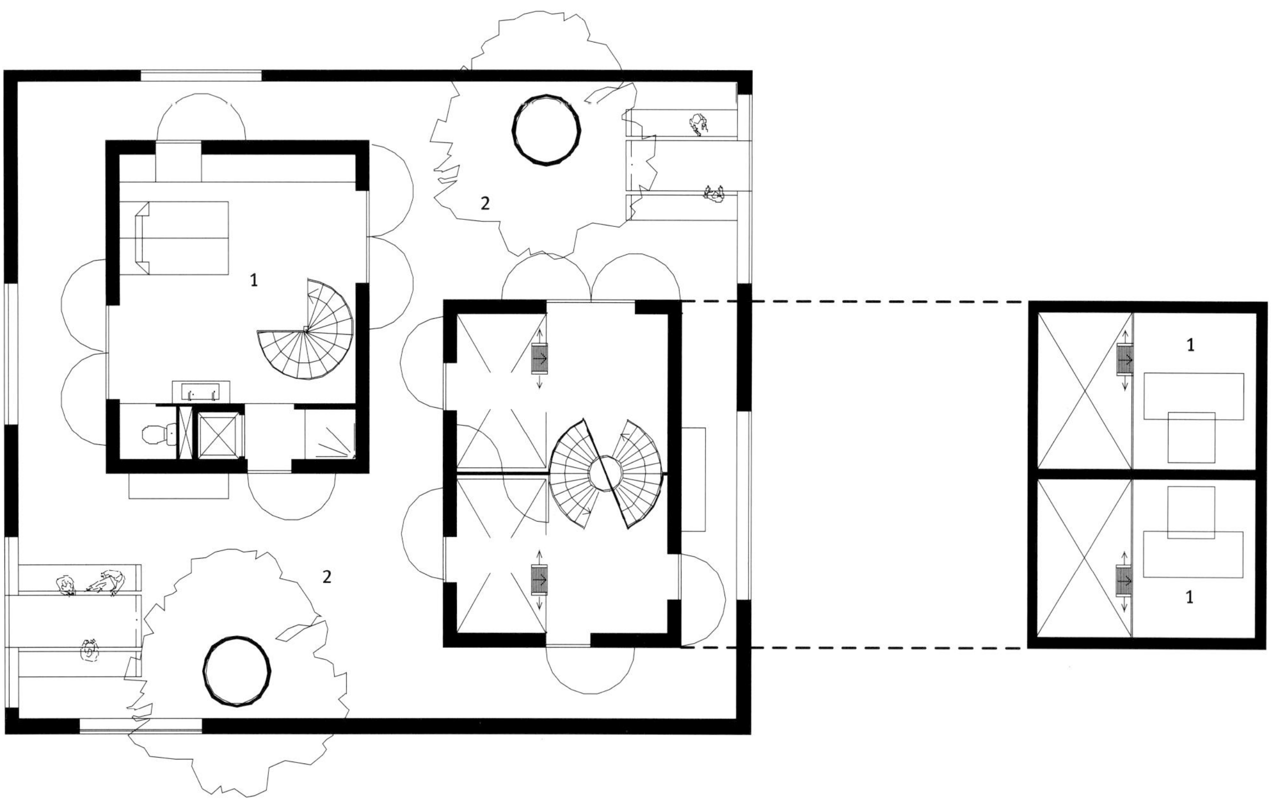

PLAN WITH EXTENSION

1. BEDROOMS
2. ROOF TERRACE — COMMON AREA

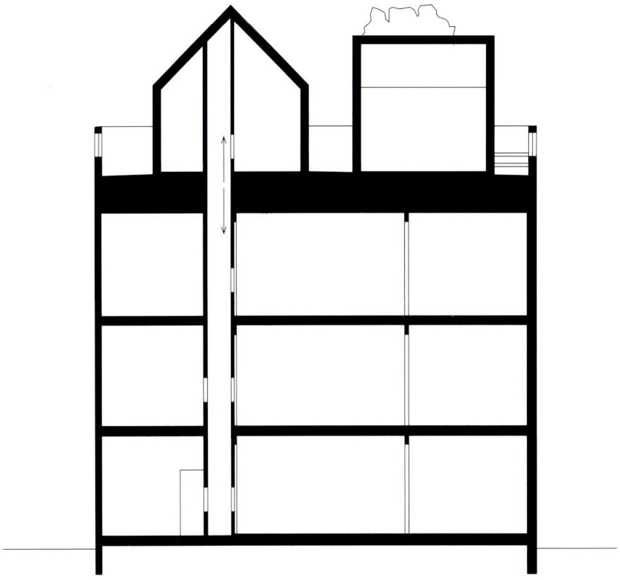

SECTION

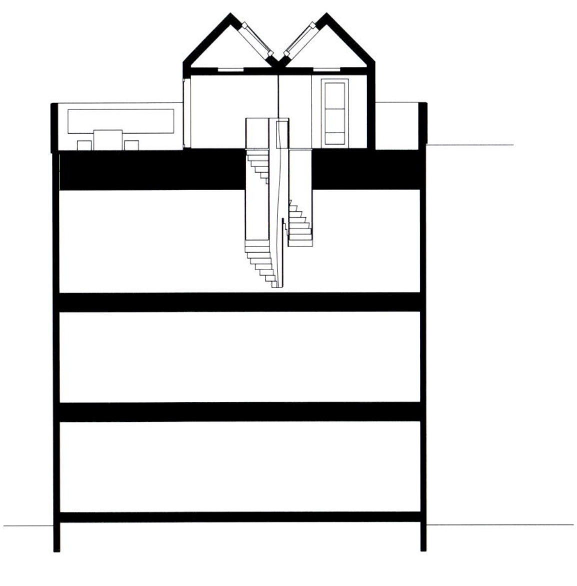

SECTION

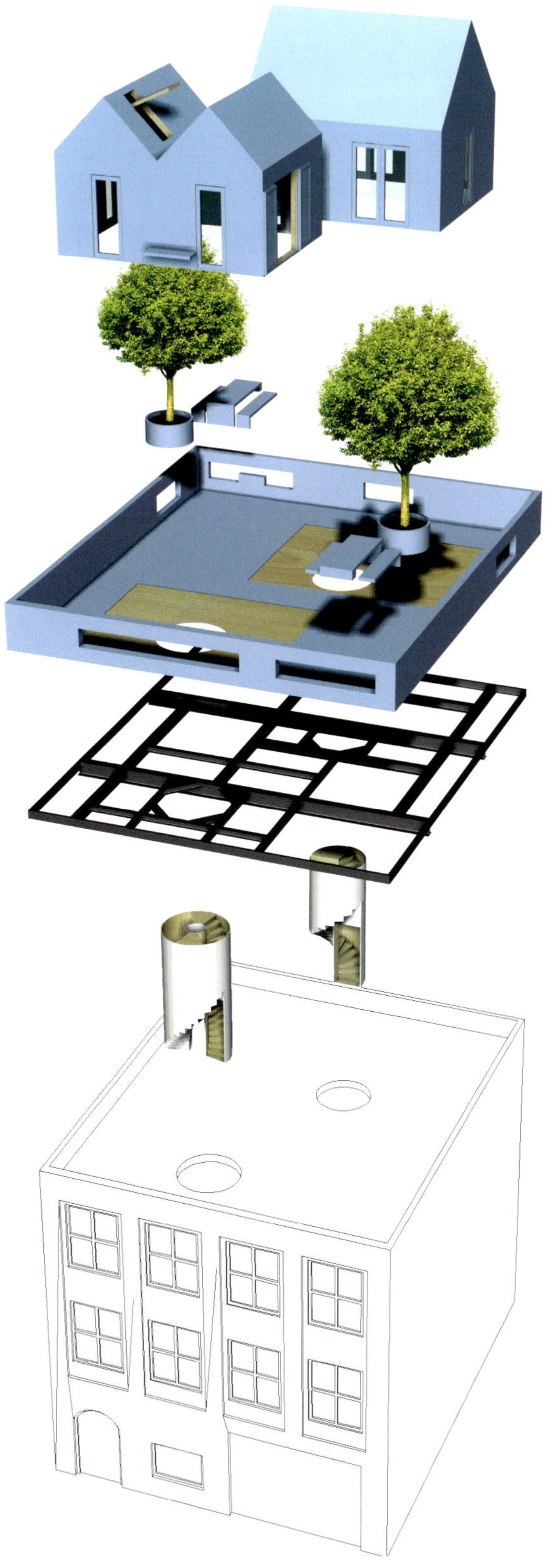

DIAGRAM OF THE CONSTRUCTION

The blue on the exterior contrasts with the red paint and pale wood on the interior. The parents' bedroom is an isolated home, while the children's rooms are arranged as semidetached houses. Each space is reached by a spiral staircase with a wooden structure that becomes the distributing axis of each room.

Atrium—University of Jussieu

PÉRIPHÉRIQUES ARCHITECTES | PARIS, FRANCE 2006

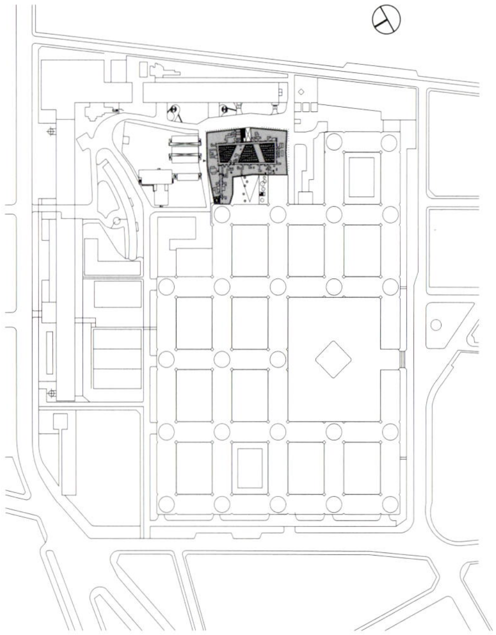

SITE PLAN

The Jussieu University campus, close to the center of Paris, is made up of a regular network of six-story buildings designed by Edouard Albert in the 1960s. Albert's planning project organized these buildings in the form of a crown—a configuration that received sustained criticism for its dispersion and the intensification of the wind blowing through the buildings. The project designed by the Périphériques team—building 16M on campus—sought, on the one hand, to form part of this scheme and, on the other, to manipulate it by inserting two patios where Albert had put just one. This is why the new building's geometry followed the orthogonal layout of the urban project and was drawn up as a standard unit from which an inner space—the central patio—has been removed.

One of the patios is covered by walkways raised on piles in which the architects gathered together the circulation of the entire complex. This gives rise to a "vertical square" that defines the routes within the atrium. The ground floor is folded over like a piece of origami to create an orange ramp that matches the level of the consolidated exterior with that of the inner patio—a strategy that establishes a fluid circulation between exterior and interior.

TYPE OF PROJECT **Classrooms and laboratories**

TOTAL SURFACE AREA **182,000 sq. ft. (16,895 m²)**

PHOTOS **© Luc Boegly**

The atrium both contrasts with the surroundings and borrows elements from it. The bright colors make it possible to identify the various uses and enhance the vertical movement between the floors. The finishing of the double skin on the interior facades is distinguished from the exterior to emphasize the building's horizontality.

BASEMENT

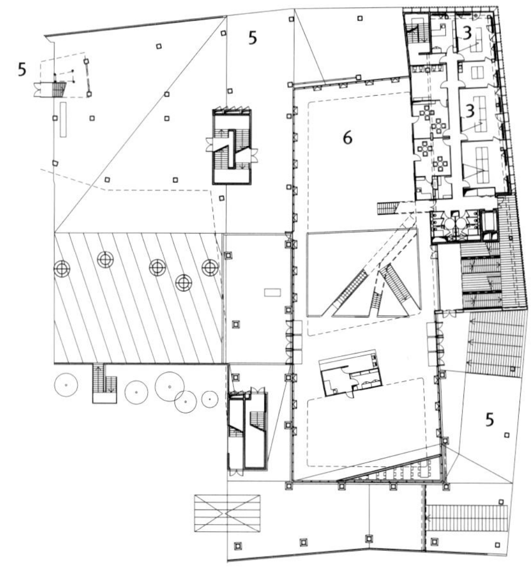

GROUND FLOOR

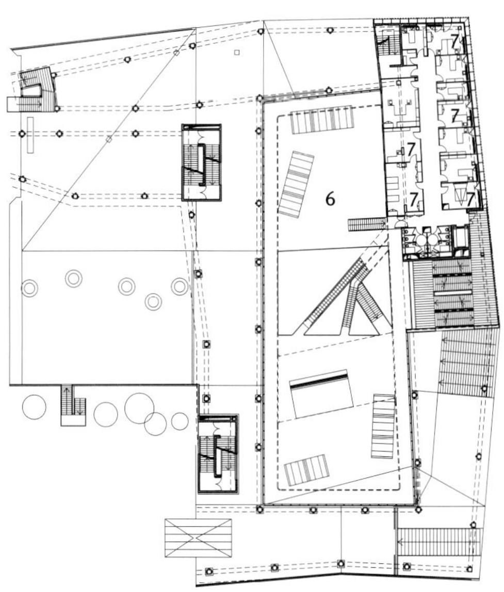

SECOND FLOOR

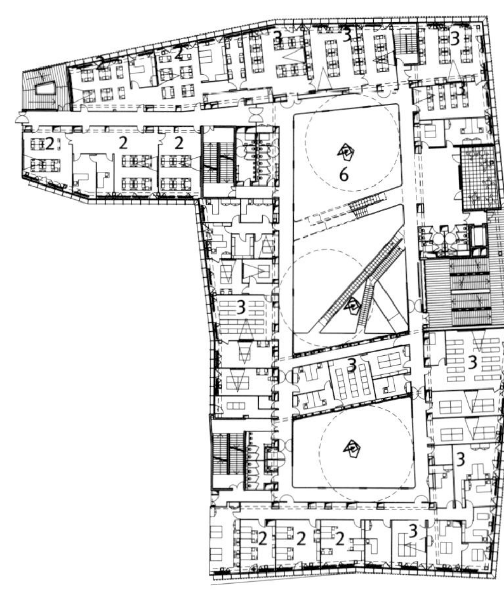

THIRD FLOOR

1, READING ROOM
2. WORKROOMS
3. CLASSROOMS
4. REST AREAS
5. ENTRANCES
6. ATRIUM
7. OFFICES

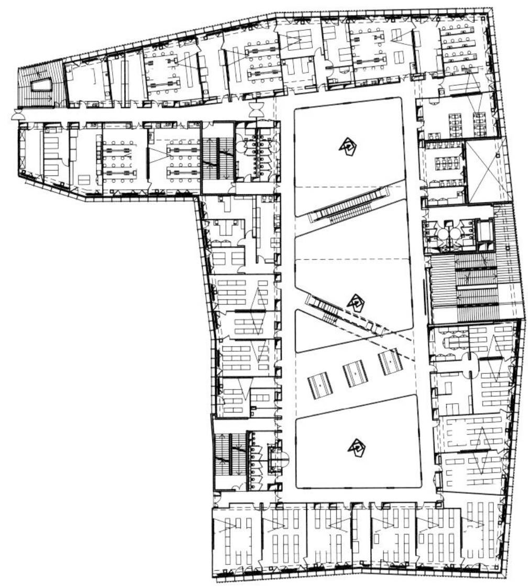

FOURTH FLOOR

FIFTH FLOOR

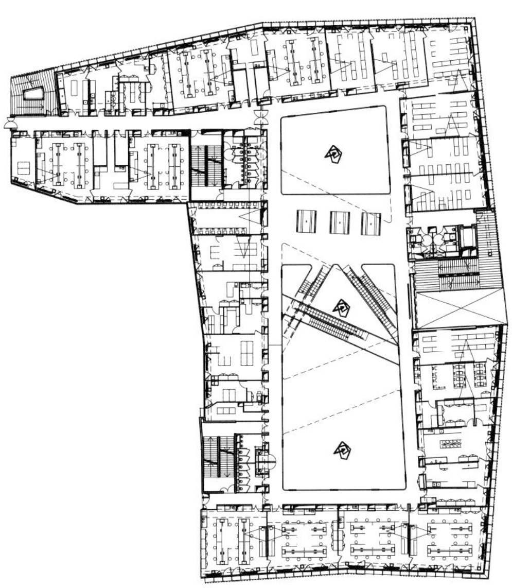

SIXTH FLOOR

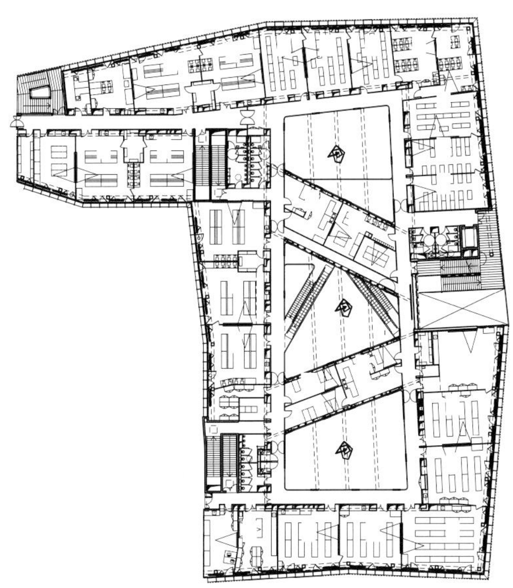

SEVENTH FLOOR

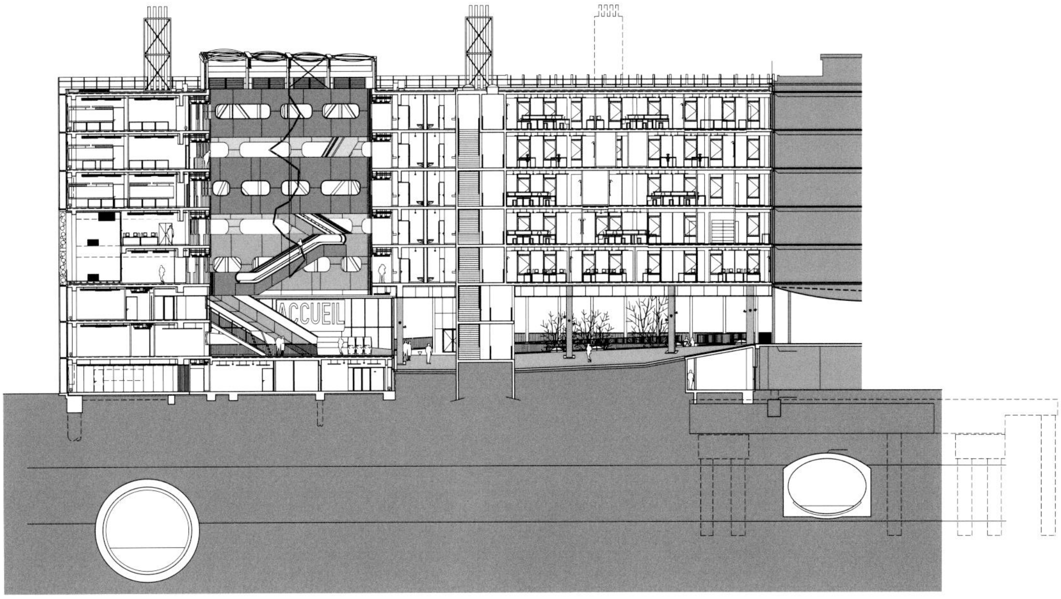

CROSS SECTION

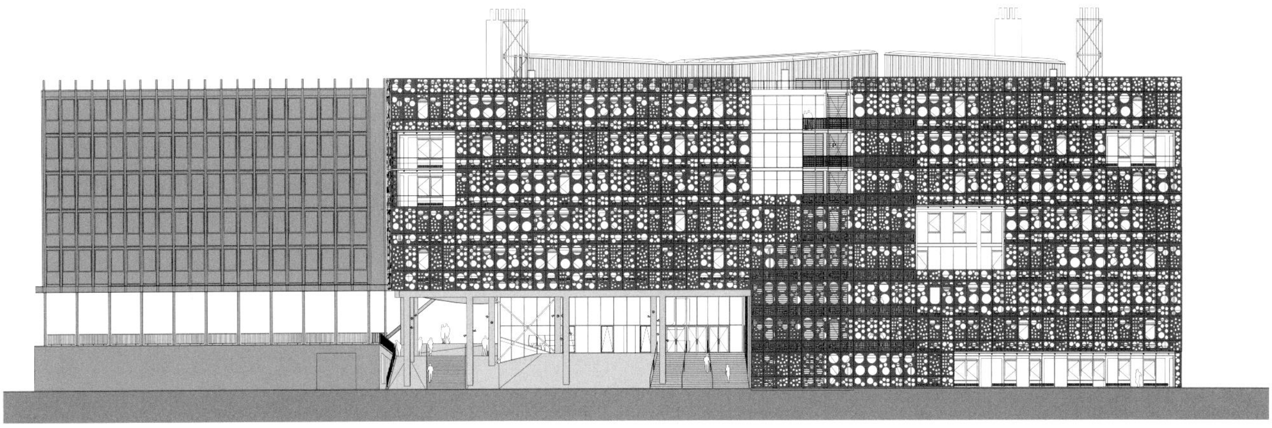

EAST ELEVATION

1. U-SHAPED STEEL OUTLINE
2. PERFORATED ALUMINUM SHEET
3. FIRE SERVICE ACCESS PANEL
4. GALVANIZED STEEL BALUSTRADE
5. GALVANIZED STEEL GRID
6. CONNECTING STEEL PLATE OUTLINE AND SUPPORT
7. STEEL SUPPORT
8. WIREWOOL INSULATION
9. SOLAR PROTECTION SHUTTERS
10. CONCRETE BLOCK

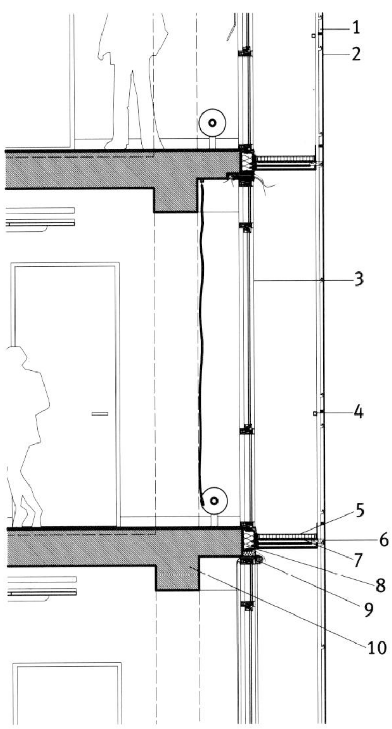

CONSTRUCTION DETAIL

1. U-UPA OUTLINE
2. METAL PEG
3. STEEL SUPPORT
4. U-SHAPE STEEL GIRDER
5. ASSEMBLAGE PLATE
6. GALVANIZED STEEL BALUSTRADE
7. PERFORATED ALUMINUM SHEET
8. GALVANIZED STEEL GRID
9. ROD SUPPORTING SHEET
10. PROTECTIVE BASEBOARD

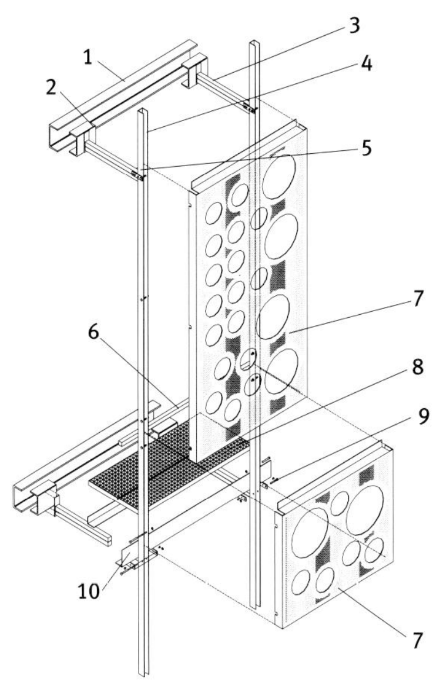

DETAIL OF FACADE

The rigidity of the circulation area contrasts with the delicacy of the facades, which are made up of two layers: one of glass, which maintains the design of the neighboring building; the other of ten types of metal panels with perforations in different sizes—a double skin that provides complexity and variation in the depth of the facades. The colors inside the various teaching areas can be distinguished from the outside, both by day and (more particularly) by night. This lighting effect is achieved by means of reflections on the glass on the facades and the holes in the metal panels. These effects of color and light serve as a reminder that the original design has been modified.

The classrooms are flexible spaces, initially intended to take in students transferred from buildings that are being renovated due to the presence of asbestos. Afterwards, the building will be reserved for postgraduate students. The architects from Périphériques decided to develop the project around the main patio, the focus of circulation, while a library, lecture halls, classrooms, multimedia and computer facilities, laboratories, administrative offices, and services comprise the functional program in the atrium building.

223
TP E
229

fire station

PHILIPPE SAMYN AND PARTNERS, ARCHITECTS & ENGINEERS | HOUTEN, NETHERLANDS 2000

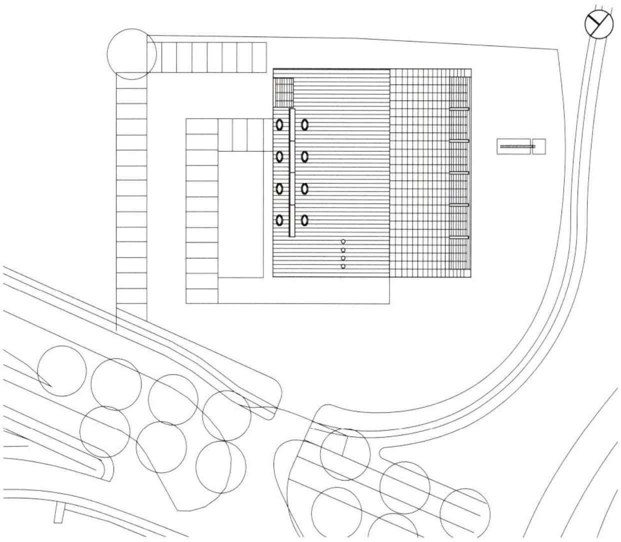

SITE PLAN

204

The fire service in the Dutch town of Houten comprises four professional firefighters and some sixty volunteers. On this basis, the firm of Philippe Samyn and Partners drew up a modern structure fitted out to receive six fire trucks. At the same time, the architects based their design on the radical separation between the roof structure and the internal organization of space. In this way, they sought to convey the idea of a shelter, independent from the building as such.

The parabolic form of the roof was chosen right from the start because the structure can be put up quickly and its elements used easily to the full. The building has two long facades facing north and south; two solar panels were set on the south side to take advantage of this placement.

The land is surrounded by empty green spaces and is set in an area marked by constant flux and strong social conflict. To alleviate these tensions, 2,200 children aged from five to seven from twenty-two local schools were asked to draw the firefighters' adventures and triumphs. These were used to create a kind of jigsaw puzzle on the interior wall, thereby establishing an emotional link between the population and the building.

TYPE OF PROJECT **Public service facility**

TOTAL SURFACE AREA **12,000 sq. ft. (1,100 m²)**

PHOTOS **© Stijn Brakkee, Daria Scagliola**

PRELIMINARY SKETCH

BRANDWEER

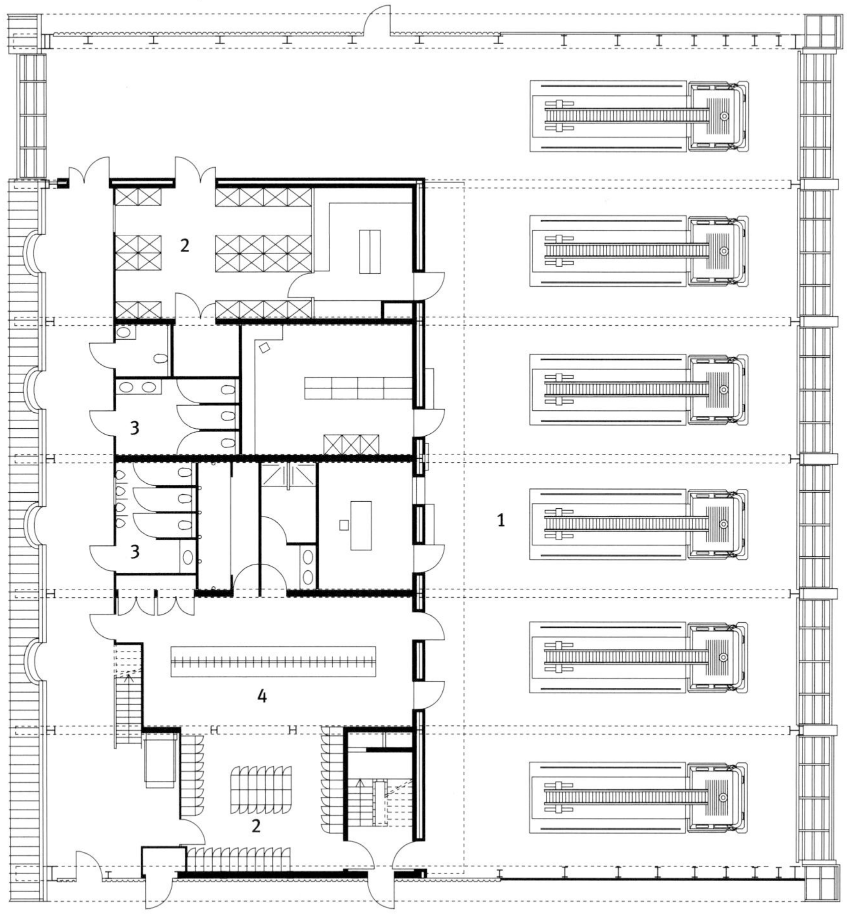

GROUND FLOOR

1. PARKING FOR TRUCKS
2. STORAGE AREAS
3. RESTROOMS
4. CHANGING ROOM
5. CAFETERIA
6. MEETING ROOM

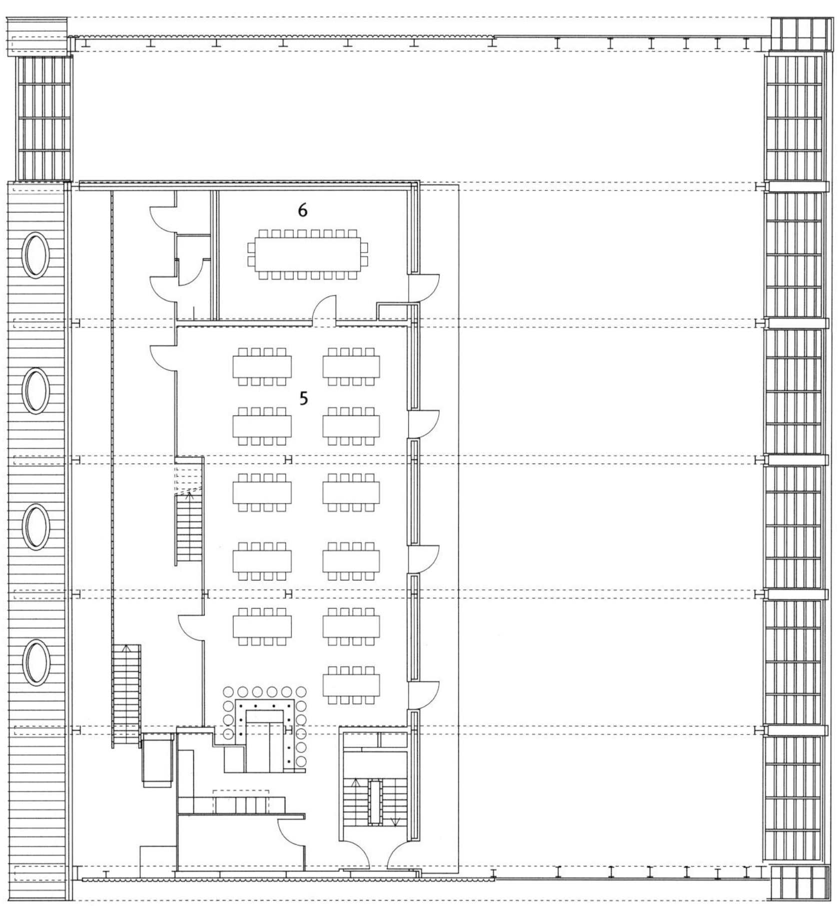

SECOND FLOOR

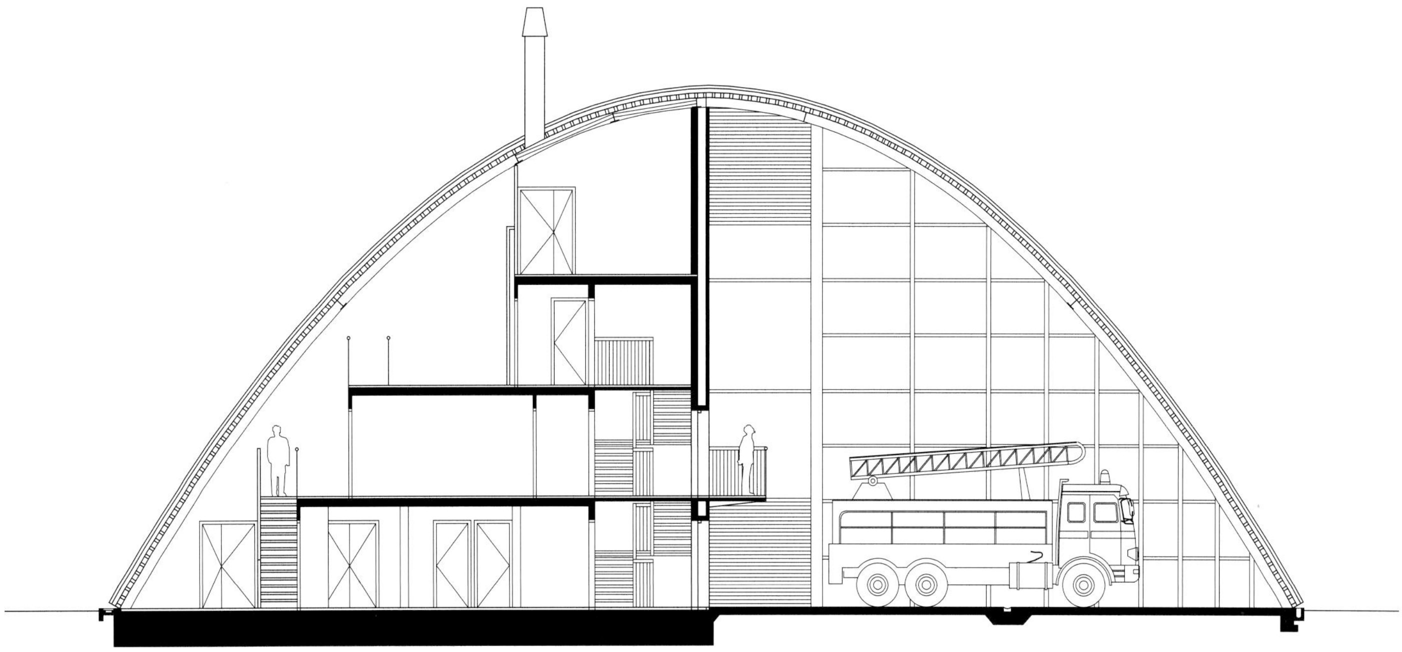

CROSS SECTION

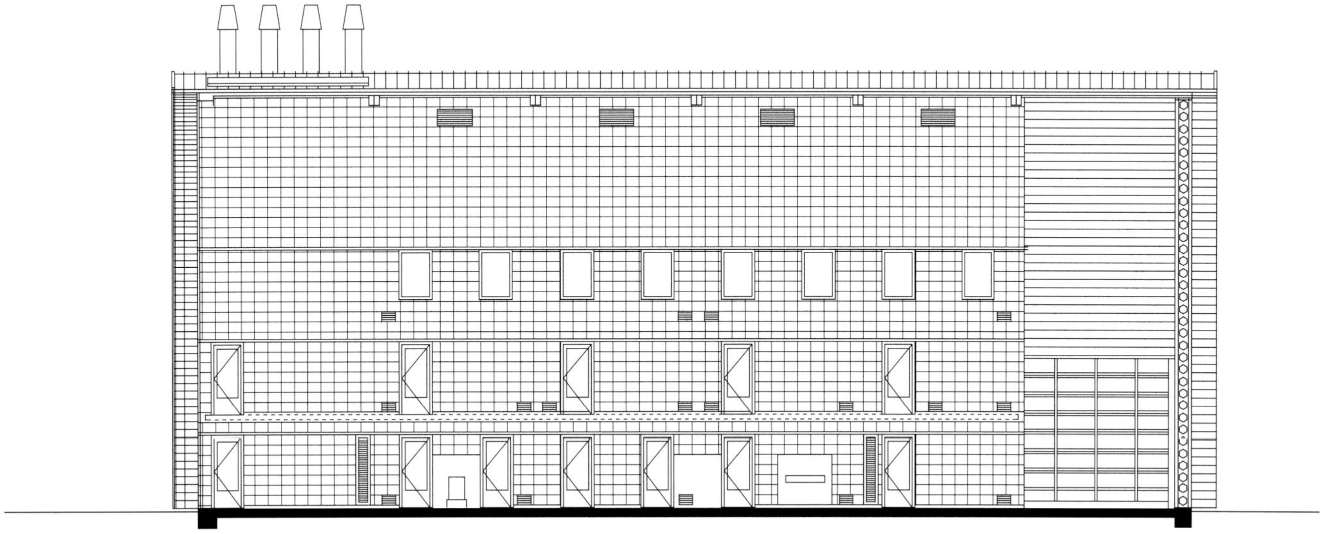

LONGITUDINAL SECTION

ALARM 112
ALARM 112

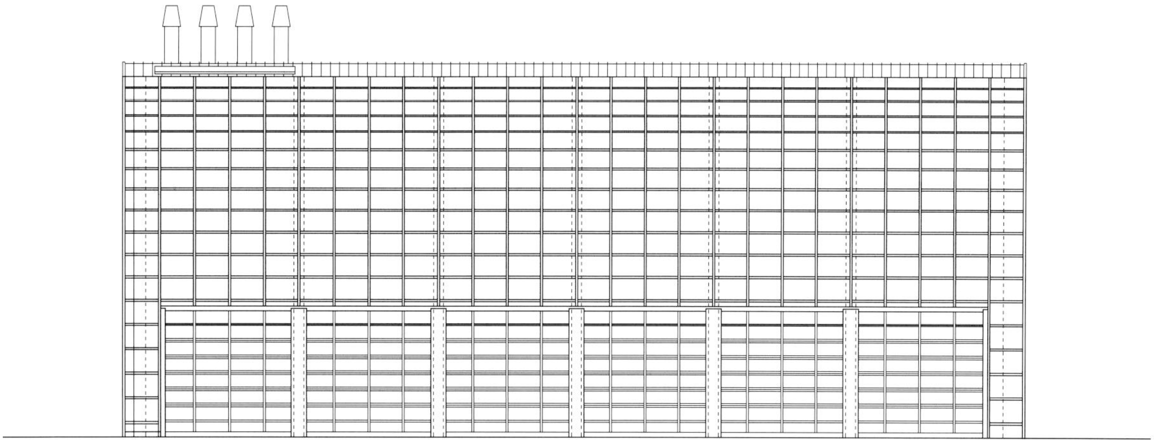

SOUTHEAST ELEVATION

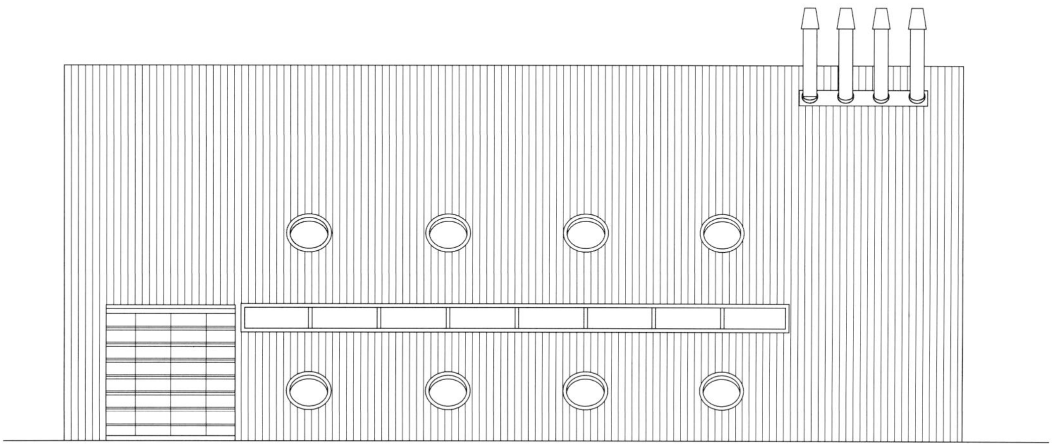

NORTHWEST ELEVATION

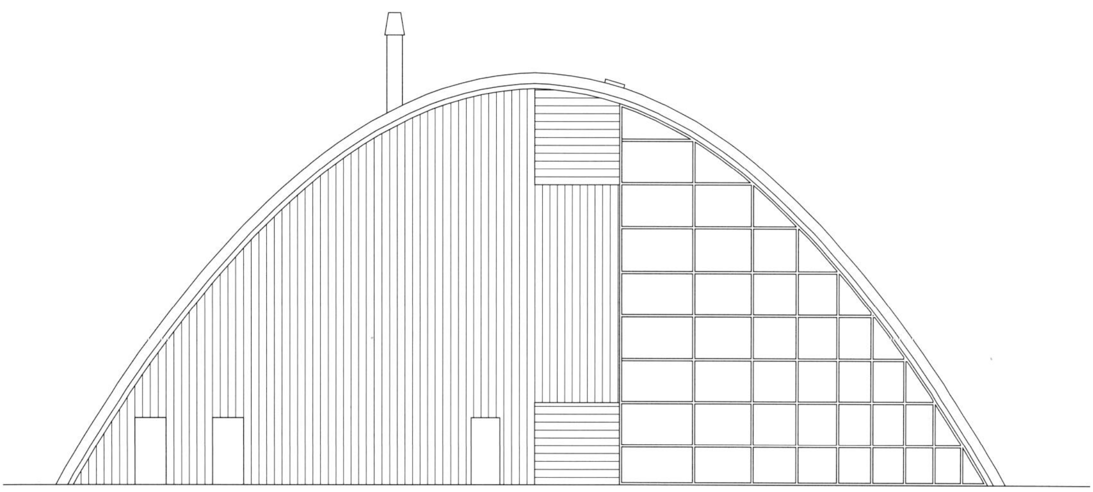

SOUTHWEST ELEVATION

The children's drawings are arranged on a brick wall dividing the building in two. The 2,200 colored panels combine to form a large flame in various colors: dark blue at the bottom, green and yellow in the middle, and orange on the top.

The interior of the fire station is divided into two parts, separated by this oversize jigsaw. The south side is a totally transparent space fronted by a glass facade; this contains the main firefighting equipment, on display to the exterior as if in a large store window. This side is largely unaffected by air conditioning, because it serves as a transitional area in both winter and summer. The trucks inside and the landscape outside are visible from the raised gallery emerging from the colored wall.

The rest of the program was set on the north side of the building. This is an independent volume, made with solid load-bearing walls. The ground floor contains the showers, changing rooms, services, and storage areas for the mechanical equipment; the next floor comprises a meeting room and cafeteria, while the offices are on the top floor.

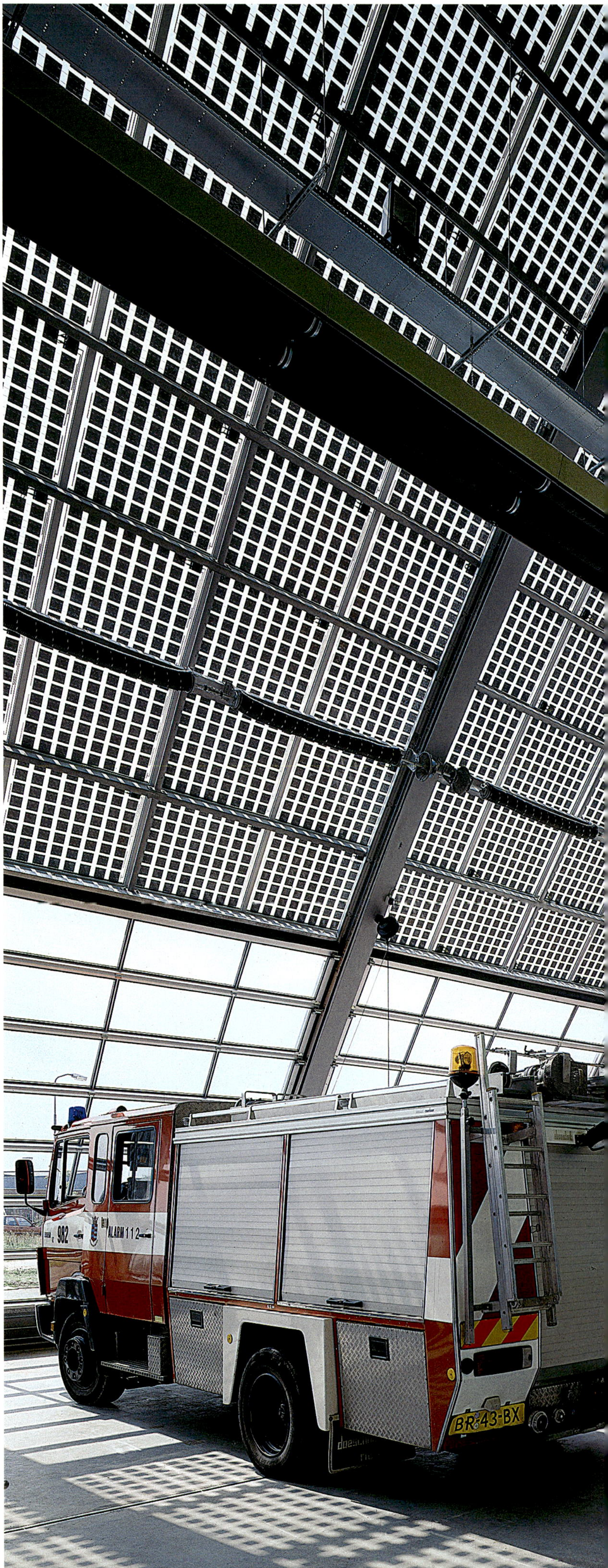

The large doors in the glass facade were designed to allow firefighters to leave quickly in case of an emergency. The interior is predominantly white, setting off the bright colors of the large flame on the central wall.

Montreal Congress Palace

TÉTRAULT, DUBUC, SAIA ET ASSOCIÉS AND HAL INGBERG | MONTREAL, CANADA 2003

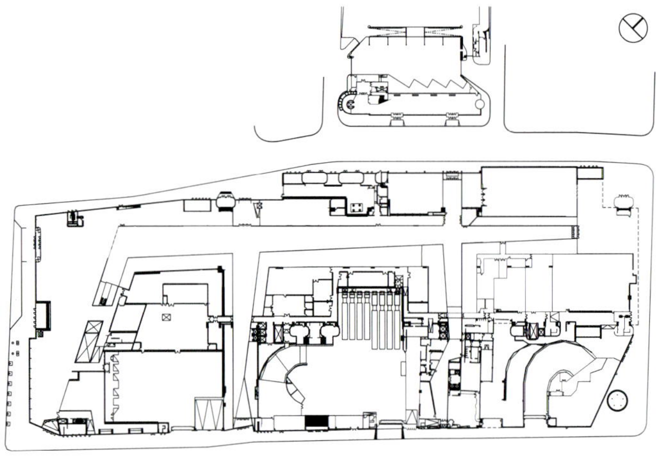

SITE PLAN

The extension of the Montreal Congress Palace demonstrates the great potential of color in architecture as a fundamental element in urban regeneration that need not interfere with historical connotations or their deep roots. The original palace was designed by Víctor Prus in 1984, set on a viaduct that separated the city's old center from its modern area. The new extension, which is known as Bleury Hall, involved the construction of a ground floor to create both public and commercial spaces that connect the building with its environment.

Bleury Hall constitutes a large urban complex with architectural features that have made it an icon of Montreal. Its multicolored glass facade alludes to the city's multicultural character and dramatically attracts the attention of passersby. A space for exhibitions and other events was built to double the preexisting expanse of conference halls. The interior of the hall combines effects that emerge from the refraction and reflection of light through transparent panels of laminated glass, creating a kaleidoscope with an orthogonal matrix of colored lights that change according to the position of the sun.

The L-shaped building, which is linked to an old pedestrian path, is made up of three rings: the outer part of each ring is given over to commercial activities, while the inner section contains service areas. Two pedestrian walkways pass between these two bands to connect old Montreal with the modern city.

TYPE OF PROJECT **Cultural facility**

COLOR **Tétrault, Dubuc, Saia et associés and Hal Ingberg**

TOTAL SURFACE AREA **3,444,000 sq. ft. (320,000 m²)**

PHOTOS **© Hal Ingberg**

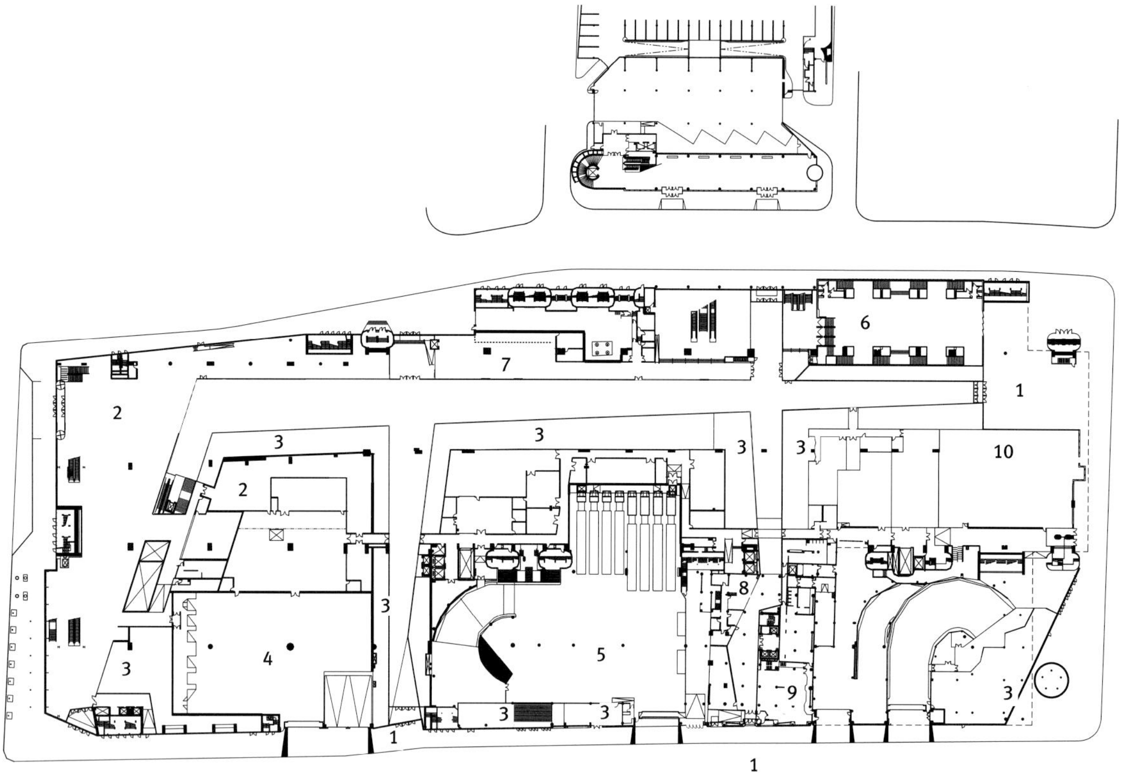

GROUND FLOOR

1. ENTRANCES
2. ATRIUM
3. COMMERCIAL PREMISES
4. BUS STATION
5. AREA FOR TRUCKS
6. SUBWAY STATION
7. COUNTER
8. SECURITY CONTROL AREA
9. POST OFFICE
10. FIRE STATION
11. EXHIBITION HALLS
12. FOYER
13. BAR
14. ESPLANADE
15. CONGRESS HALLS
16. KITCHENS
17. OBSERVATION POINT
18. RESTAURANT
19. TERRACE
20. TANKS AND TECHNICAL SERVICES

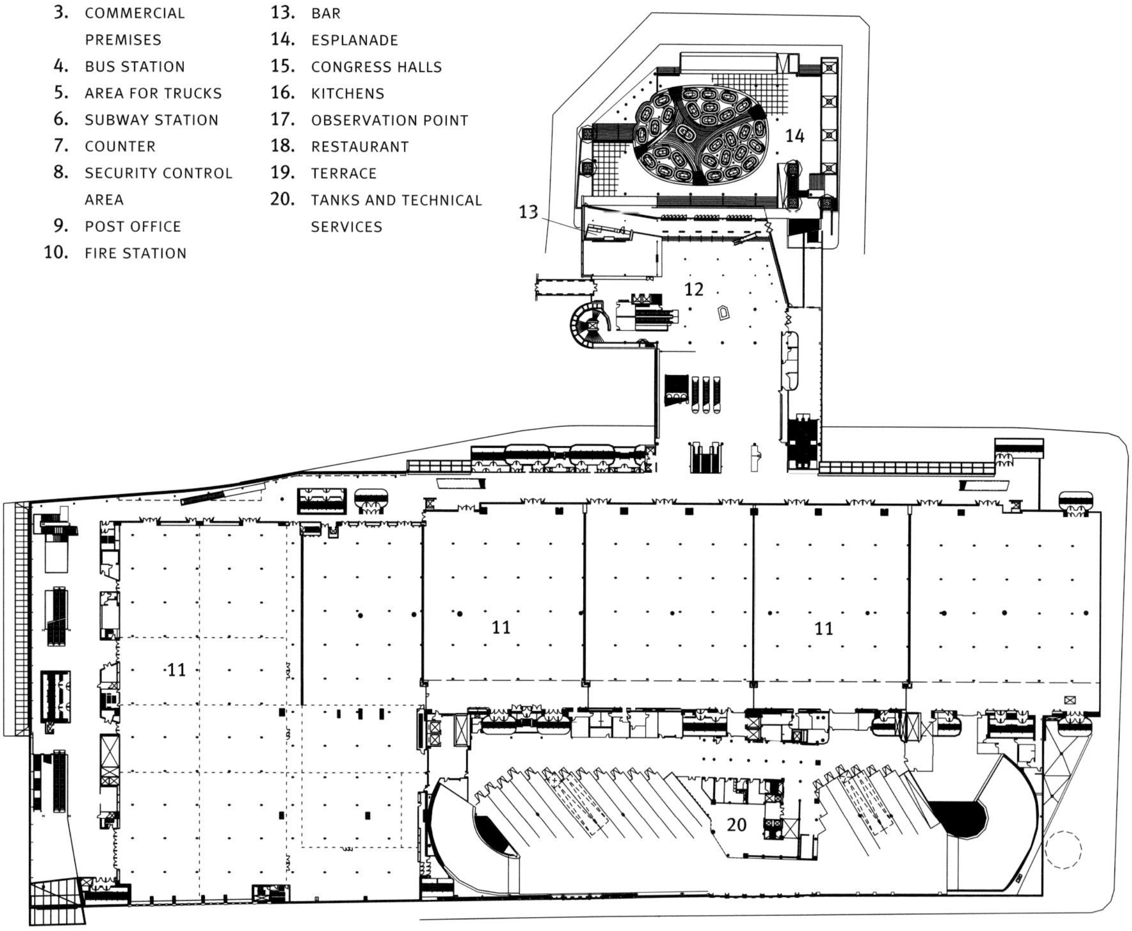

THIRD FLOOR

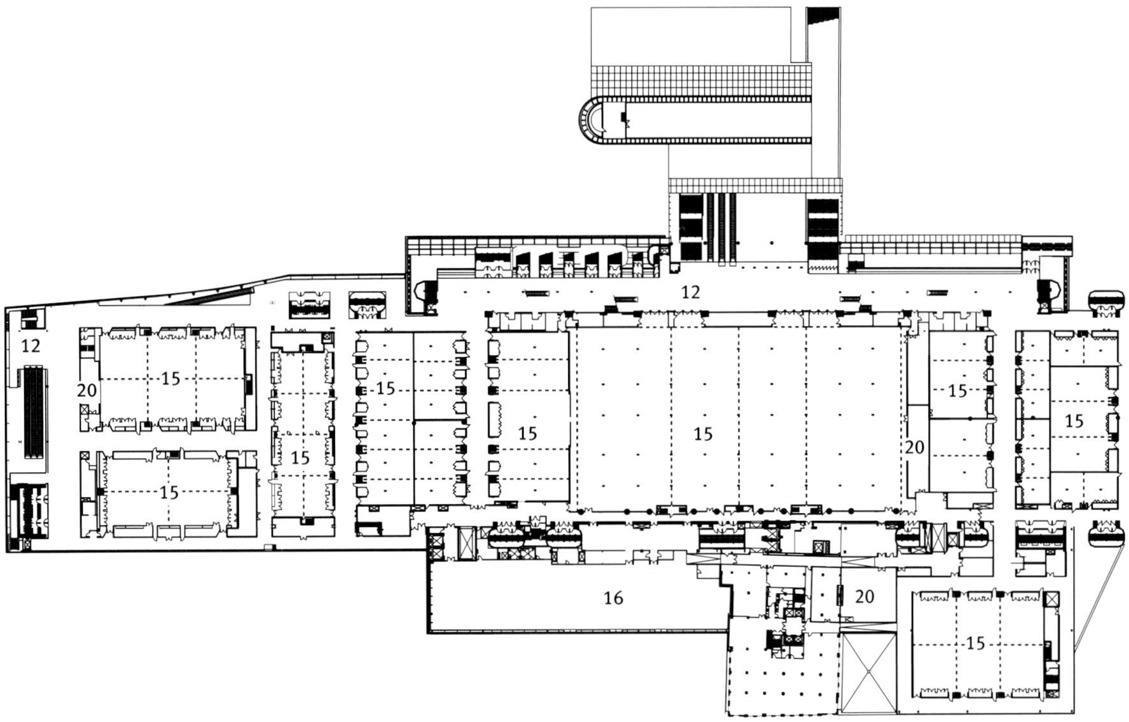

SIXTH FLOOR

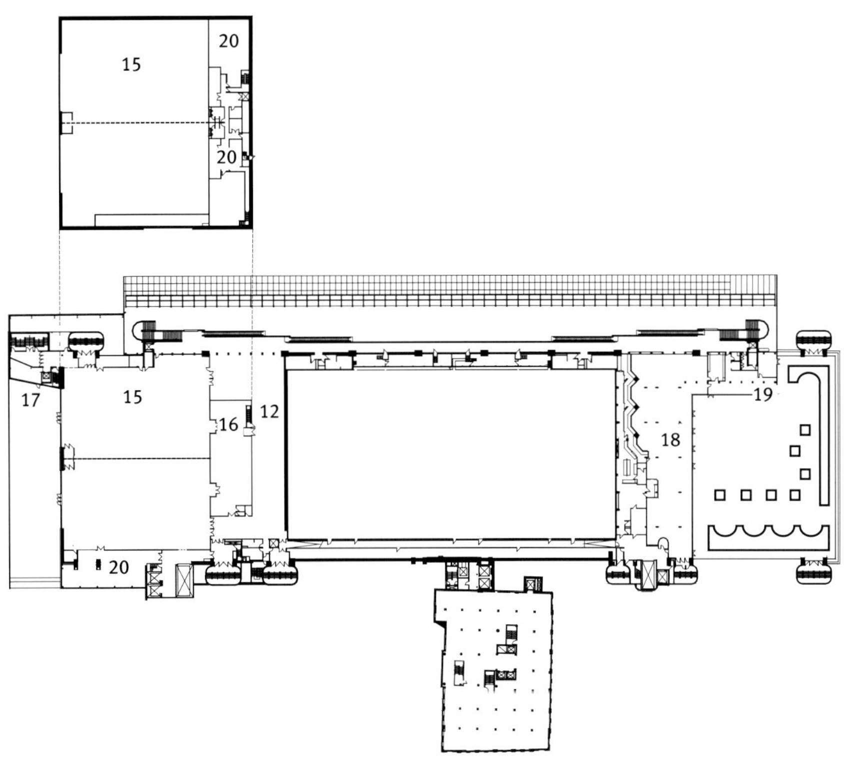

EIGHTH AND NINTH FLOORS

The placement of the new extension to the Congress Palace took into consideration the height of existing buildings in the area so that it would not disrupt the skyline. So, despite the contrast provided by the colorful facade, the extension was conceived as a structure that blends into its surroundings.

The colored glass panels establish a marked difference between interior and exterior. The interior becomes an almost immaterial, dreamlike space, while the exterior renders the building an urban landmark that radiates color amidst the gray of its surroundings.

Rez-de-chaussée

7
6
5
4
3
2
1
Congrès

Els Colors kindergarten

RCR ARQUITECTES | MANLLEU, SPAIN 2004

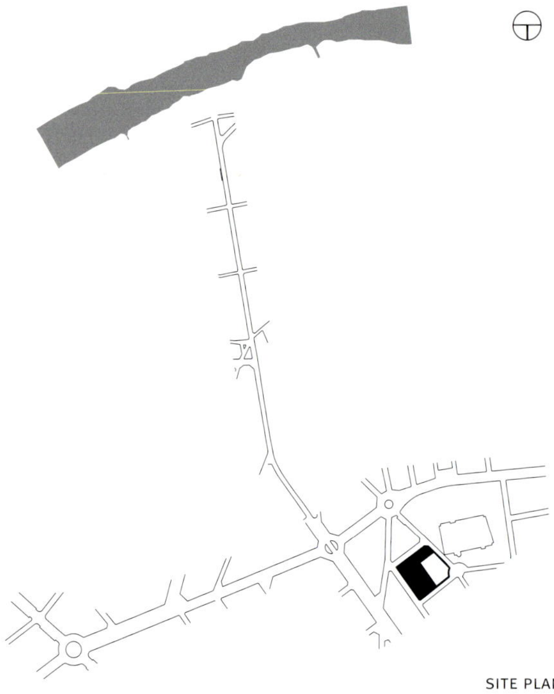

SITE PLAN

Manlleu is a Catalan town situated 50 miles (80 km) to the north of Barcelona. Manlleu Town Hall commissioned the firm run by Rafael Aranda, Carme Pigem, and Ramon Vilalta to design a kindergarten for children aged between four months and three years. The program drawn up by the architects is for a simple construction based on the repetition and superimposition of a single module, and this simplicity is set off by the colors used on the exterior cladding and inside. They came up with a building marked by clear lines and a powerful personality that stands out from its environment instead of blending in with it.

The children's spatial perception was a determining factor in configuring the spaces: the architects sought to help children get around by means of colors and fluid boundaries that allow them to relate freely both to each other and to their immediate environment. The program is organized as two rectangular volumes, separated from each other by a large interior patio and connected by a multifunctional space perpendicular to them. The rooms follow the modulation and are distributed into blocks according to the age of the children, with the general services (kitchen, laundry, and closets) set in the northern area of each block.

The structure consists of vertical metal elements and horizontal concrete elements. The colorful facades are made of red, orange, and yellow glass with a finish that is two-thirds acid-treated and one-third transparent. The interior divisions are metal structures clad with metacrilate panels 1/8 in (3 mm) thick, in the same colors as those on the exterior.

TYPE OF PROJECT **Educational facility**

COLOR **RCR Arquitectes**

TOTAL SURFACE AREA **9,989 sq. ft. (928 m²)**

PHOTOS **© Eugeni Pons**

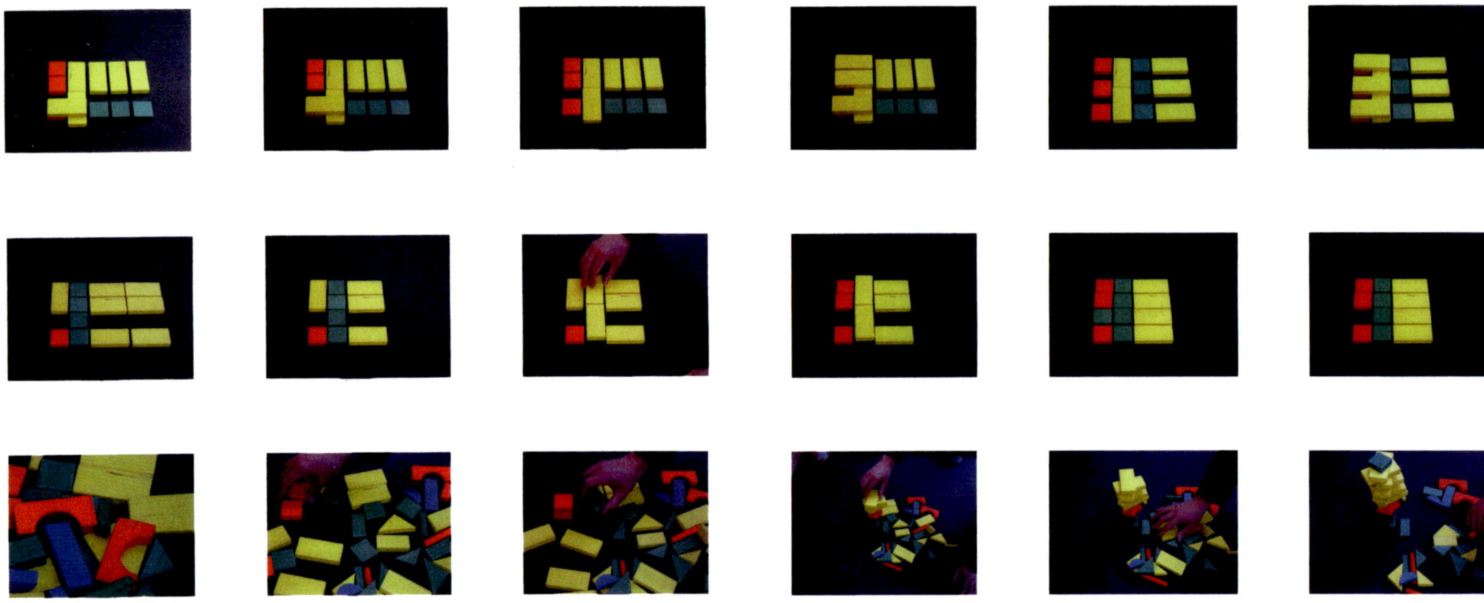

PRELIMINARY REPRESENTATION OF THE DISTRIBUTION OF USES AND SELECTION OF COLORS

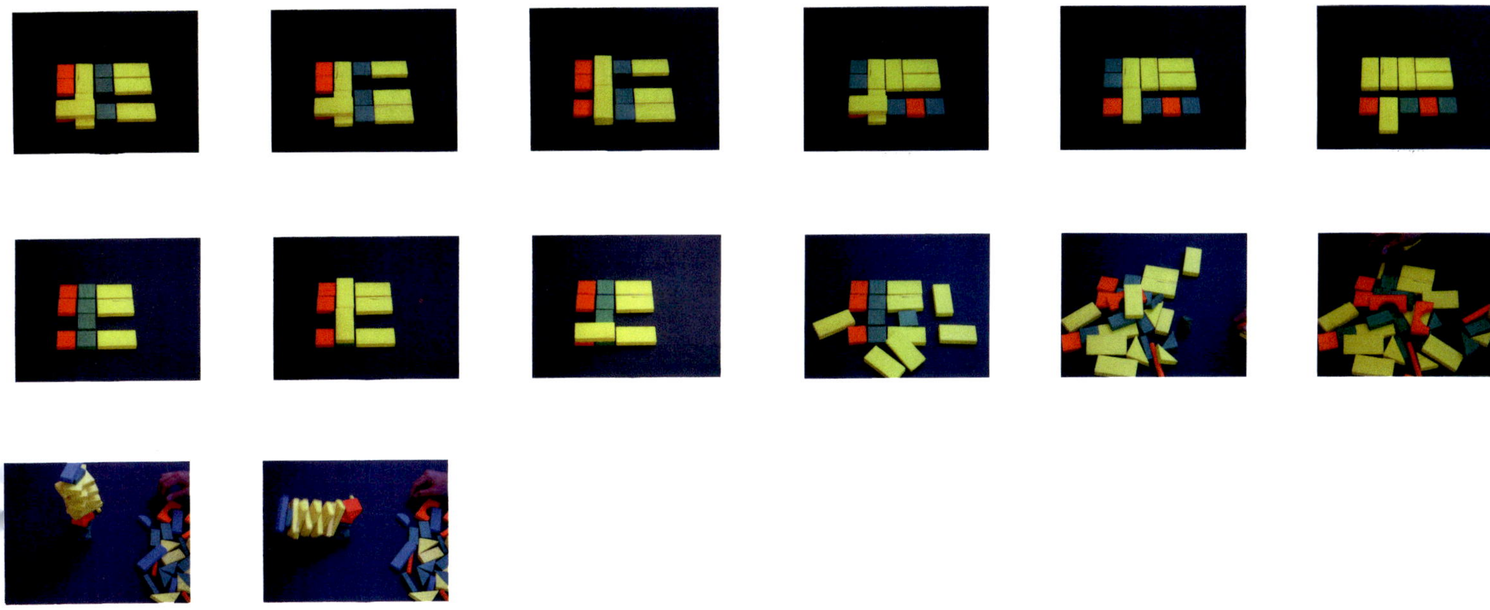

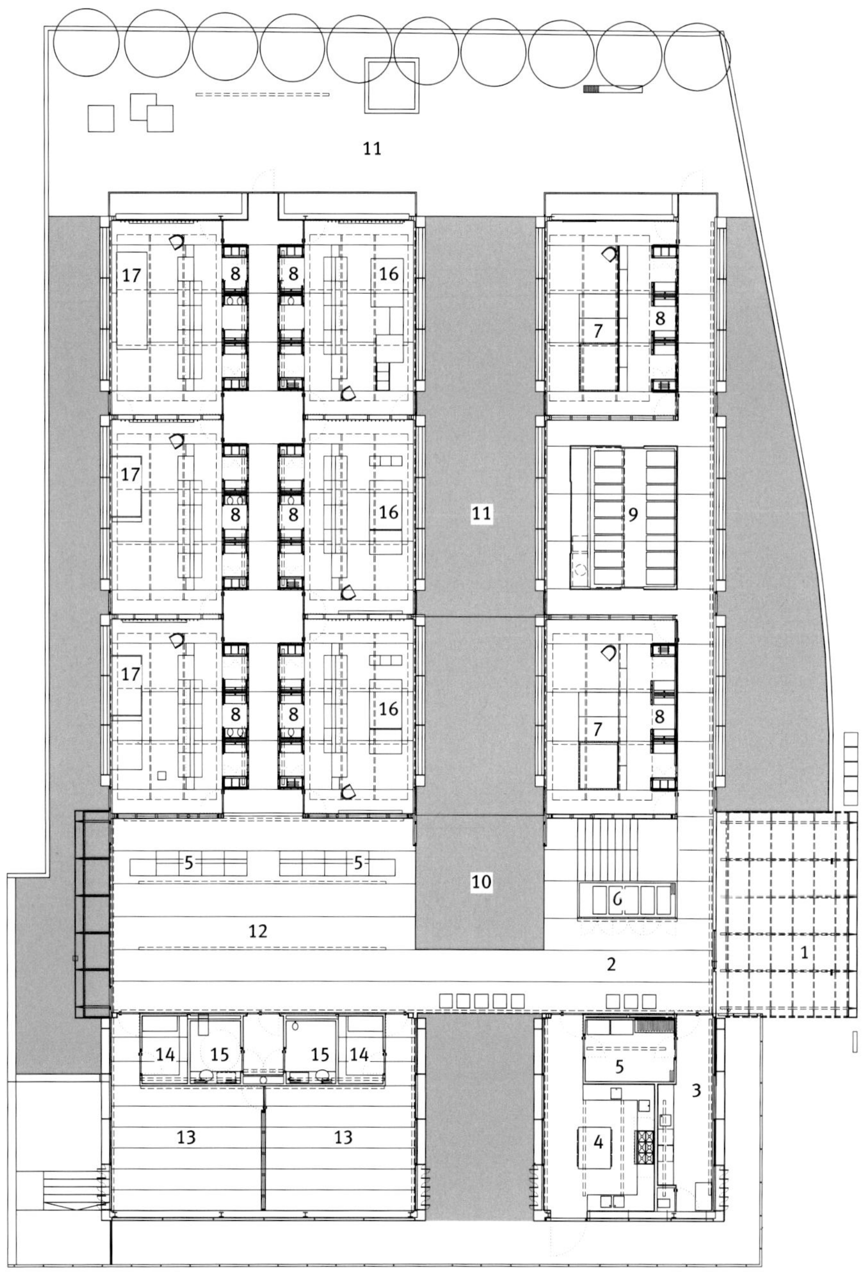

GROUND FLOOR

1. ENTRANCE
2. ENTRANCE HALL
3. LAUNDRY
4. KITCHEN
5. STORAGE AREAS
6. CLOSET FOR STROLLERS
7. CLASSROOMS 0–1 YEAR
8. CHANGING AREAS
9. DORMITORY
10. PORCH
11. PATIOS
12. MULTIPURPOSE ROOM
13. DORMITORIES/ROOMS
14. STORAGE AREAS FOR EDUCATIONAL MATERIALS
15. SERVICES
16. CLASSROOMS 1–2 YEARS
17. CLASSROOMS 2–3 YEARS
18. TEACHERS' ROOM
19. DRESSING ROOMS AND RESTROOM
20. ADMINISTRATIVE OFFICE

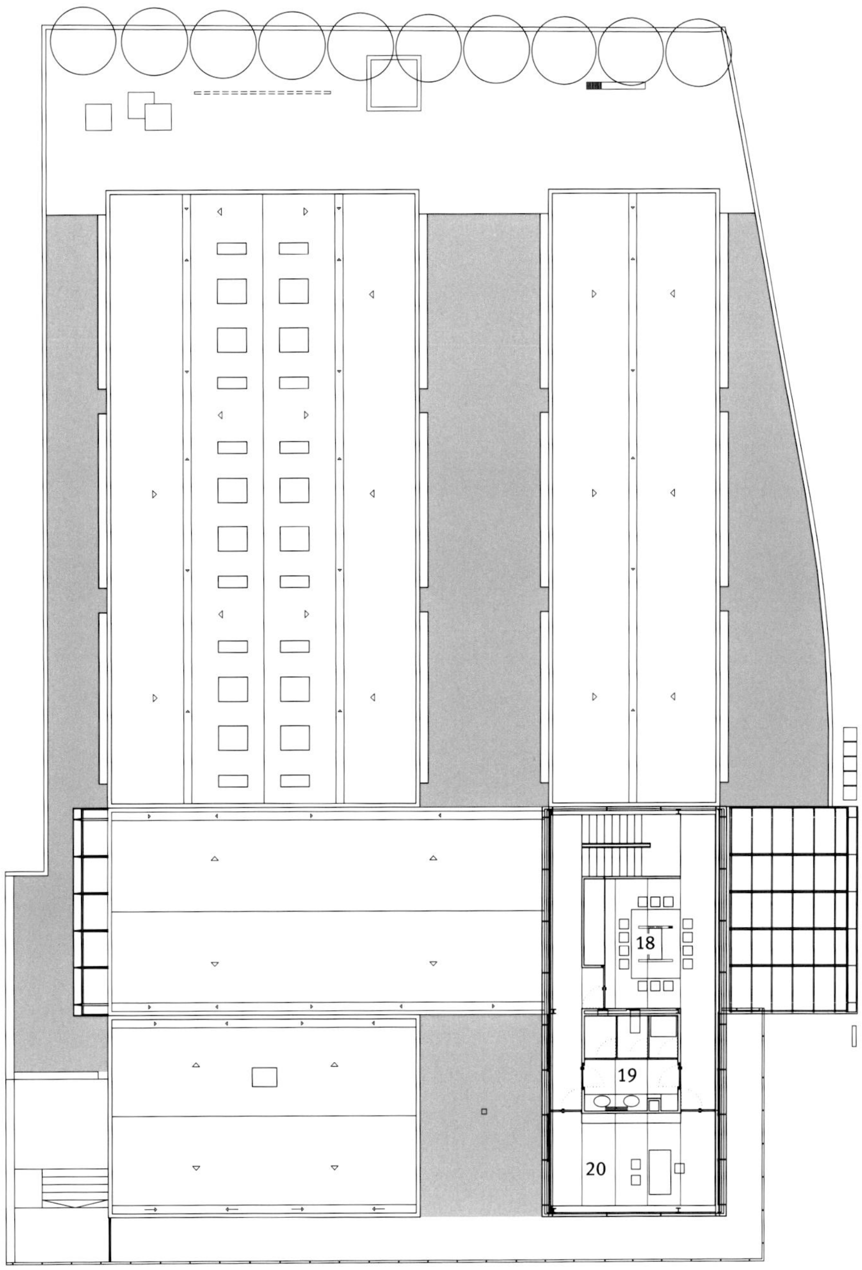

SECOND FLOOR

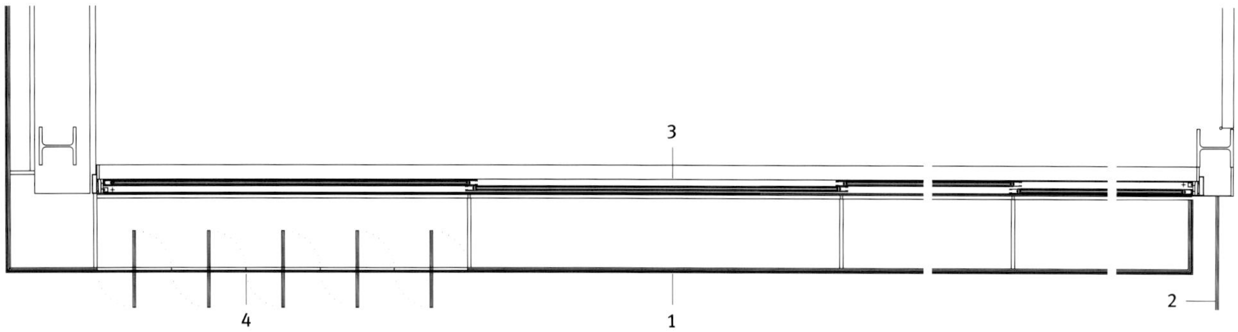

PLAN OF THE FACADE

1. PARASOL: METALLIC PLATE STRUCTURE, FINISHED WITH LAMINAR GLASS AND COLORED MATT PVB
2. LAMINAR GLASS AND TRANSPARENT PVB
3. INTERIOR ENCLOSURE: ALUMINUM AND TRANSPARENT LAMINAR GLASS
4. PARASOL: U-SHAPED OUTLINE, LAMINAR GLASS, AND COLORED WORKABLE MATT PVB
5. ANCHORING METAL PLATE STRUCTURE
6. DOOR: ALUMINUM STRUCTURE FINISHED WITH GALVANIZED SHEET METAL AND THERMAL INSULATION

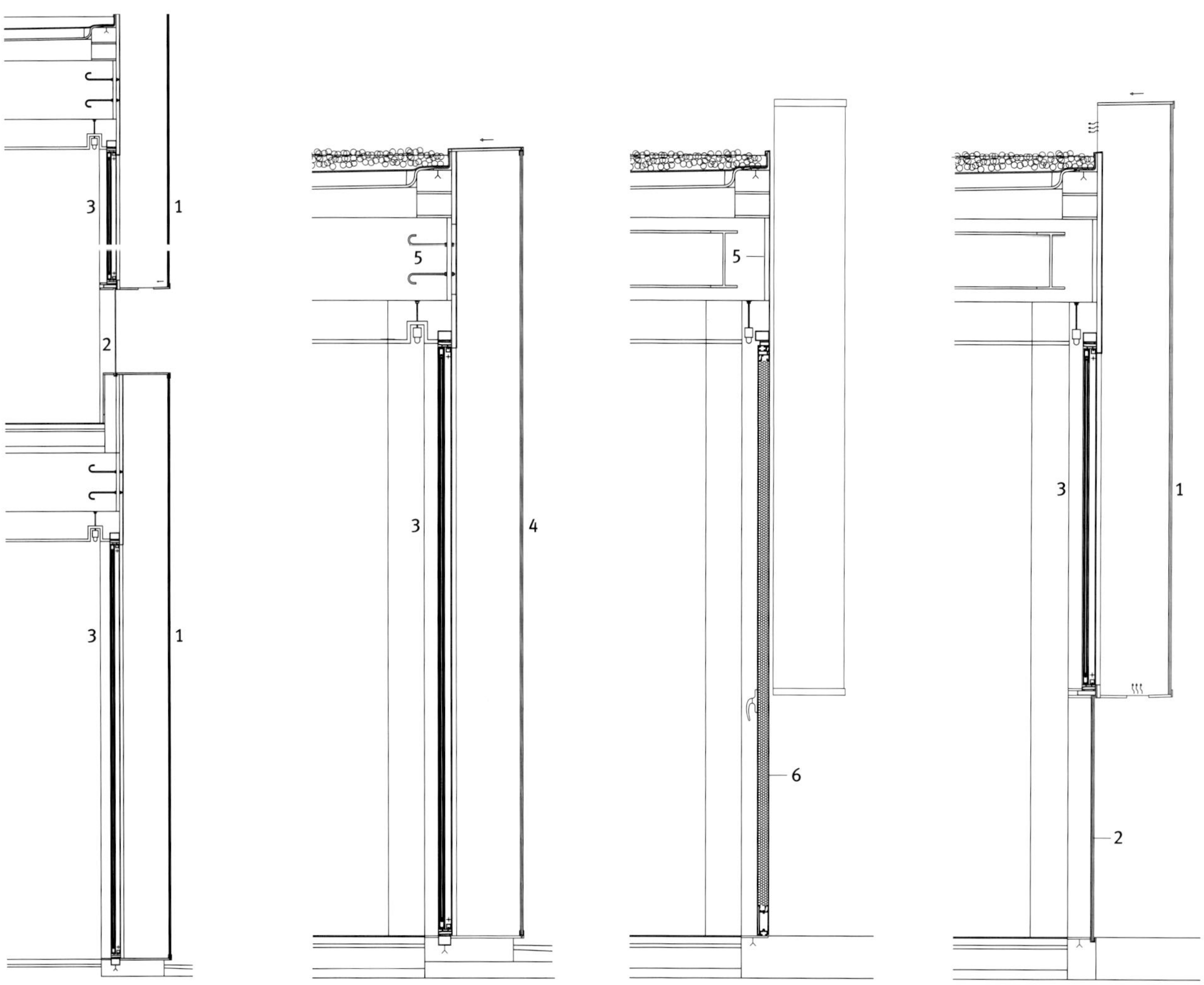

FACADE SECTIONS

NORTHEAST ELEVATION

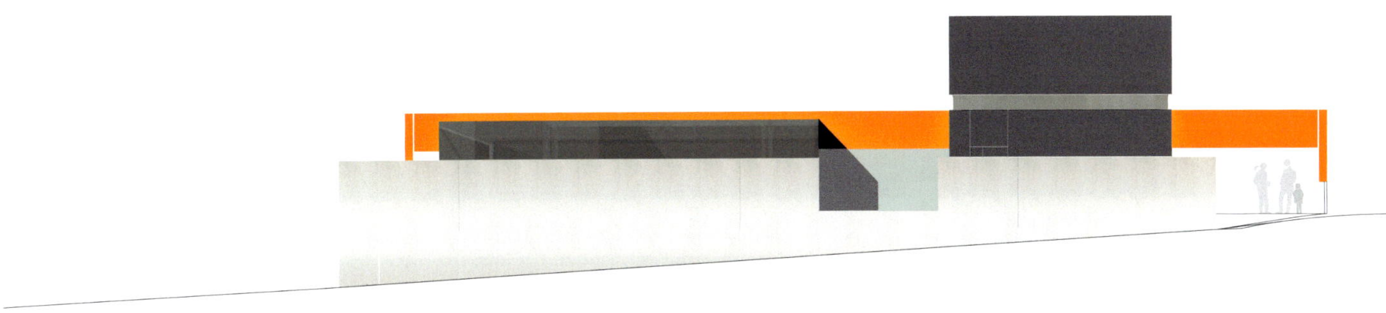

SOUTHEAST ELEVATION

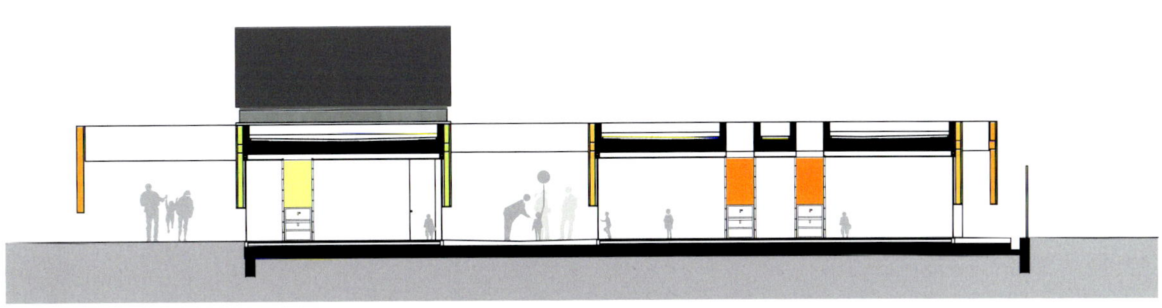

LONGITUDINAL SECTION — ENTRANCE

The Reece School

PLATT BYARD DOVELL WHITE ARCHITECTS | NEW YORK, NY 2006

SITE PLAN

The Reece School is devoted to children with learning difficulties. It is set on the Upper East Side in New York City. The project drawn up by Platt Byard Dovell White was intended to blend discreetly with its residential surroundings, dominated by brownstone houses. So, the construction fit in with the block by following the line of its facades, although it also introduced colored glass to break up the uniformity of the setting.

The glass facade traps sunshine from the exterior and creates multicolored patches of light in the rooms inside. The architects adopted a color scheme that allows pupils to find their way around and recognize the classrooms as their own. The glass enclosure has an anodized aluminum structure, while the panes themselves are laminated with PVB sheets in four different colors.

The architects considered the task of designing a school for children with special needs as a stimulating challenge. They sought the advice of therapists, social workers, and teachers in order to understand the workings of such an institution and appreciate the requirements of staff and pupils alike. They finally came up with a five-story building with twelve classrooms and various complementary spaces, as well as special therapy rooms, offices for psychologists and counsellors, and flexible areas that can be adapted to the needs of the moment.

TYPE OF PROJECT **Educational facility**

TOTAL SURFACE AREA **21,043 sq. ft. (1,955 m²)**

PHOTOS **© Jonathan Wallen**

238

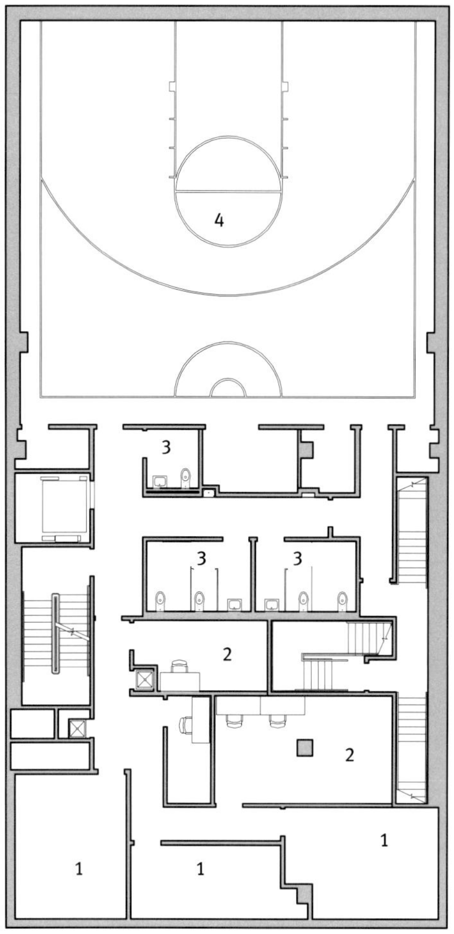

BASEMENT

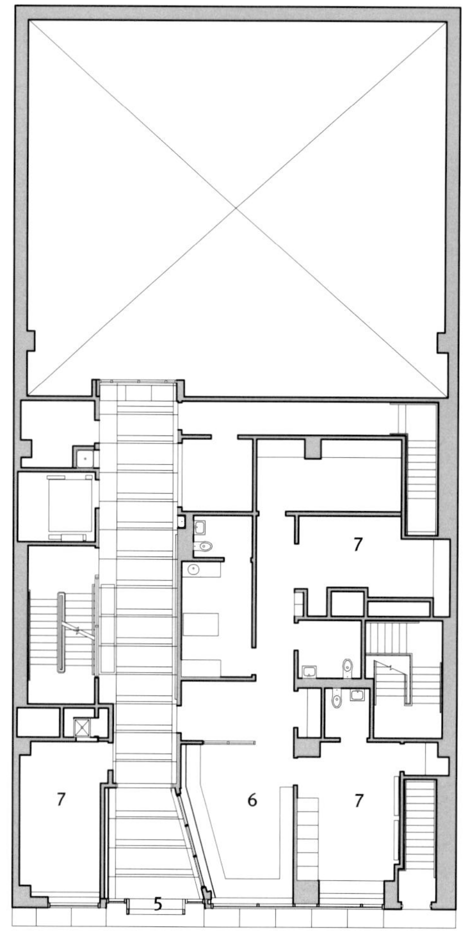

GROUND FLOOR

1. INSTALLATIONS
2. ARCHIVES
3. RESTROOMS
4. GYM
5. ENTRANCE
6. RECEPTION
7. OFFICES
8. CLASSROOMS
9. CUBBIES
10. SPECIAL ROOMS
11. TERRACE

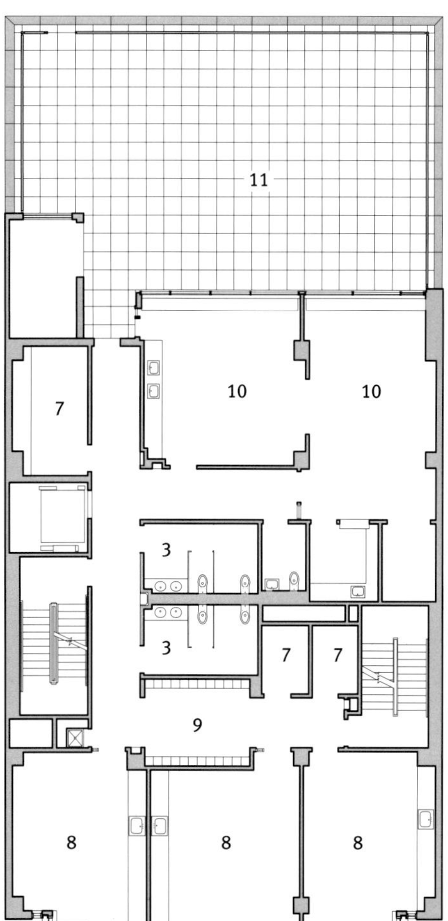

SECOND FLOOR

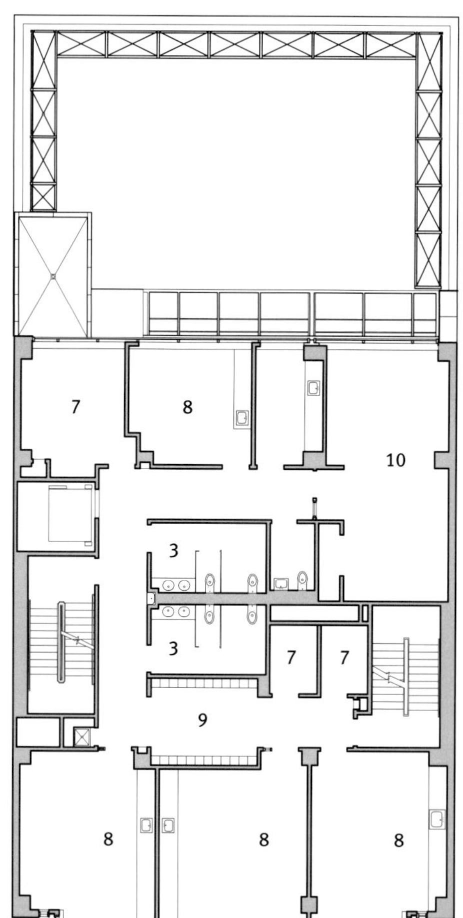

THIRD FLOOR

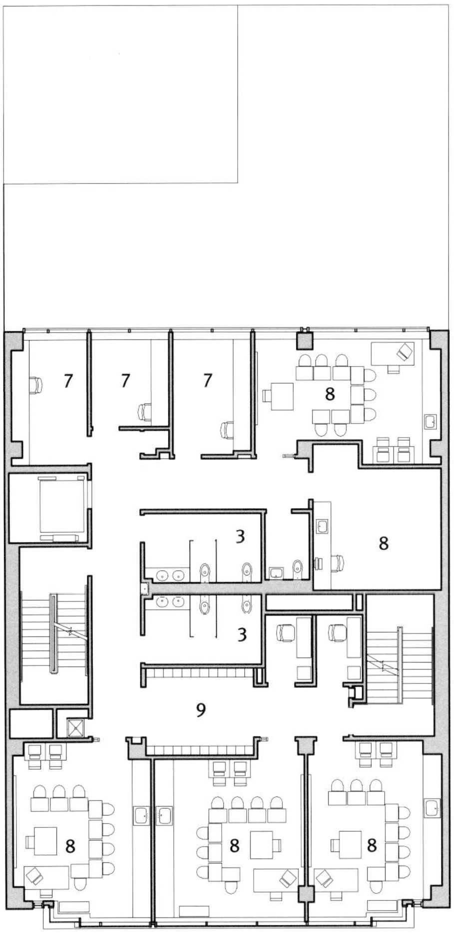

FOURTH FLOOR

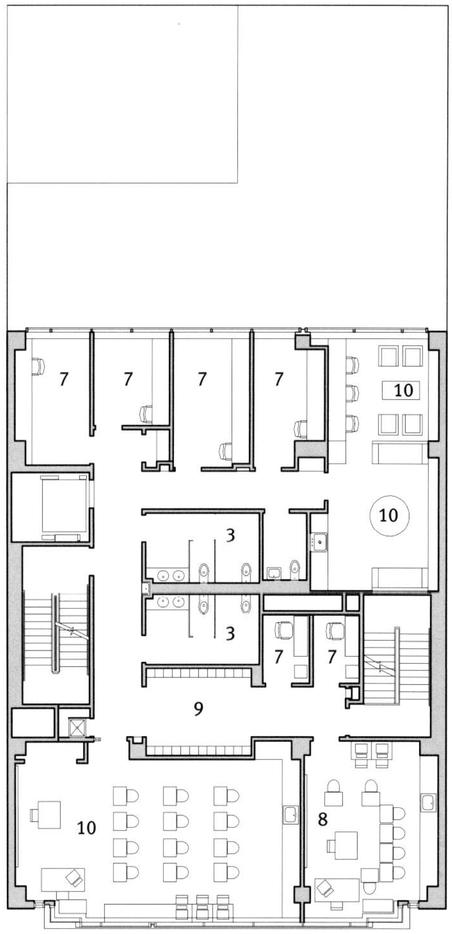

FIFTH FLOOR

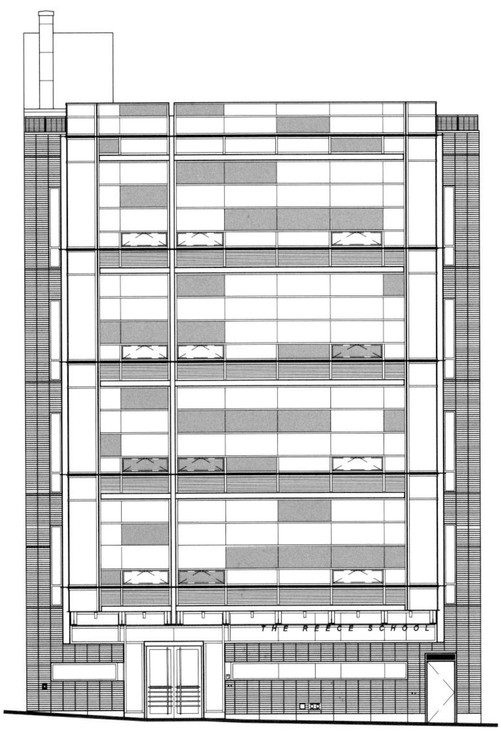

ELEVATION

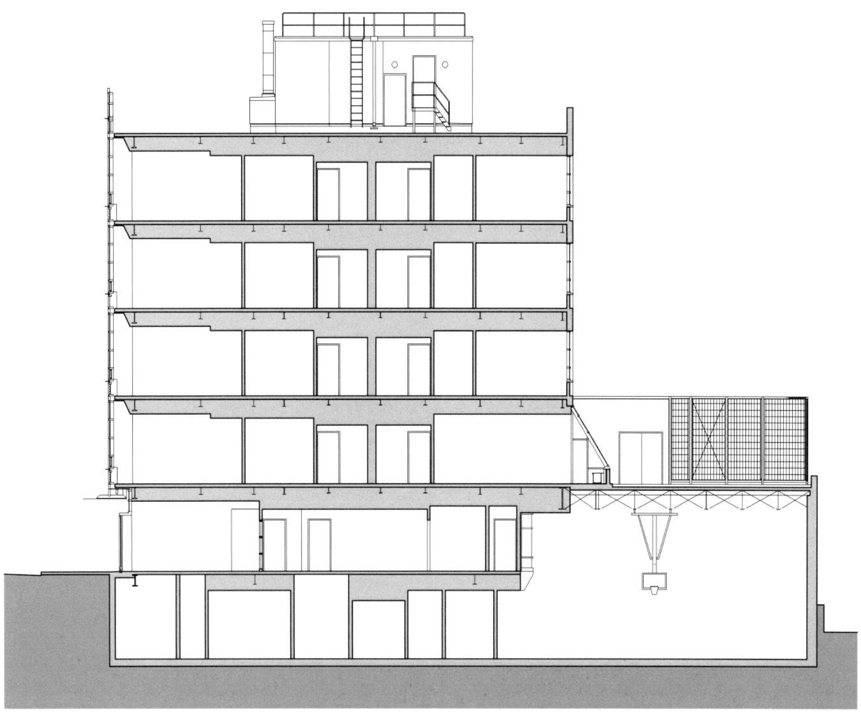

LONGITUDINAL SECTION

THE REECE SCHOOL

MONOPOLY
Boggle
Twister
Charades for Kids
Connect Four

The scale of the neighboring buildings was maintained in the interior spaces, thus creating classrooms measuring 301 sq. ft. (28 m²) that enhance the personal interaction between teachers and pupils.

Moreover, The Reece School has satisfied the conditions for LEED certification of sustainable construction for the use of approved wood and recycled materials, as well as the appropriate handling of waste during construction.

taquilla

Parque Explora

ALEJANDRO ECHEVERRI RESTREPO | MEDELLÍN, COLOMBIA 2008

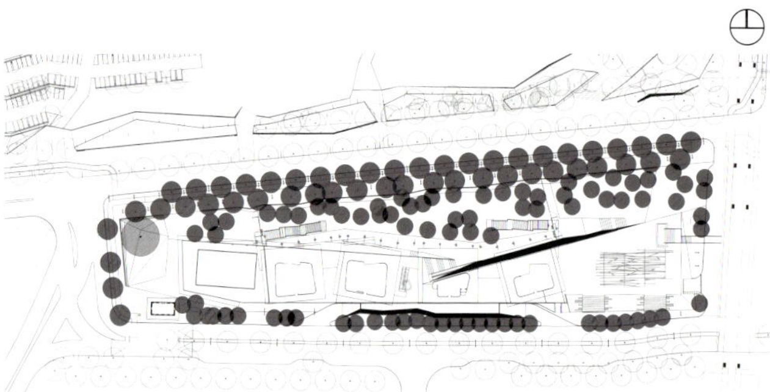

SITE PLAN

In order to create a museum of science and technology for children and young people that avoided well-worn academic formats and was timeless, dynamic, and flexible, the team from Medellín Town Hall, headed by the architect Alejandro Echeverri Restrepo, opted for forms and colors that correspond to "the festive spirit of the program without turning it into an ephemeral, fast-consumption fairground." So, Parque Explora is structured around a combination of open and closed spaces in constant touch with both its urban setting—nearby neighborhoods in the process of being developed—and its natural surroundings—the Andes Mountains. The main components are four red boxes that house the museum's interior, and a large square on the ground level that serves as the main entrance and plays host to various scientific games in an outdoor setting of young trees.

The new museum is set in the north of Medellín, in an area called the New North that is currently experiencing a social and physical transformation embodied by this iconic building. The upheavals of this urban process are reflected in the constant movement of visitors along the open spaces and through the red boxes.

TYPE OF PROJECT Interactive museum of science and technology

TOTAL SURFACE AREA 296,000 sq. ft. (27,476 m²)

PHOTOS © Sergio Gómez, Carlos Tobón

Parque Explora has become a catalyst for new activities in a run-down area currently in the process of being redeveloped. The project's colorful architecture makes the building stand out as a landmark visible from all over the city. The simple materials used on the exterior, such as concrete and red galvanized steel sheets, contrast with the complexity of the activities underway inside.

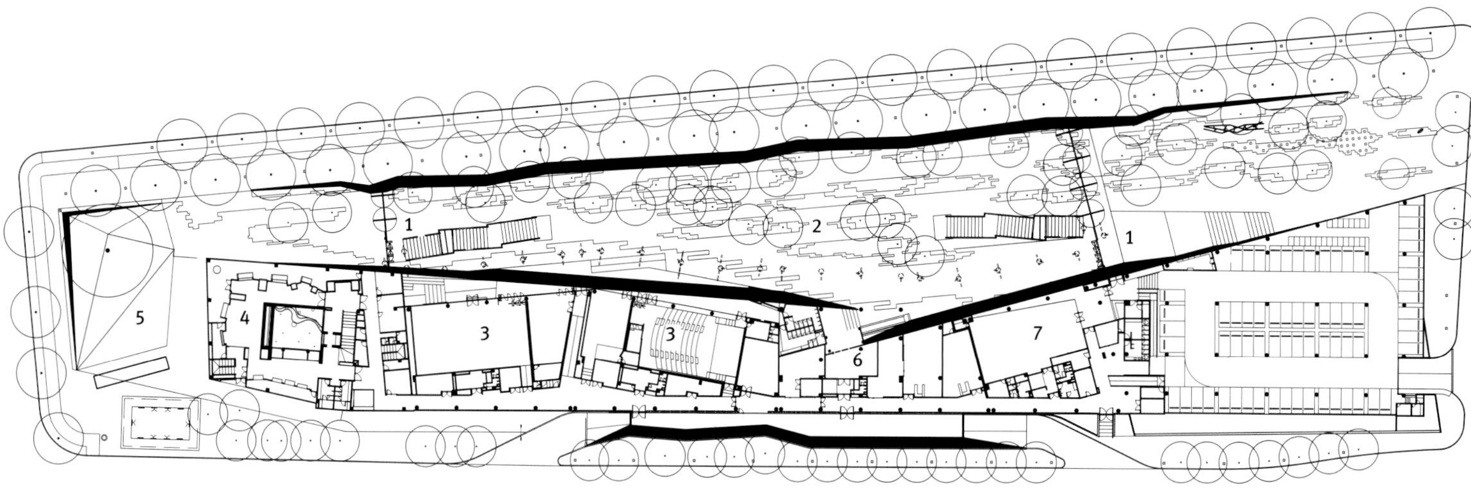

STREET LEVEL PLAN

1. ENTRANCES
2. OPEN HALL
3. CLASSROOMS
4. AQUARIUM
5. STATION PARK
6. RESTROOMS
7. STORE AND RESTAURANT
8. FOOD SQUARE
9. MEDELLÍN SUBWAY
10. BALCONY
11. LIVING PHYSICS HALL
12. LIFE CONNECTION HALL
13. GEODIVERSE COLOMBIA HALL
14. DIGITAL TERRITORY

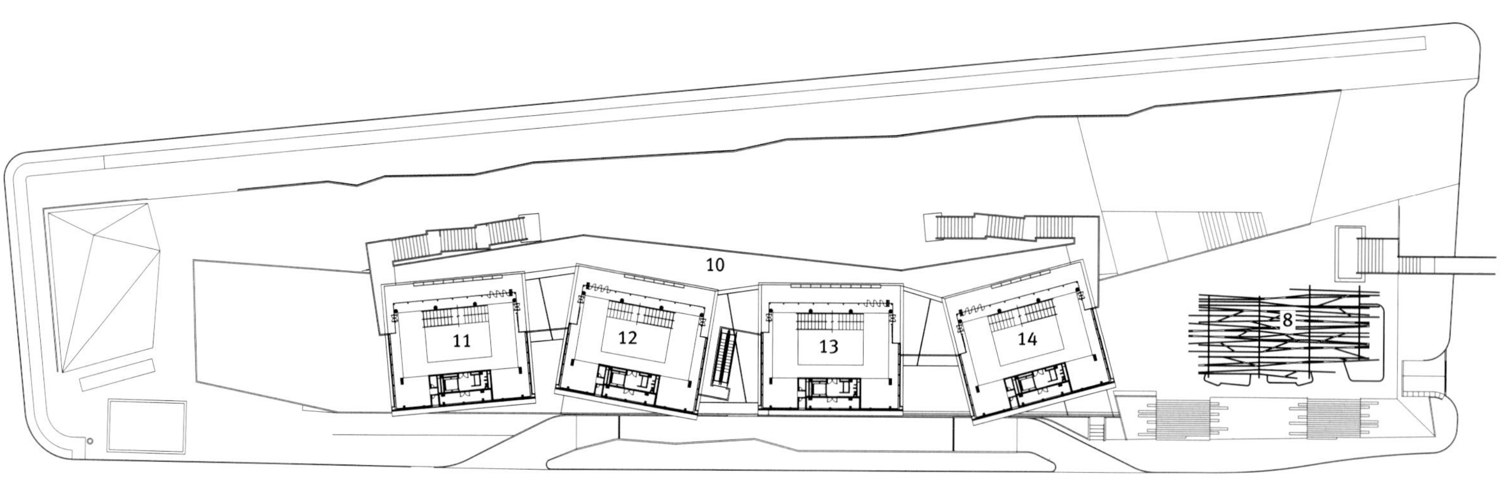

HALL LEVEL PLAN

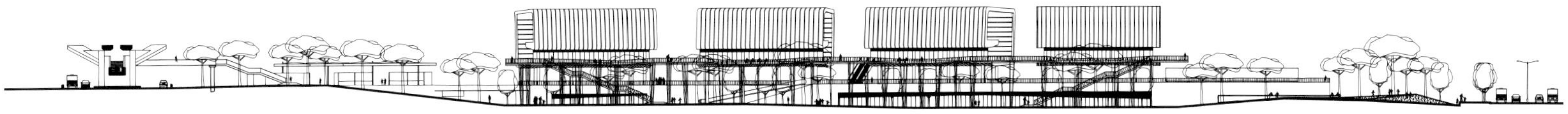

LONGITUDINAL SECTION — OPEN HALL

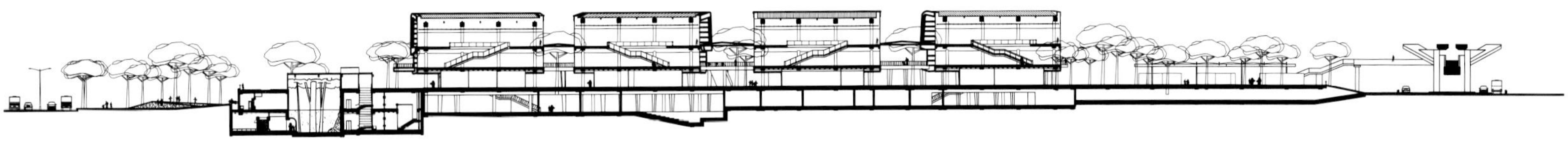

LONGITUDINAL SECTION — AQUARIUM

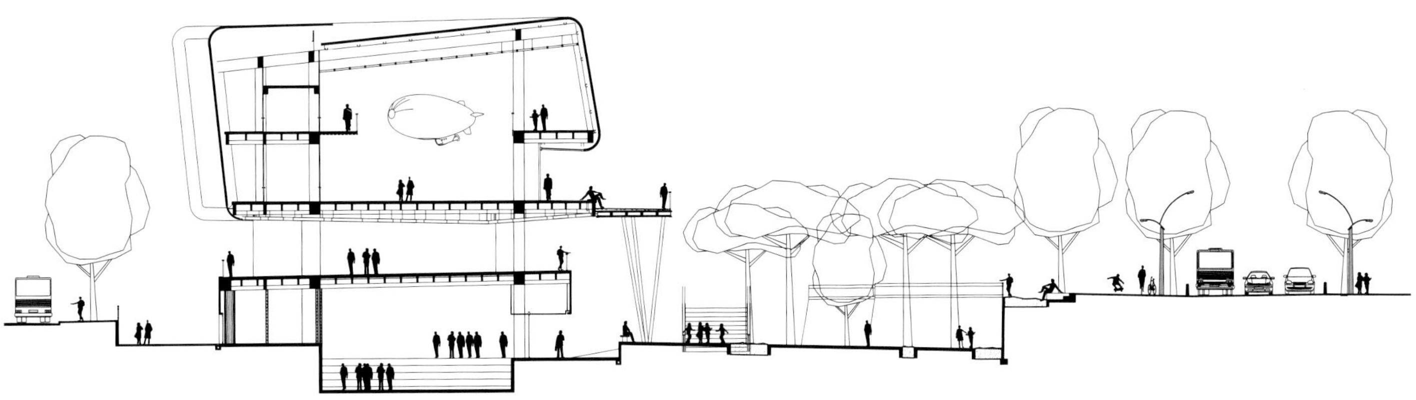

CROSS SECTION — LIFE CONNECTION HALL

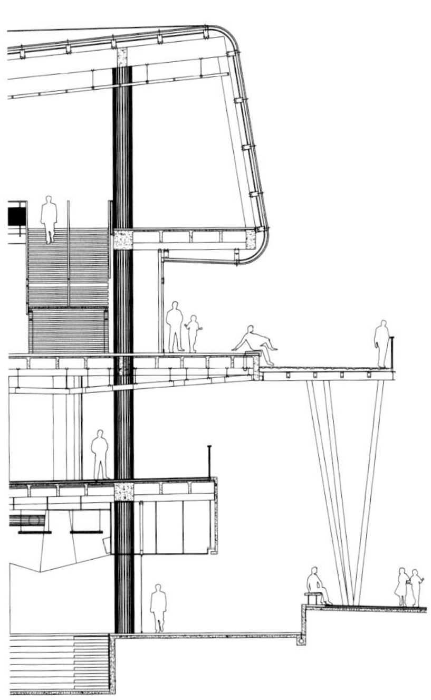

CONSTRUCTION DETAIL OF THE FACADE

The architect has created a new topography of fissures and undulations to form the silhouette of a museum that has become one of the city's most visible buildings from every angle. Parque Explora was designed to present science as a field directly related to everyday life. Visitors participate actively and freely in their own scientific apprenticeship. Users interact with a microworld, allowing them to discover physical phenomena and relate them to their own life. The museum also proclaims the diversity of the natural environment, with special emphasis on Colombia.

The open square owes its fairground atmosphere to the attractions on offer as extensions to the enclosed spaces. This area is further complemented by technological games set on the first floor, between the square and the red boxes; an aquarium, a digital movie theater, a TV studio, administrative offices, and technological services are included. On the top level, the museum's core spaces are found inside the red boxes: Living Physics, Connection of Life, Geodiverse Colombia, and Digital Territory. These closed spaces are connected via a long raised walkway, supported by a large metal structure that forms the nexus of the entire project.

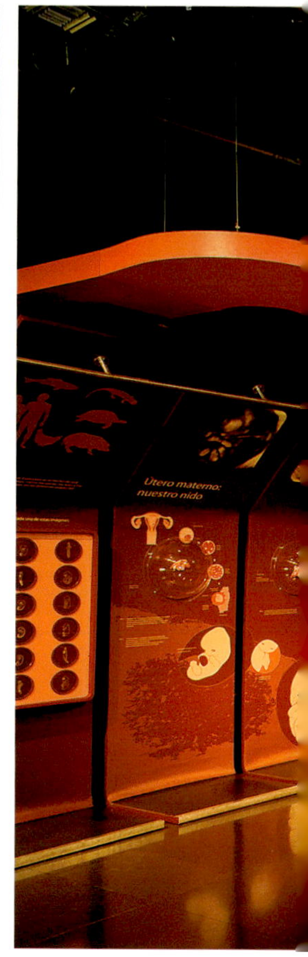
Útero materno:
nuestro nido

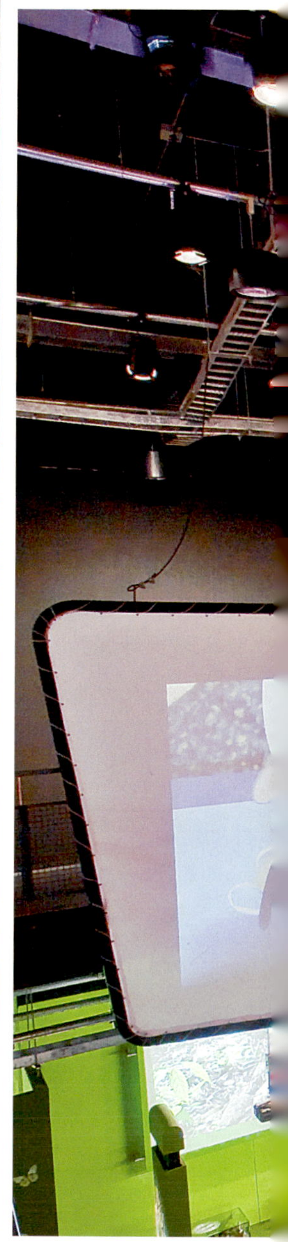

The installations in the large interior spaces are left exposed to view, while the state-of-the-art technology of the scientific games interacts with the basic systems in the construction. The interiors echo the simplicity of the materials, combining with the constant movement of users and activities to complete the project's program.

Netherlands Institute of Sound and Vision

NEUTELINGS RIEDIJK ARCHITECTEN | HILVERSUM, NETHERLANDS 2006

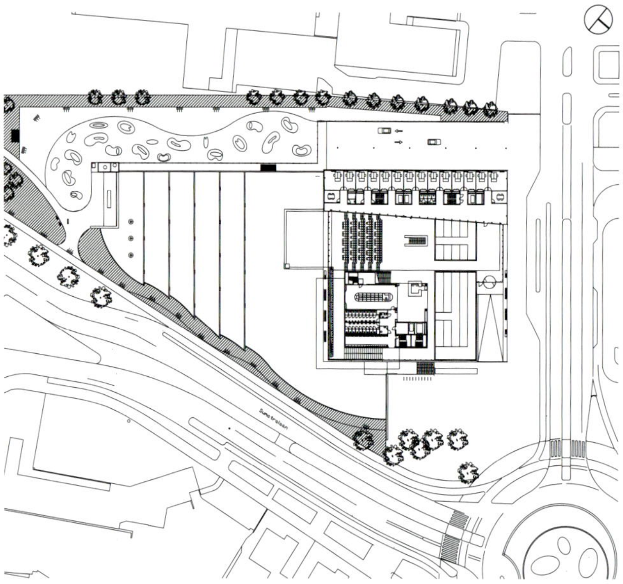

SITE PLAN

Hilversum is situated 19 miles (30 km) south of Amsterdam and forms part of the Randstad, a large conurbation known as Media City, as it groups together the main Dutch radio and television corporations. The Netherlands Institute of Sound and Vision fits into this context by preserving all the archives covering the history of Dutch radio and television, and the architects conceived the building as a large TV set paying tribute to the national memory. So, working in collaboration with the artist Jaap Drupsteen and a research team from TNO Eindhoven and Saint-Gobain, they turned the facades into a tactile surface made of glass panels enhanced by reliefs.

Still images retrieved from TV broadcasts were chosen to represent the variety of archives in the institute; in all, 748 images were applied to 2,100 glass panels. Each photogram was transferred to a particular section by applying ceramic paste to the glass, while the relief was created by using a CNC (computerized numerical control) milling machine with a small bit that runs along an MDF wooden board. The glass was treated with a layer of ceramic paste, put into a sand mold, and then inserted into an oven heated to 1508°F (820°C) C. At this temperature, the glass takes on the form of the mold and the paste sticks the image on it.

TYPE OF PROJECT **National broadcasting archives**

TOTAL SURFACE AREA **377,000 sq. ft. (35,000 m²)**

PHOTOS **© Daria Scagliola, Stijn Brakkee**

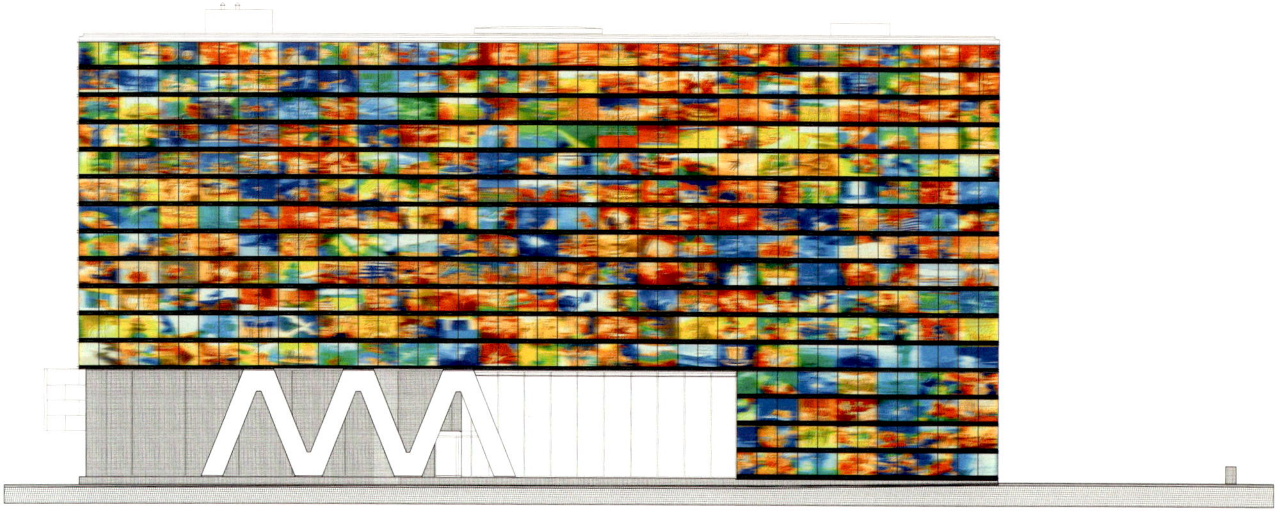

NORTH ELEVATION

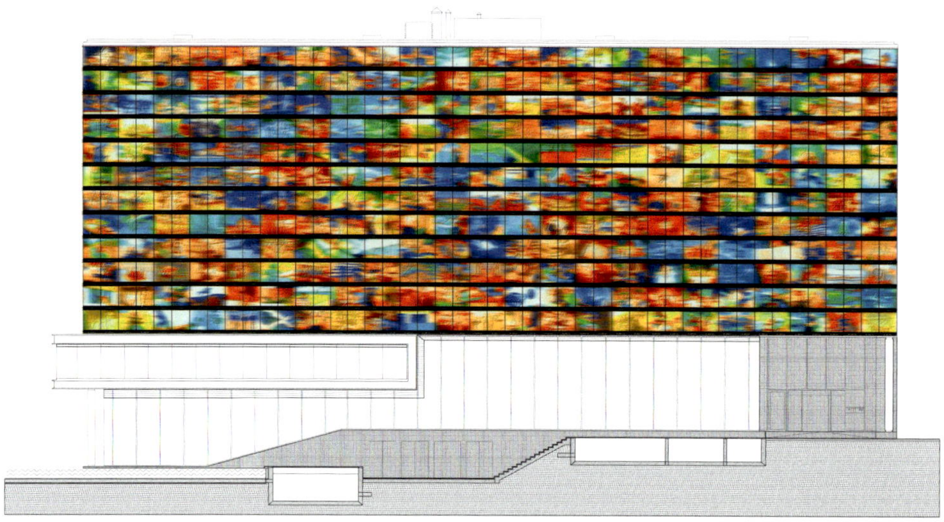

EAST ELEVATION

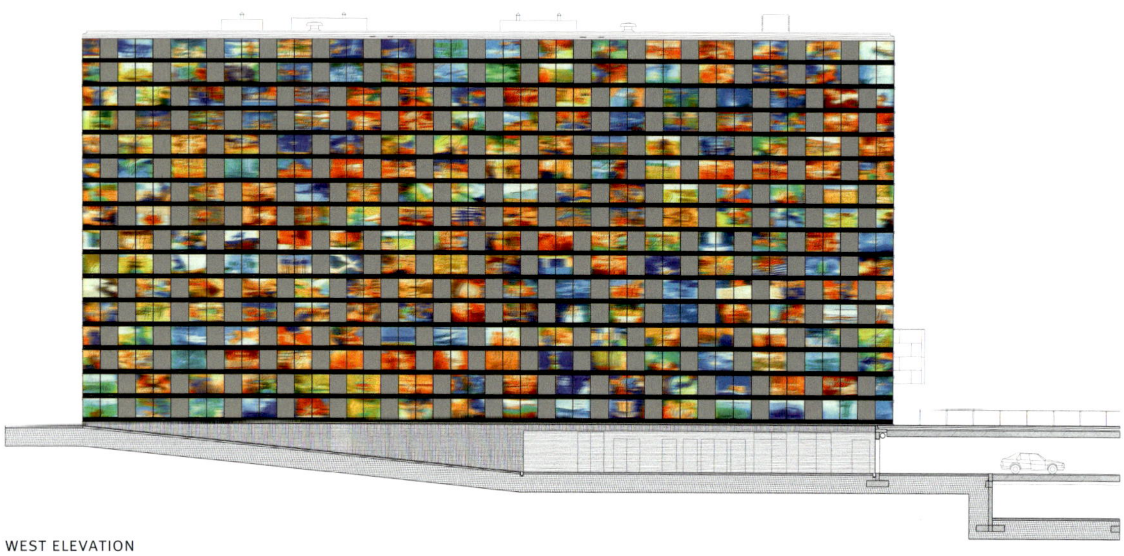

WEST ELEVATION

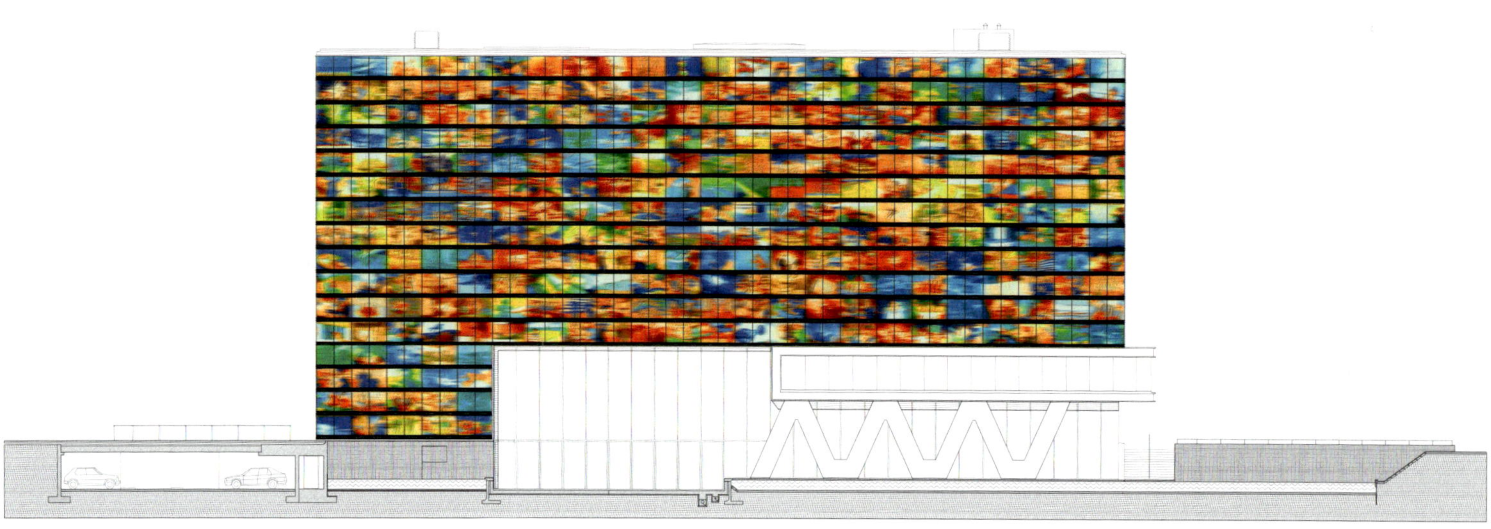

SOUTH ELEVATION

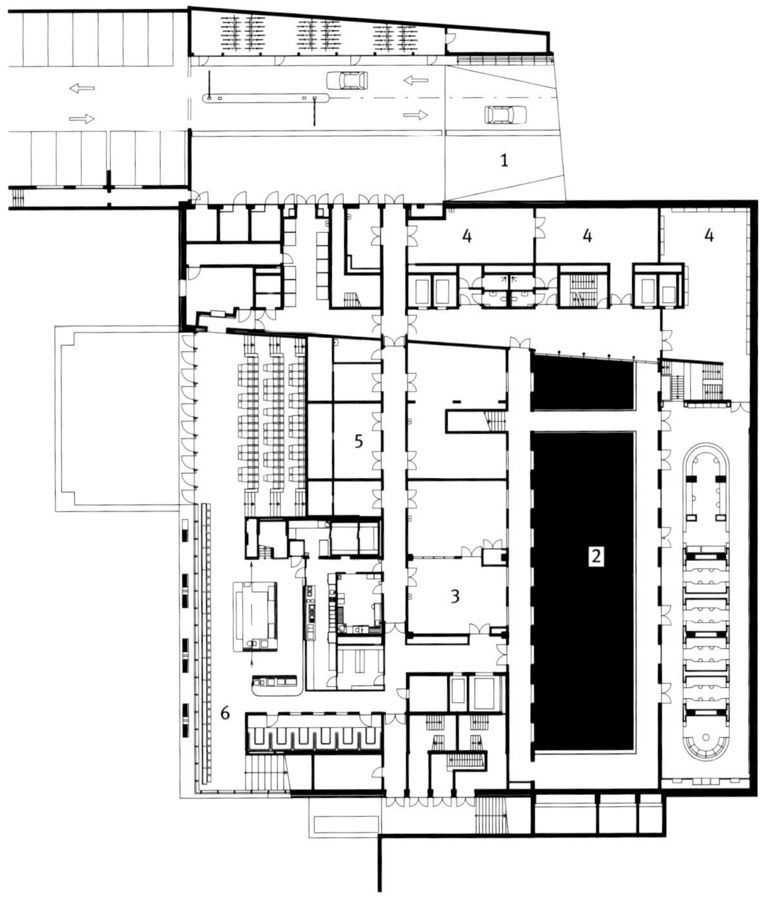

FIRST BASEMENT PLAN

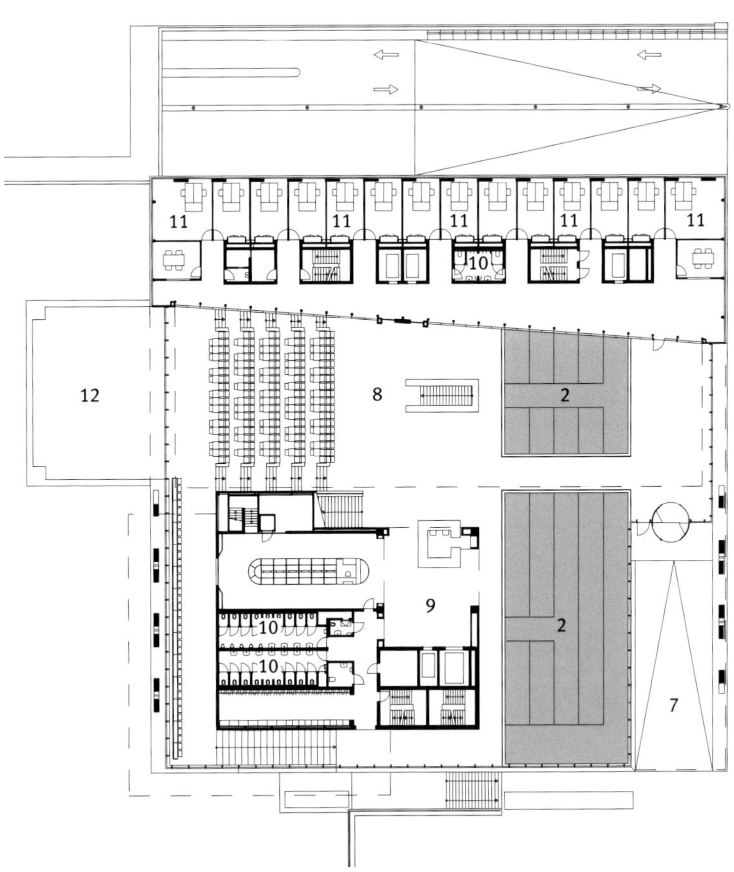

GROUND FLOOR

1. GARAGE ENTRANCE
2. INNER COURTYARD
3. WORKSHOPS
4. ARCHIVES
5. STORAGE AREAS
6. CAFETERIA
7. PUBLIC ENTRANCE
8. ATRIUM
9. FOYER AND STORE
10. RESTROOMS
11. OFFICES
12. TERRACE

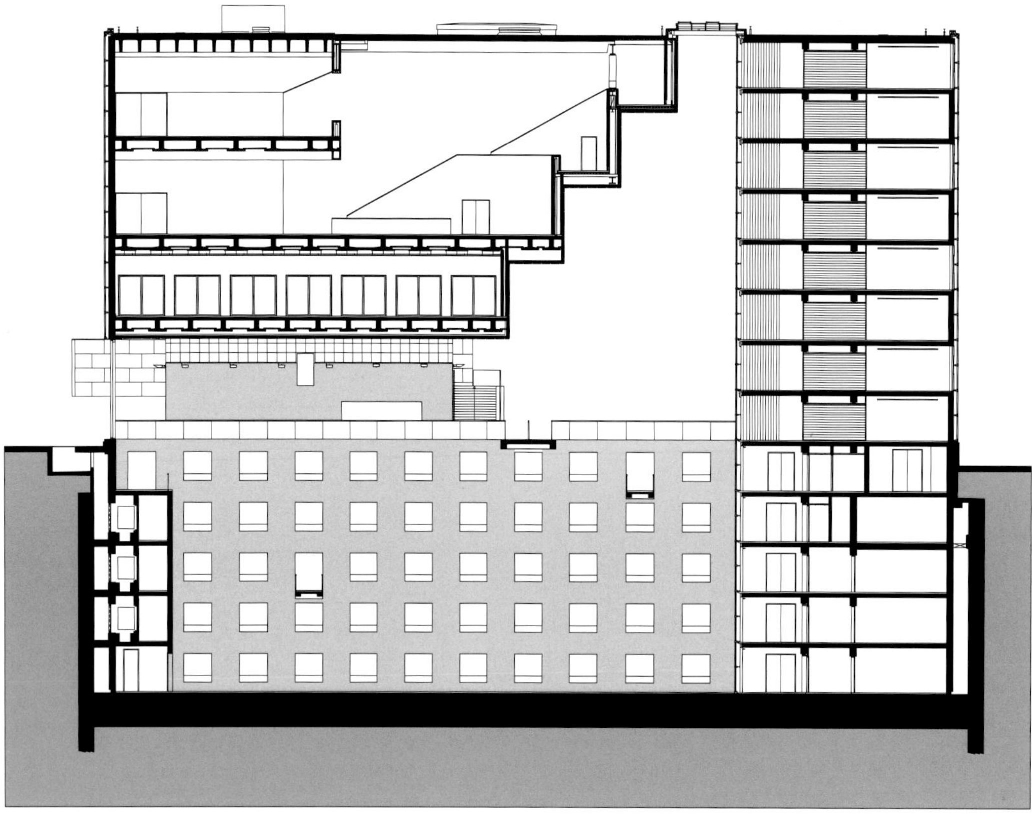

LONGITUDINAL SECTION—INNER COURTYARD

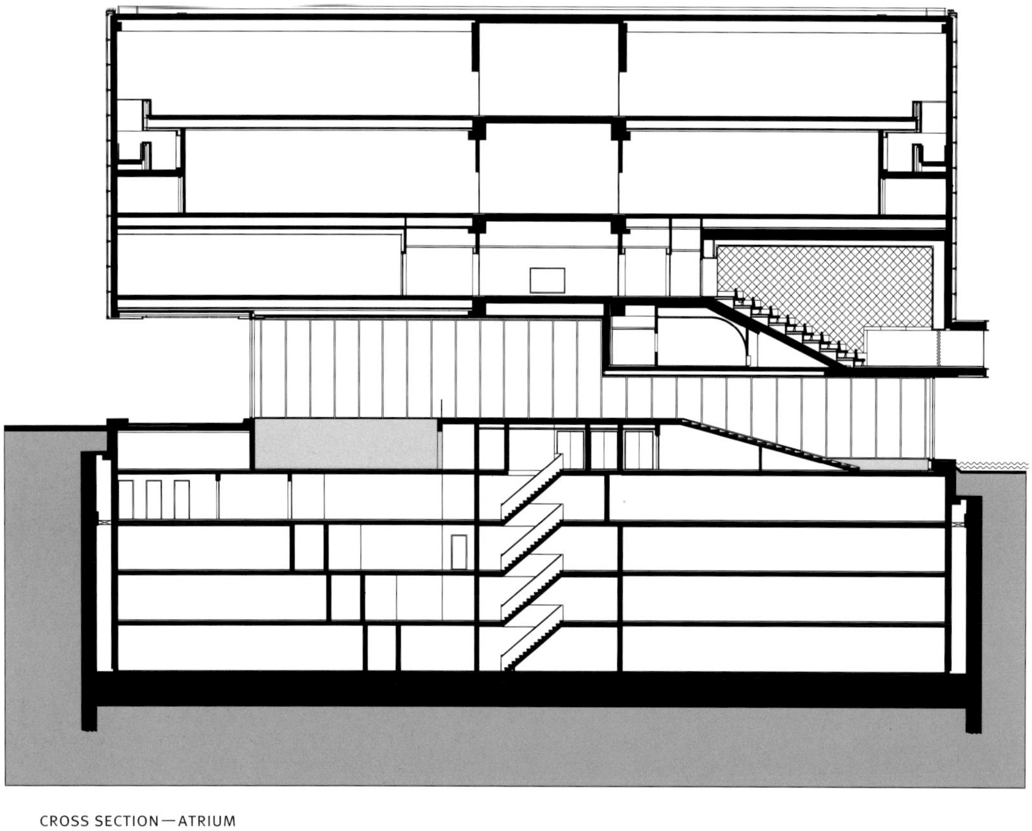

CROSS SECTION—ATRIUM

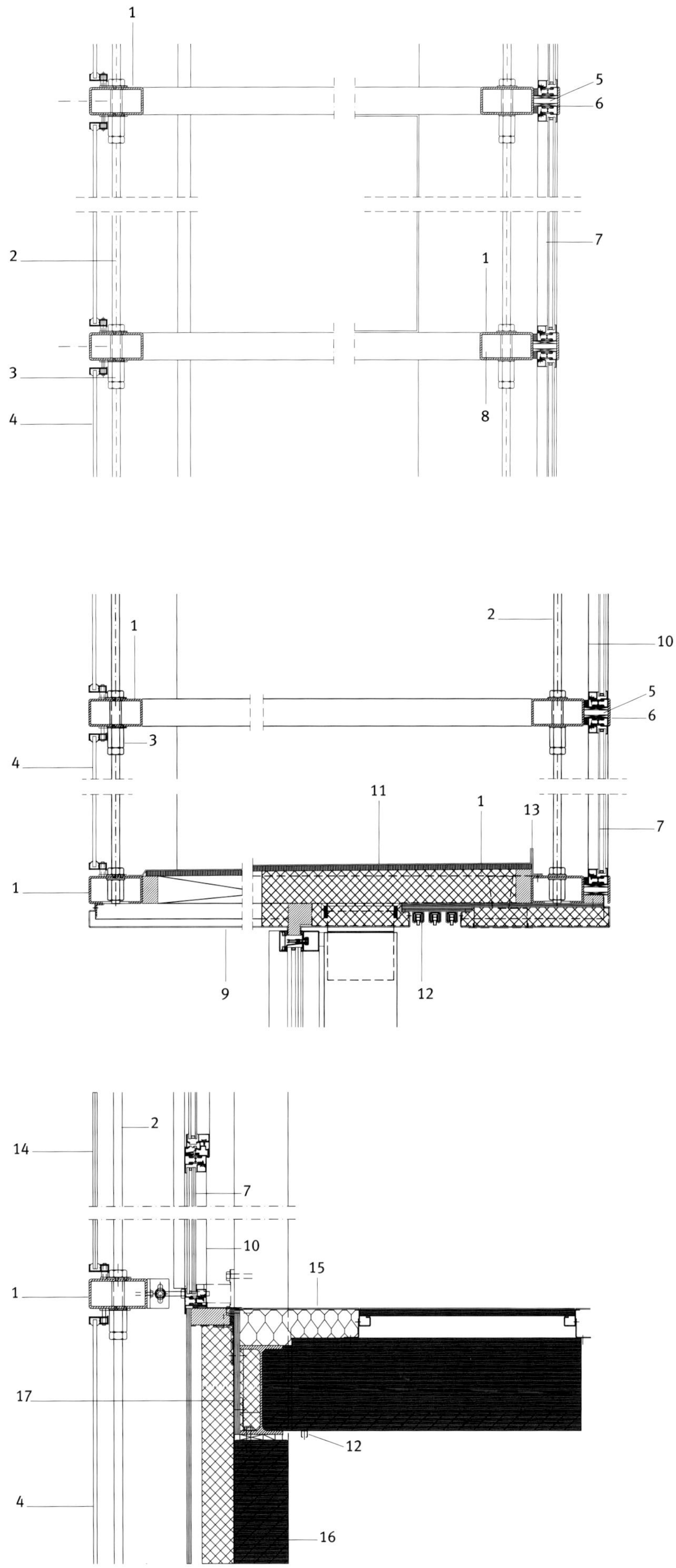

1. 5 x 3 in. (120 x 80 mm) steel crossbeam
2. 1 in. (24 mm) suspended steel tube
3. Nut joint
4. Tempered glass with relief
5. Wear strip
6. Steel plate
7. Clear glass with chamber
8. Support for steel crossbeam
9. Galvanized steel plate
10. Steel insulating frame
11. Synthetic resin cladding
12. Rails for drapes
13. Steel sheet covered with plastic
14. Clear tempered glass
15. 1/8 in. (4mm) linoleum floor
16. Prefabricated concrete
17. Cement-fiber cladding

CONSTRUCTION DETAILS

The building is spread over two volumes that are clearly visible in the elevation. The archive is set underground, while the theaters are located in the upper section; the reception area, services, and public spaces link the two. The core of the construction comprises a large central hollow running from the foundations to the roof to create a nexus for the building's five component elements: the archives, museum, offices, reception, and services.

Agora Theater

UNStudio | LELYSTAD, NETHERLANDS 2007

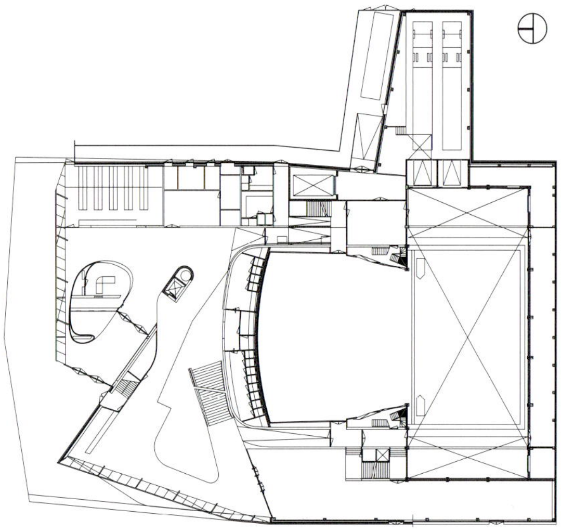

SITE PLAN

The new Agora Theater, designed by the studio of Ben van Berkel and Caroline Bos, forms part of the renovation plan for Lelystad's urban center, drawn up by West 8. UNStudio's building replaces a theater that opened in 1976 and was knocked down in 2004. The new construction was required to breathe new life into this new town—planned after World War II—in an appropriately theatrical way: capturing spectators' attention through pranks and stories, education, and encouragement for reflection. This approach led to the decision to create geometry in both the interior and the exterior that would simulate a kaleidoscope, echoing the experience of being on stage.

The theater design explores the integration of the arts and the new media into a single sculptural form, thereby turning the exterior into a landmark in the city. The facades, distinguished by their sharp angles and arched planes, are covered with sheets of glass and steel painted yellow and orange. At night, the colors on the exterior are set off by meticulously calculated lighting, created with the input of Arup as a design consultant.

The shape of the exterior also responds, for obvious acoustical reasons, to the need to separate two auditoriums on different levels. The plan embraces two theater spaces (with 725 and 200 seats, respectively), various foyers, dressing rooms, multifunctional rooms, a café and restaurant. Inside, the colors become more intense: the main auditorium is red, while the color scheme for the staircase running from the center of the foyer on the ground floor spans white, pink, violet, and various shades of red.

TYPE OF PROJECT **Cultural facility**

COLOR **UNStudio**

LIGHTING **Arup Lighting**

TOTAL SURFACE AREA **63,400 sq. ft. (5,890 m²)**

PHOTOS **Agora Theater, 2007, UN Studio © Christian Richters**

The theater has become a landmark in the town that emphasizes the diagonal route running from the central station.

The movement of the planes on the facades has made it possible to create spaces in which the perspective of the audience intersects with that of the performers: an area set above the main entrance, reserved for the theater staff, allows them to look through a large sloping window and watch members of the public entering the building.

PRELIMINARY STUDY

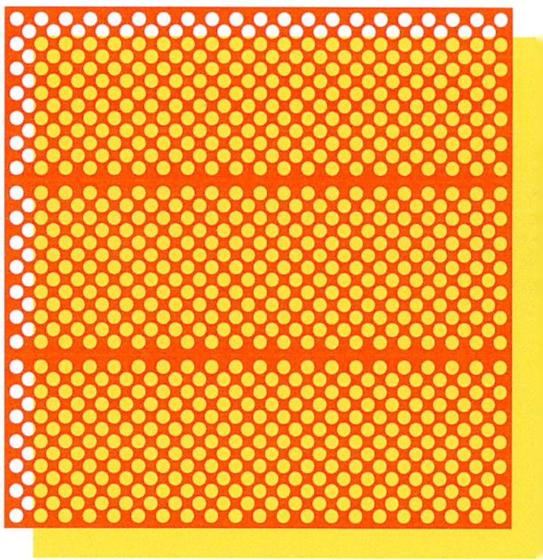

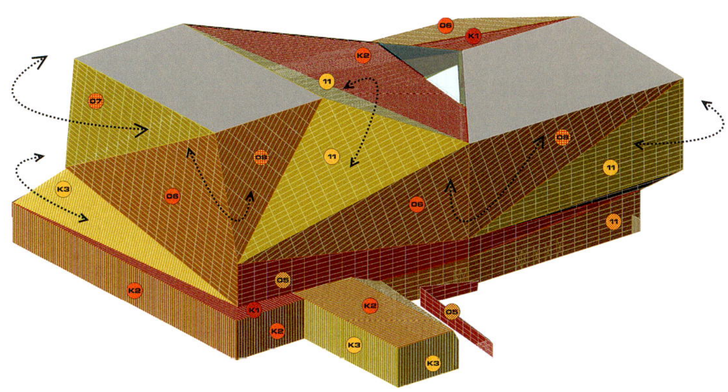

NORTHWEST VIEW

SOUTHWEST VIEW

DISTRIBUTION OF THE COLORS ON THE FACADES

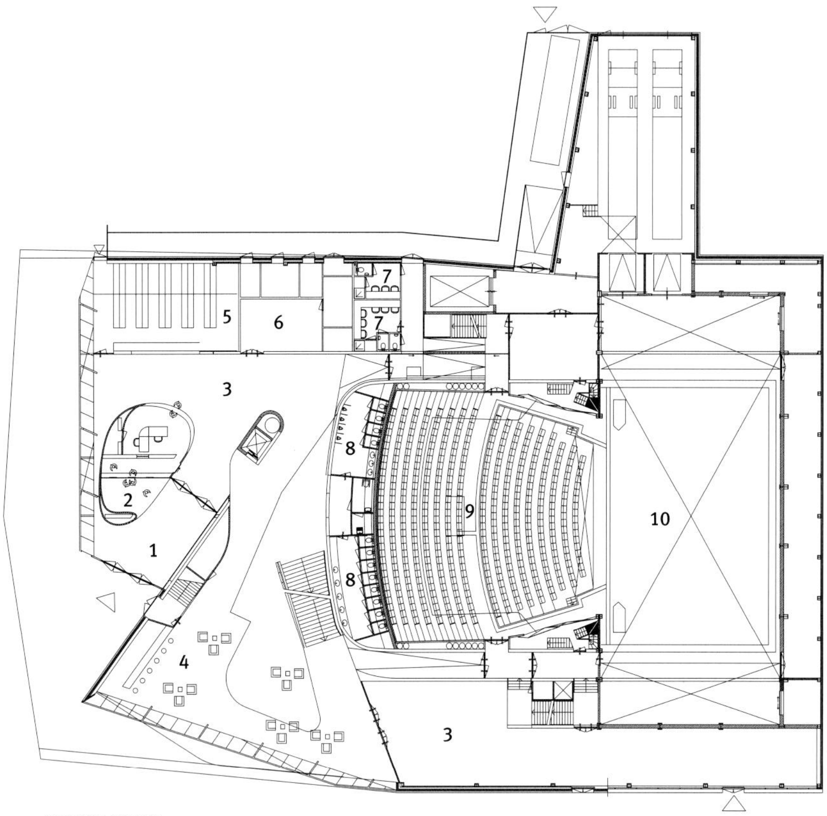

GROUND FLOOR

1. MAIN ENTRANCE
2. COUNTER
3. FOYER
4. BARS
5. CHECKROOM
6. OFFICES
7. DRESSING ROOM
8. SERVICES
9. LARGE THEATER
10. STAGE AND INSTALLATIONS IN THE LARGE THEATER
11. SMALL THEATER
12. BALCONY OBSERVATION POINT
13. MULTIPURPOSE HALLS
14. STORAGE AREA

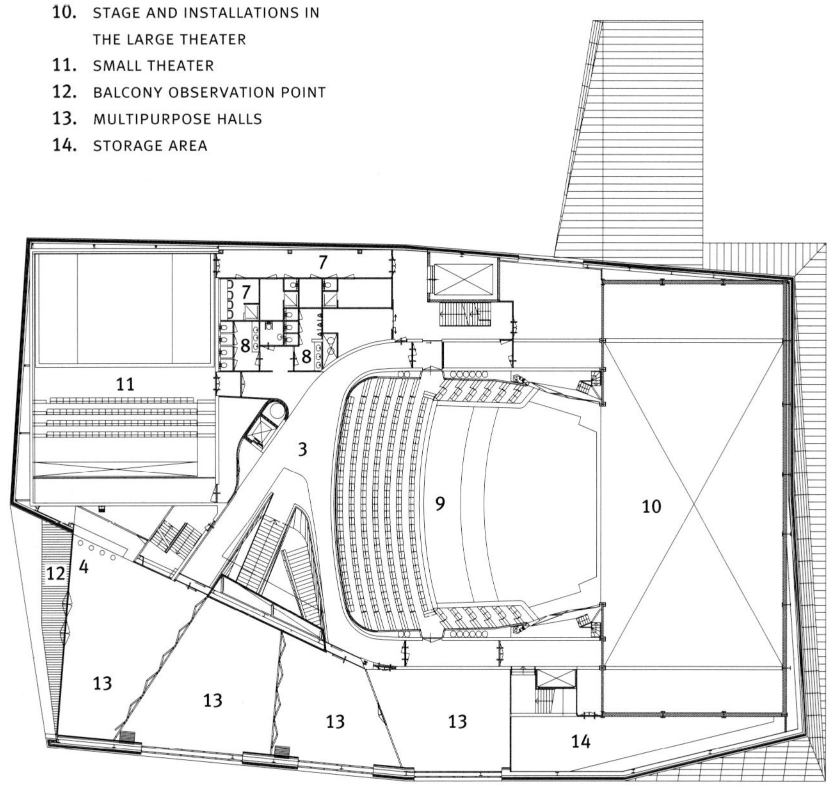

SECOND FLOOR

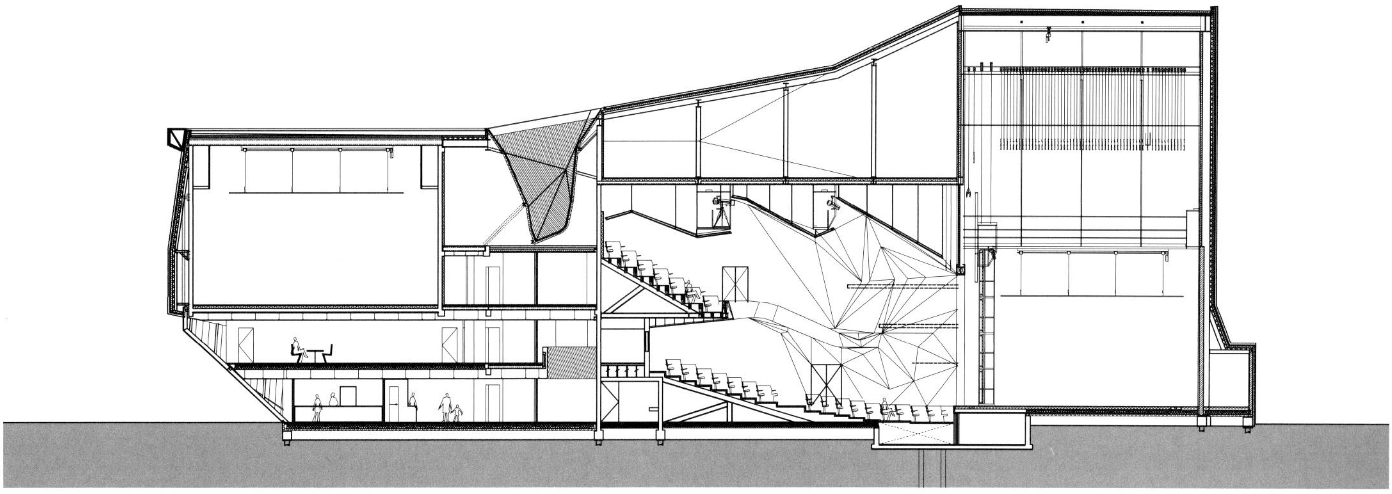

CROSS SECTION—COUNTER

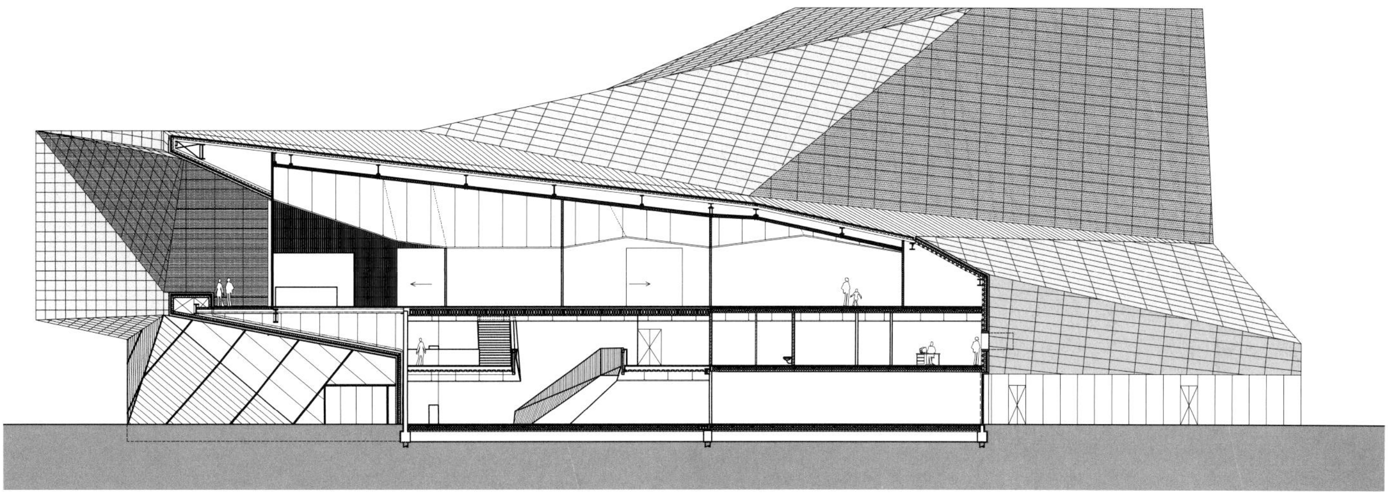

CROSS SECTION—MAIN ENTRANCE

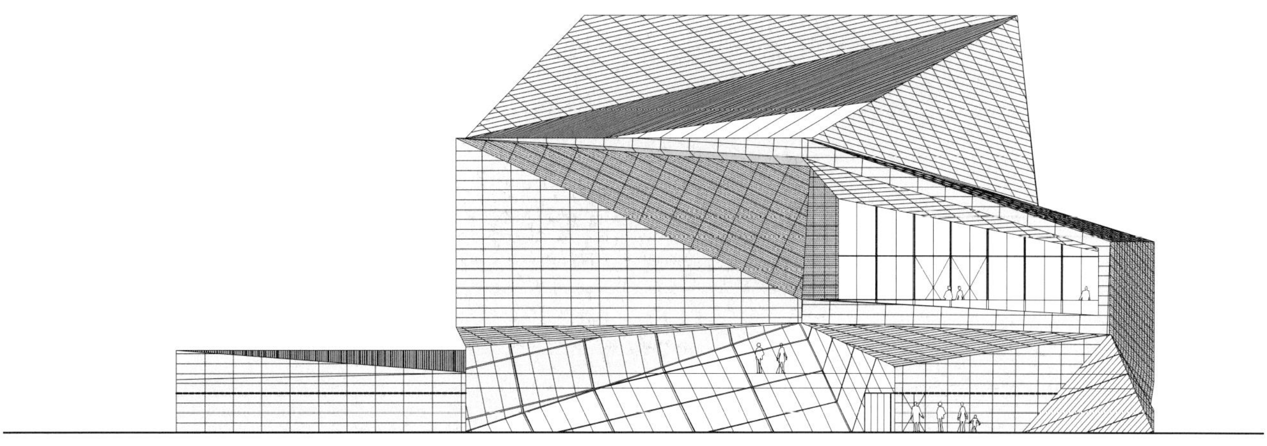

NORTH ELEVATION

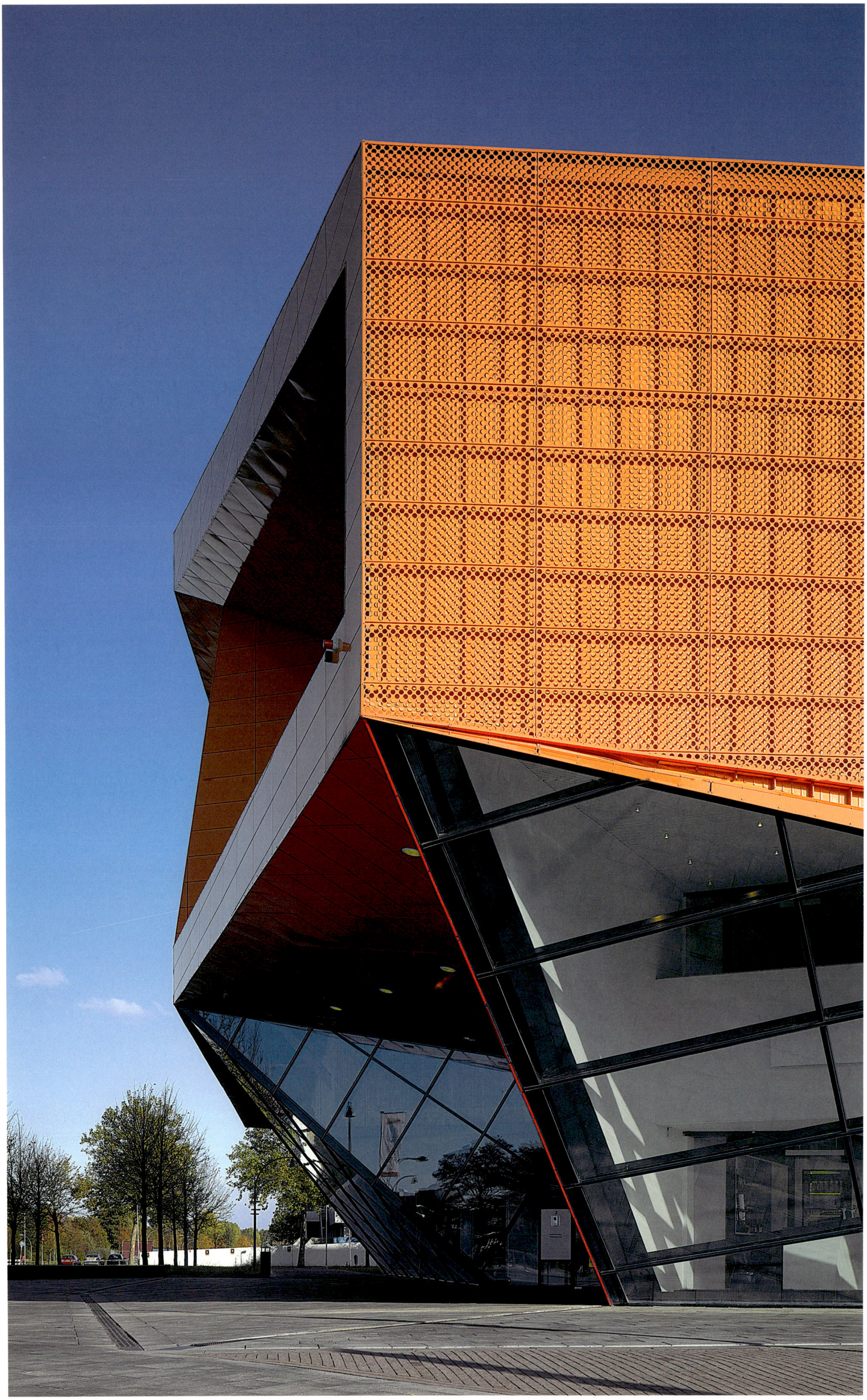

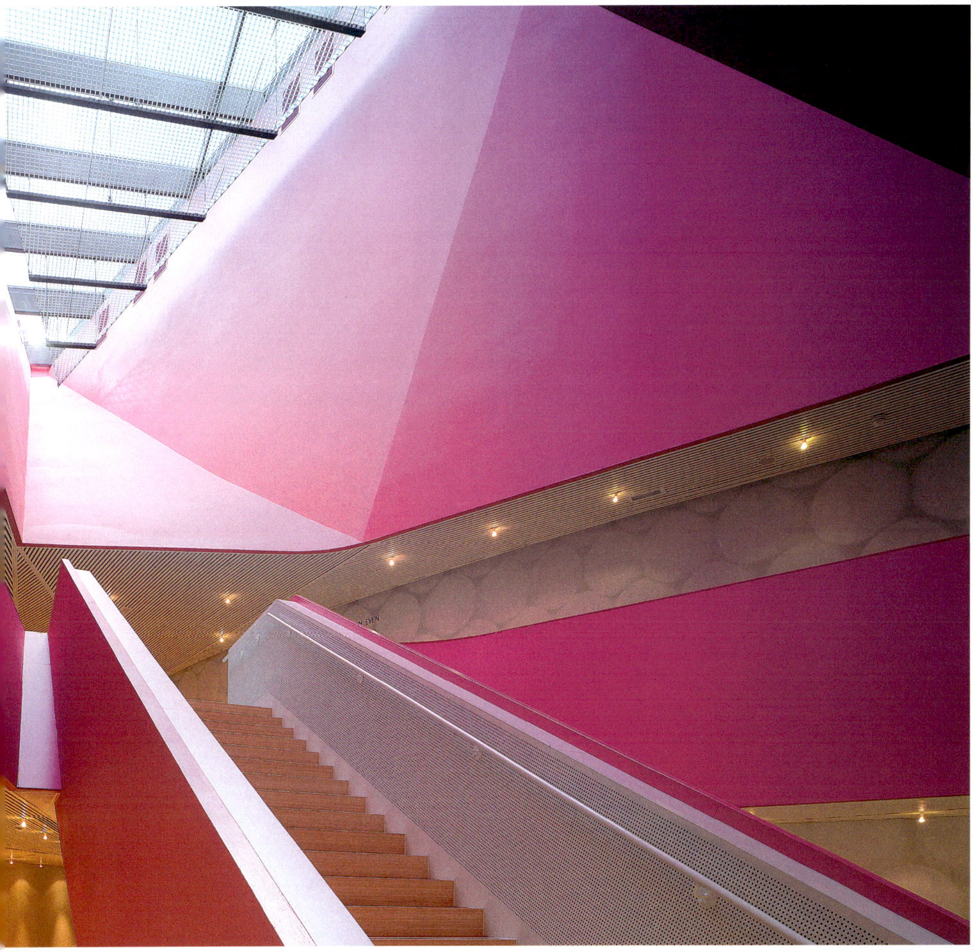

Bearing in mind the innovations witnessed by theatrical architecture in recent years, the team from UNStudio sought to endow the Agora with a clear, open organization in order to achieve a multifunctional theater of flexible, transparent, and intelligent design.

So, inside, the staircase leading from the main foyer reflects the building's complexity by serving as a link between auditoriums on different floors.

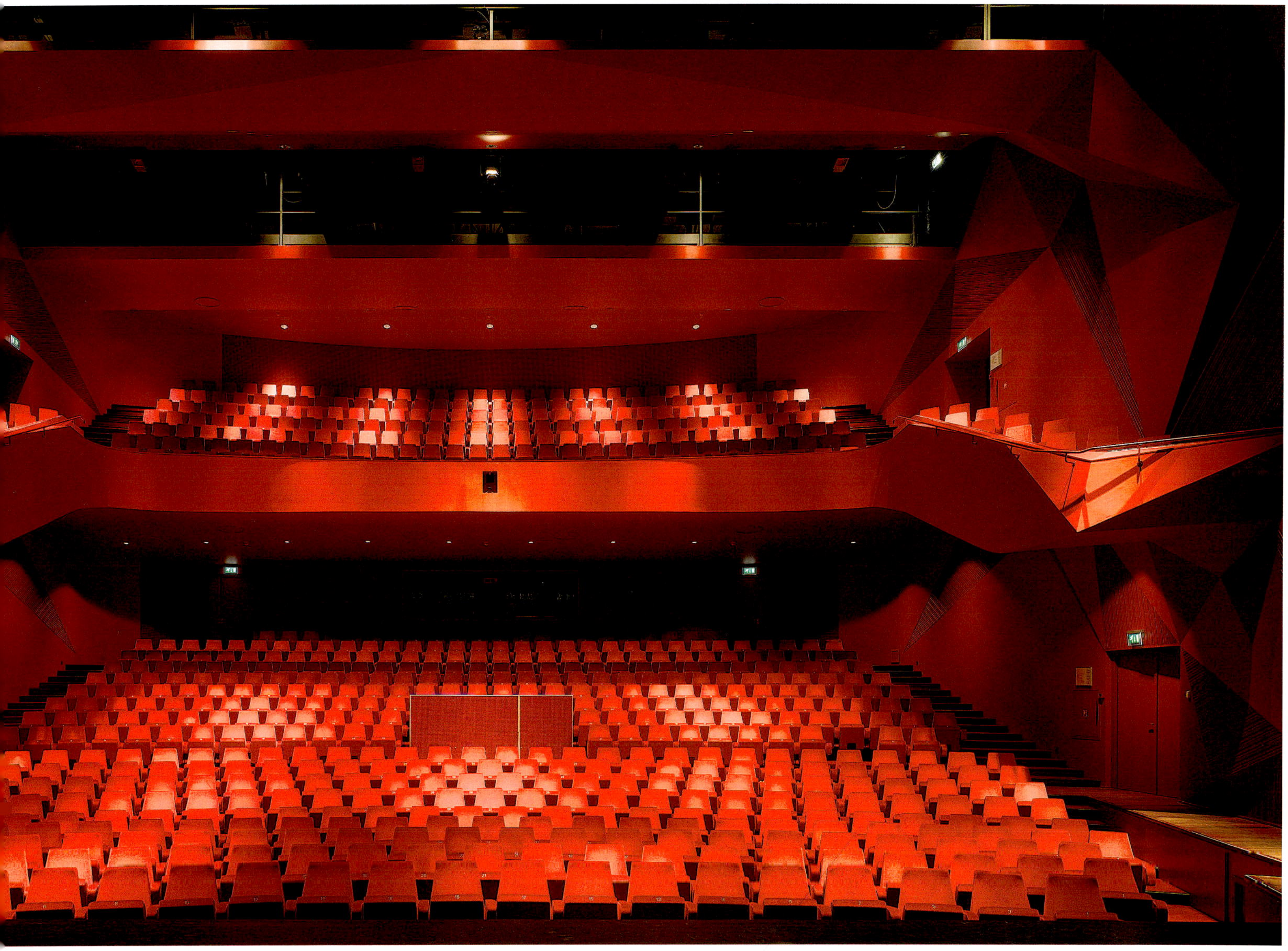

sound

278
Windshape | Lacoste, France
nARCHITECTS

288
Sonic Forest | Zaragoza, Spain
Christopher Janney

298
Center for the Dramatic Arts | Taipei, Taiwan
B+U

310
Low Rez / Hi Fi | Washington, DC, United States
Höweler + Yoon Architecture

318
Chant de bambous | Chaumont-sur-Loire, France
N+B Architectes

324
Kofmehl | Solothurn, Switzerland
ssm architekten

Windshape

nARCHITECTS | LACOSTE, FRANCE 2006

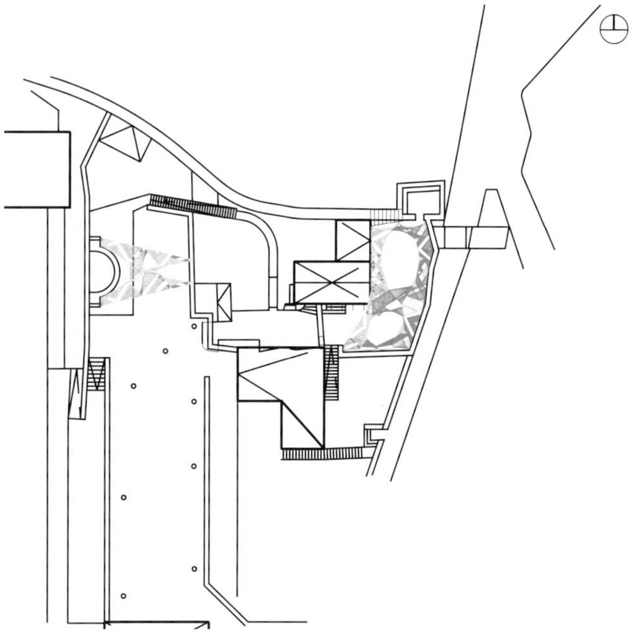

SITE PLAN

280

The University of Arts and Design Savannah (SCAD) commissioned nArchitects to design a reunion center near its French campus in Lacoste, a picturesque medieval town with cobbled streets and vernacular architecture, built on a mountaintop in Provence. This small town, complete with a castle once occupied by the Marquis de Sade in the eighteenth century, seems to have been carved out of the mountain, while the fields of vines and lavender that stretch out at its feet form a luminous, gently rolling landscape that is constantly changing. The architects created a space that owes its external form to the town's angular geometry and the dynamism inherent in the surrounding countryside.

During the summer of 2006, the town welcomed a new public space for concerts, exhibitions, and a range of performances. The architects worked with a group of students from SCAD to put up Windshape in just five weeks, thanks to a new construction method that facilitated the use of some predetermined and some undefined elements to create pavilions with stacked, tiered tripods. The final outcome was a simple structure made up of groups of three white plastic tubes that comprised the tripods, joined together by strips of aluminum. Polypropylene cords, also white, were woven together in situ and the structures were placed on top of each other; once they had been mounted, further cords were woven together and strung between the tripods.

TYPE OF PROJECT **Temporary installation**

TOTAL SURFACE AREA **18,500 sq. ft. (1,720 m²)**

PHOTOS **© nArchitects, Daniela Zimmer**

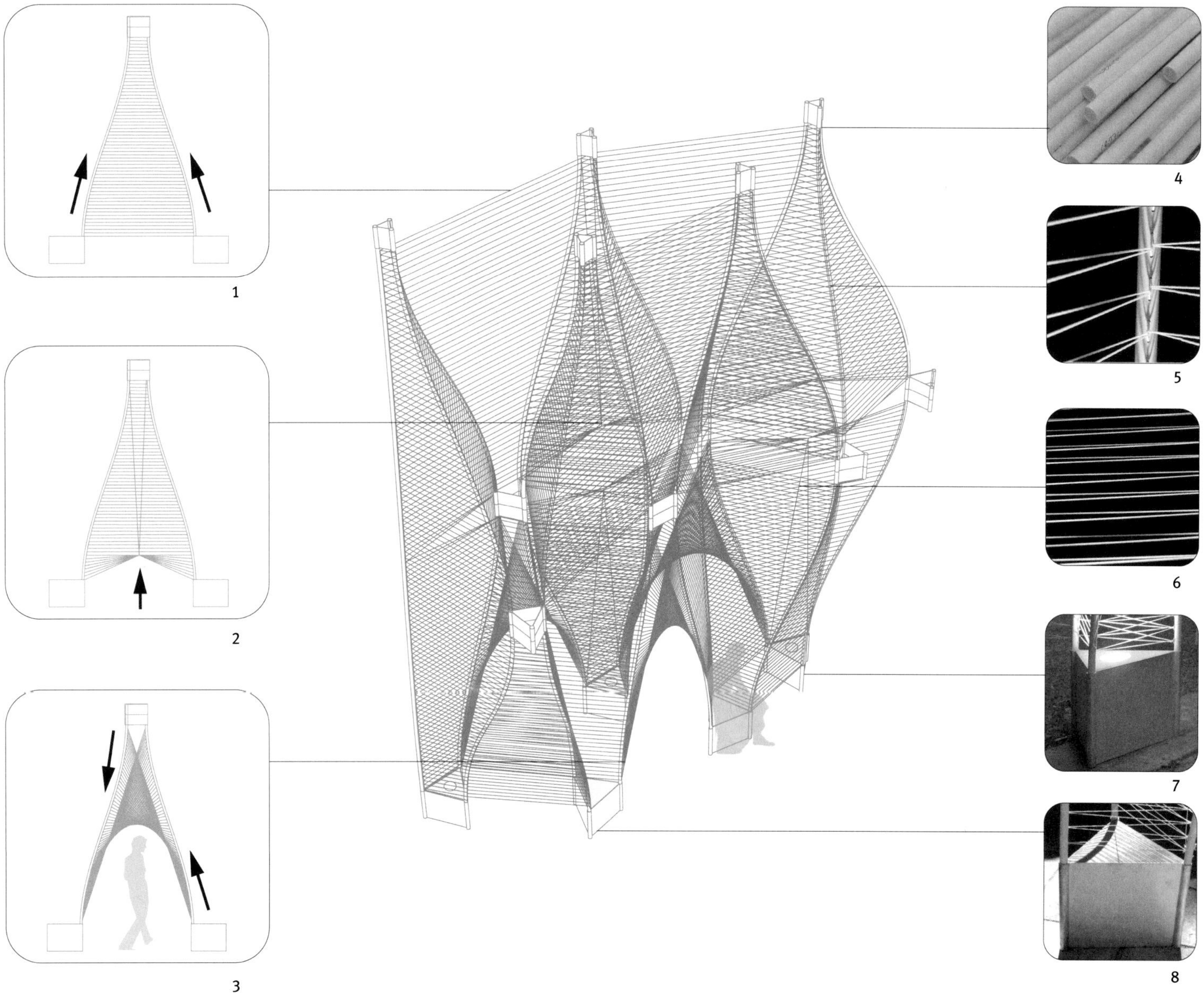

DIAGRAM OF STRATEGIES FOR WEAVING AND MATERIALS

1. STANDARD WEAVE
2. GATHERED WEAVE
3. PARABOLIC WEAVE
4. PLASTIC TUBES
5. BASIC STITCHING
6. COMPLEMENTARY WEAVE
7. TRIPOD BASE AND LAMP
8. TRIPOD BASE AND SEAT

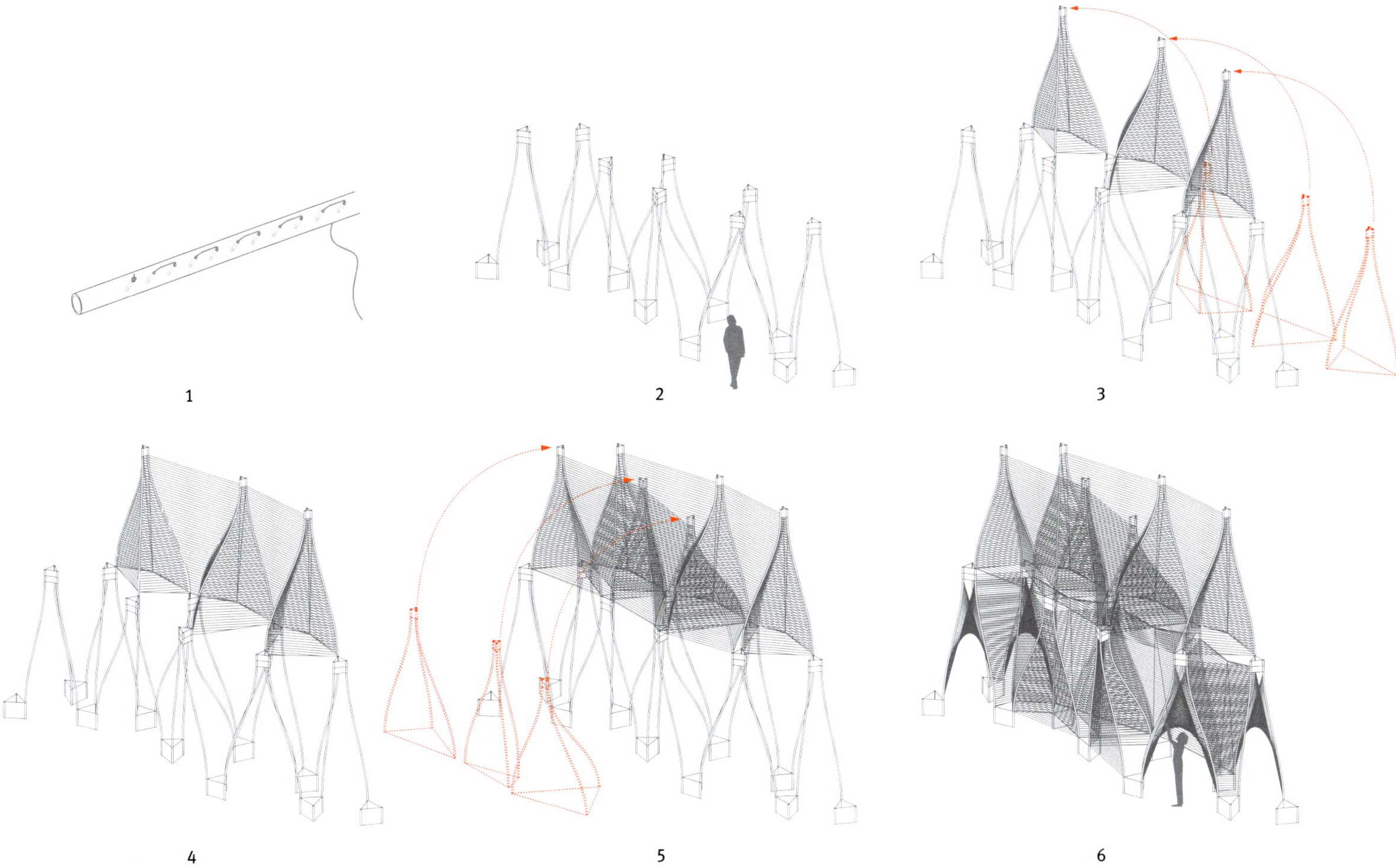

CONSTRUCTION SEQUENCE

1. STITCHING ON THE PLASTIC TUBES
2. MOUNTING THE BASE TRIPODS
3. PRE-BRAIDING AND MOUNTING THE UPPER TRIPODS
4. WEAVING BETWEEN THE TRIPODS
5. MOUNTING THE UPPER TRIPODS AND WEAVING BETWEEN THEM
6. BRAIDING THE BASE

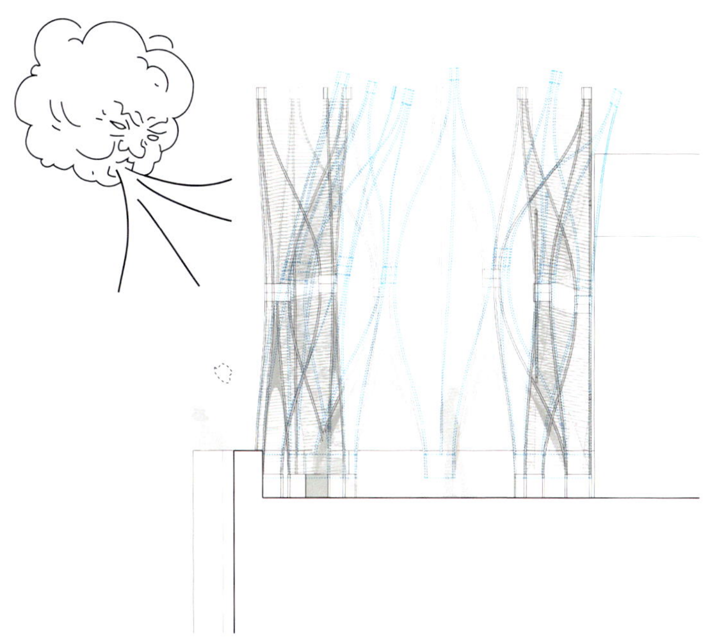

COMPLETE STRUCTURE

284

nARCHITECTS, founded in 1999 by Eric Bunge and Mimi Hoang, seeks to create receptive, flexible architecture that results in structures subject to change. The experience of building Windshape allowed them to investigate the idea of a building that would respond to natural stimuli. This temporary installation consisted of 26-foot (8-m) high pavilions that changed constantly in accordance with the speed of the wind. By altering the tension in the cords, the wind set up rhythmic undulations and rapid vibrations, causing the pavilions to take on different forms as they swelled up or shrunk. The installation was lit up at night, with the marquis de Sade's castle as a backdrop, and it could be seen 3 miles (5 km) away.

31 miles (50 km) of polypropylene cords were used to make Windshape, threaded through the structure to create densely woven surfaces which offered spaces that served for sitting on and other, more fluid areas that formed doors and windows. The characteristics of these thin, fragile materials were exploited to create an elastic structure, so that the curved tubes and taut cords formed a flexible shell, which moved with the oscillations of the wind. Thus, the structure combined purpose-built pieces with others built in situ.

CHIMÈRES

The architects developed a construction method that enabled them to combine regular and irregular manufacturing systems. The cords, tubes, and aluminum strips were already defined and digitally modelled, but additional elements were incorporated as the structure was going up.

Sonic Forest

CHRISTOPHER JANNEY | ZARAGOZA, SPAIN 2008

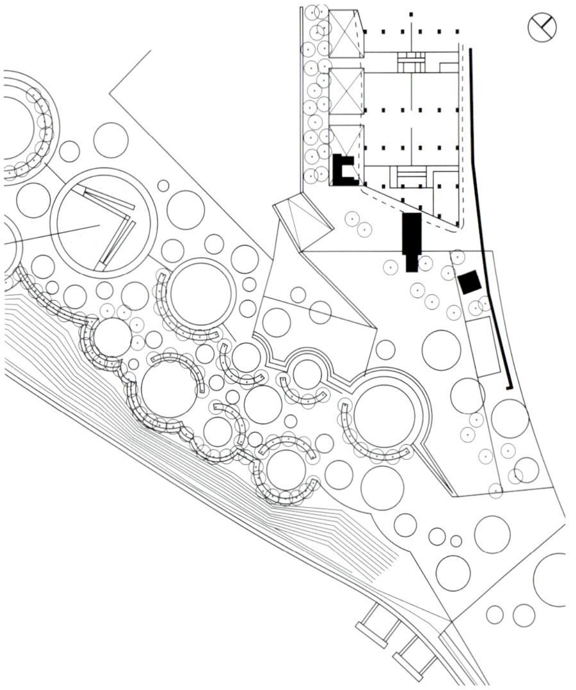

SITE PLAN

Christopher Janney's project for the 2008 Zaragoza Expo was one of the "urban musical instruments" that he has been creating since his student days to enliven built-up settings by means of sound and light. His first Sonic Forest was installed in 1994 on the square in front of the PPG Building in Pittsburgh and in front of Lincoln Center in New York; that version comprised twenty-five aluminum trees, each 8 feet (2.44 m) high. In 2004, he came up with a new and more refined version for Union Square and, once again, Lincoln Center, both in New York. The following year, this installation was mounted again for the Bonnaroo Music Festival in Manchester, Tennessee.

The installation sought to bring a human dimension back to the public space by making the trees 10 inches (25 cm) smaller than the onlookers, thereby weaving the Sonic Forest into the urban fabric. Each column is fitted with electronic sensors that imitate the human eye, 4-inch (10-cm) loudspeakers, and MR16 lamps. The spectators' movements around these columns set off a variety of preprogrammed sound and lighting effects. The installation can fit in anywhere as its columns can be inserted into the ground.

TYPE OF PROJECT **Permanent installation**

TOTAL SURFACE AREA: 1,000 sq. ft. **(93 m²)**

PHOTOS **Javier Belver © Expo Zaragoza 2008**

The version designed for the Zaragoza Expo 2008 consists of twenty-one columns that not only respond to the movements of onlookers but are also programmed to reactivate after 10 seconds of inactivity. In keeping with the Expo's themes of water and sustainability, the speakers in this particular Sonic Forest emit the sound of whales and porpoises communicating in order to evoke an underwater environment.

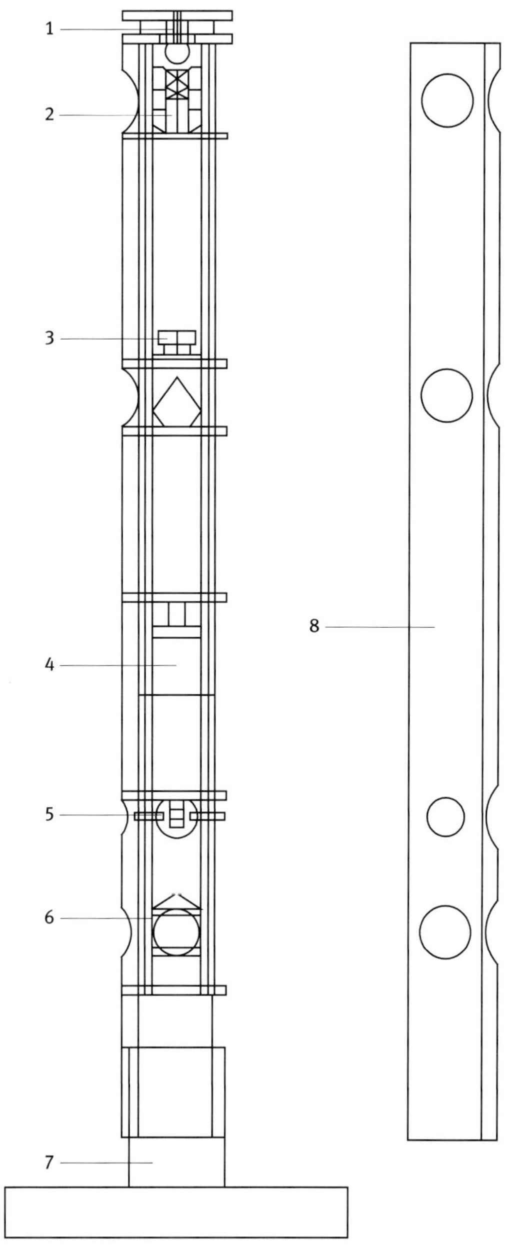

SECTION AND ELEVATION—COLUMN

1. STROBOSCOPIC LIGHT
2. 4 MR16 LEDS
3. LOUDSPEAKER
4. CIRCUIT BOARD
5. PHOTOELECTRIC CELL
6. INCANDESCENT NIGHTLIGHT
7. CONCRETE BASE
8. ACCESS PANEL

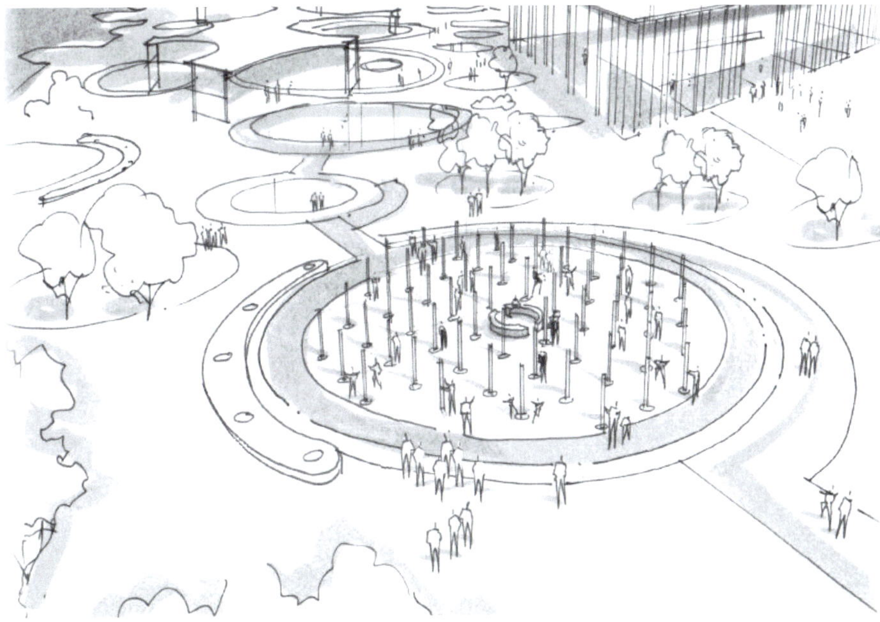

PRELIMINARY SKETCH

295

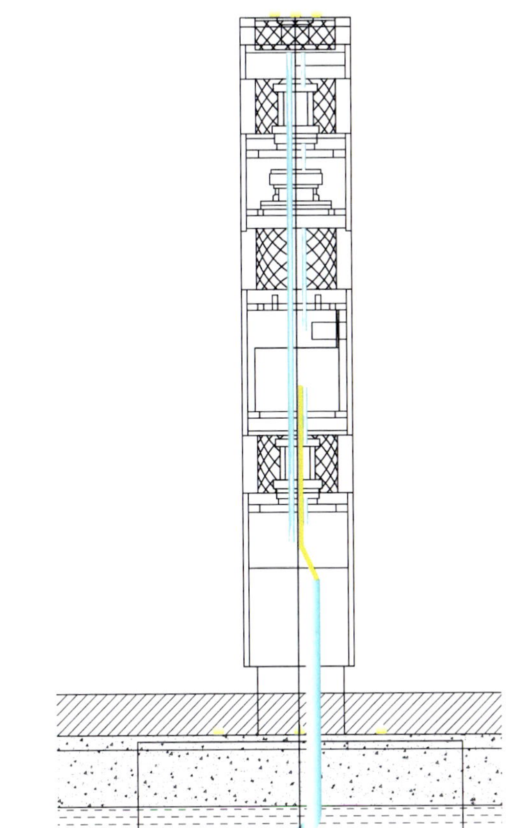

CONSTRUCTION SECTION

The Sonic Forest was one of the projects devised by Expo 2008 to enliven the area around the Ebro River, and it is the first installation of its kind to find a permanent home outside the United States.

Each tree in the Zaragoza installation reproduces different sounds from nature, as well as musical instruments and short melodies; these sounds are mixed at random to create an overall effect that is never quite identical.

acciona

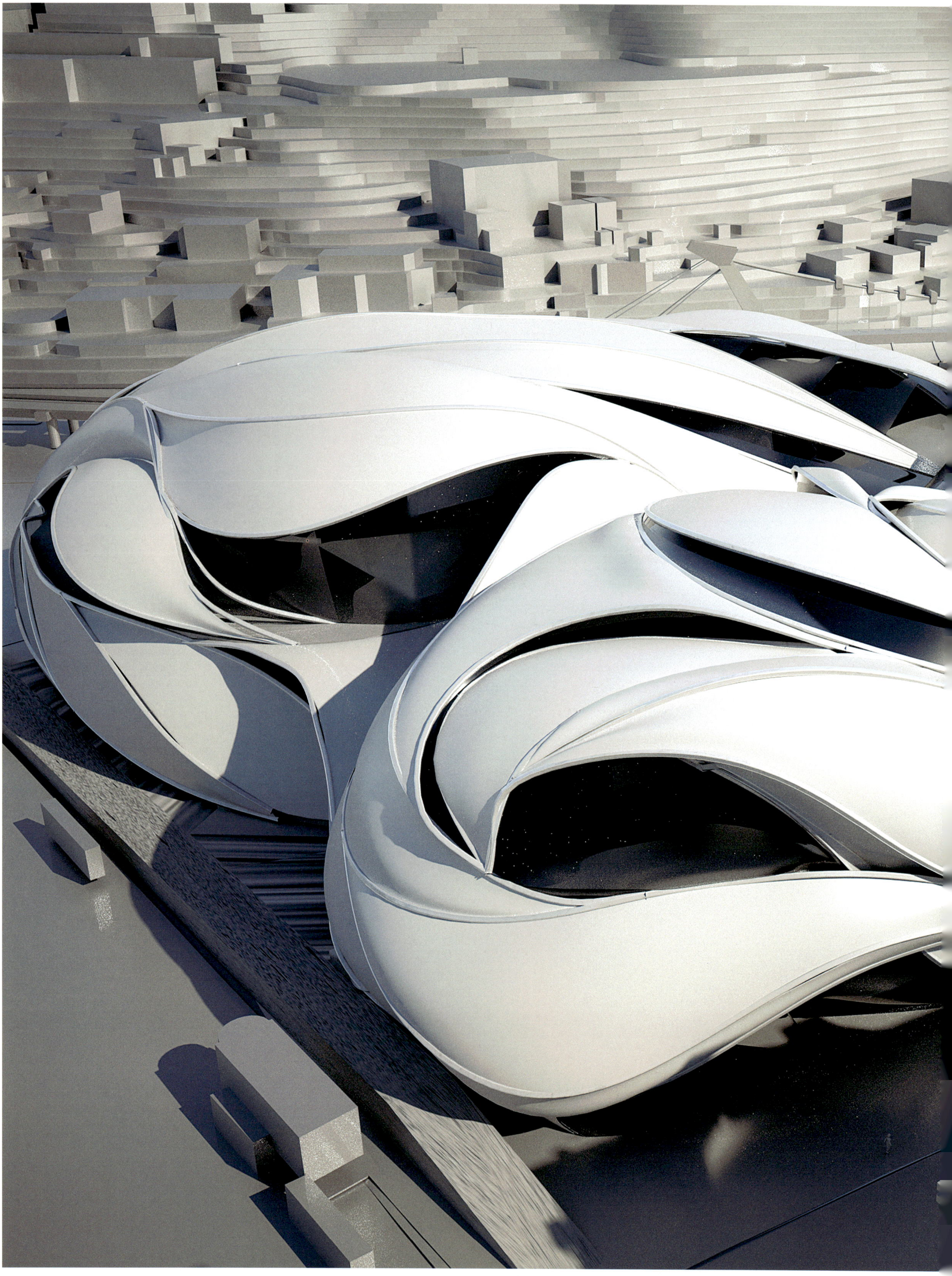

Center for the Dramatic Arts

B+U | TAIPEI, TAIWAN 2008 (UNBUILT PROJECT)

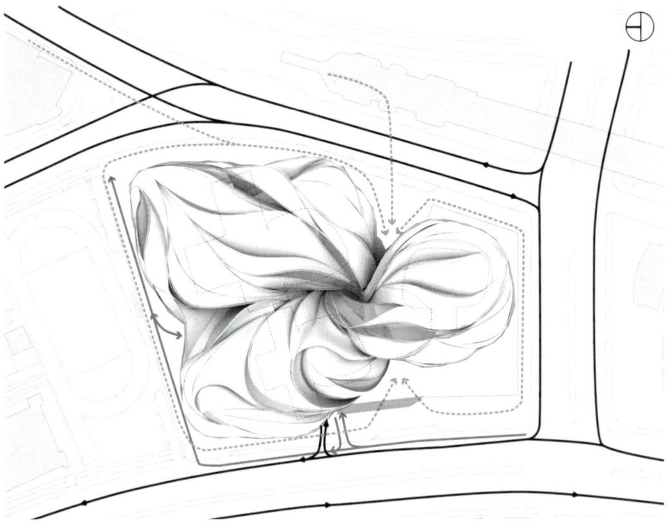

SITE PLAN

The members of the B+U team combine their musical training and architectural experience to come up with projects that involve both musical composition and digital media. They have created software that enables them to experiment with three-dimensional forms based on sonograms and sounds. Accordingly, their project for the competition to build the Center for the Dramatic Arts in Taipei was based on sound. They analyzed sound waves to transform them into vectors that provide the structure and exterior form of the building. In this way they sought to enhance the richness and diversity of an institution that has to serve as a reference point for the city. The glass and metal used on the exterior emphasize the wavy lines of the three volumes and offer glimpses of the activities underway inside.

The building's location is a link between the Shilin nighttime market and the Jiantan train station. Bearing in mind that this nexus is destined to be a large square, the architects decided to raise the building above the ground. This approach links the streets in the vicinity and structures the central entrance onto the main foyer and the three theaters. On the level of the square itself, an area covered by the large roof of one of the theaters contains stores and restaurants, which can be reached from both the square and adjacent streets.

TYPE OF PROJECT **Cultural facility**

TOTAL SURFACE AREA: **430,000 sq. ft. (40,000 m²)**

RENDERS: **© B + U**

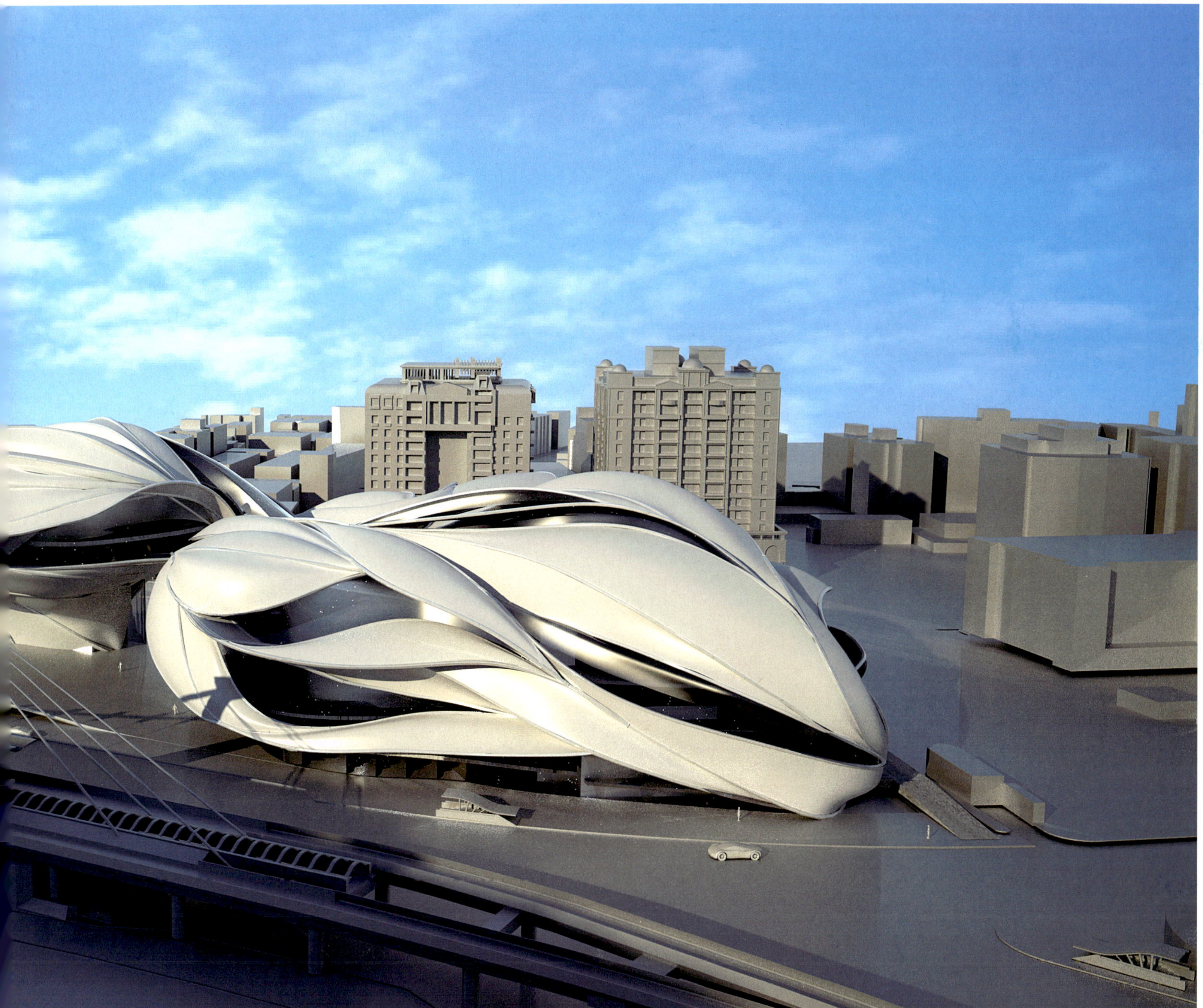

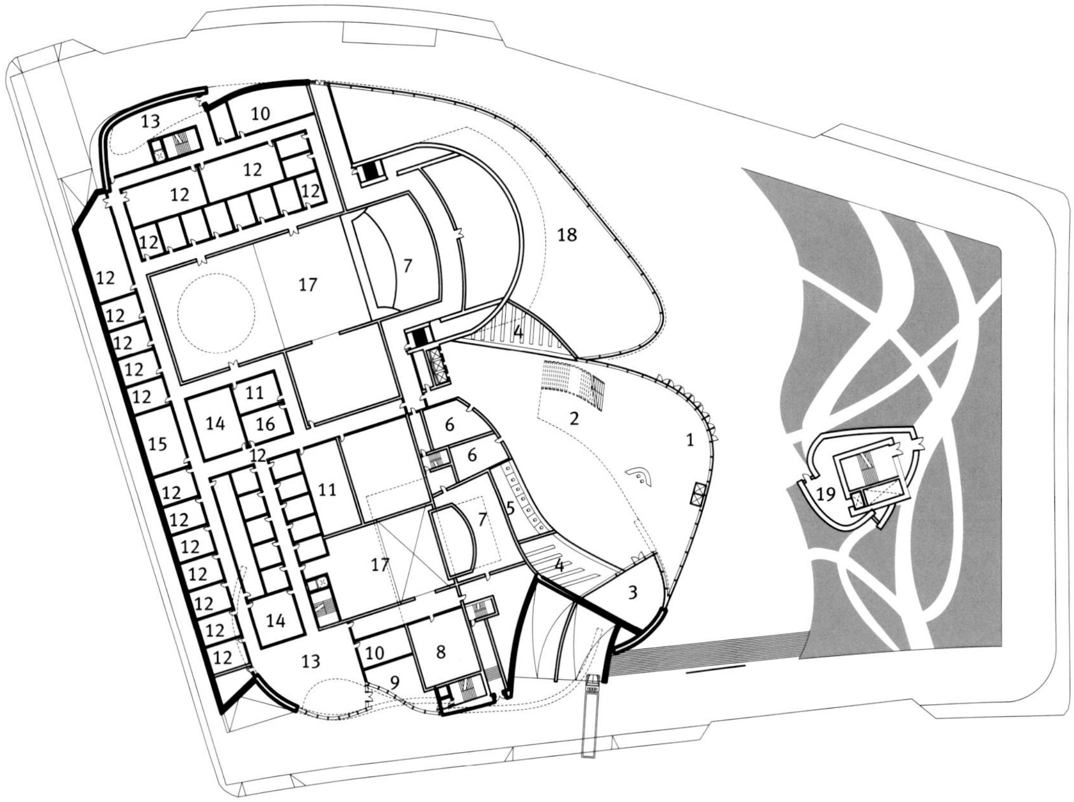

GROUND FLOOR

1. ENTRANCE
2. FOYER
3. SECURITY CABINS
4. CLOAKROOM
5. COUNTER
6. RESTROOMS
7. STORAGE AREAS
8. MACHINE ROOMS
9. OFFICES
10. MEETING ROOMS
11. BATHROOMS
12. LOCKER ROOMS
13. RECEPTIONS
14. DRESSING ROOMS
15. LAUNDRY
16. FIRST AID
17. LOWER STAGE
18. SHOPPING GALLERY AND RESTAURANTS
19. SECURITY ENTRANCE
20. PROSCENIUM
21. MAIN STAGE
22. PLAYHOUSE
23. GRAND THEATER
24. SCENERY CONSTRUCTION
25. REHEARSAL ROOMS
26. RESTAURANT
27. BAR
28. TECHNICIANS' ROOM
29. KITCHEN
30. EMERGENCY CONTROL
31. MULTIFORM THEATER
32. GREEN ROOM

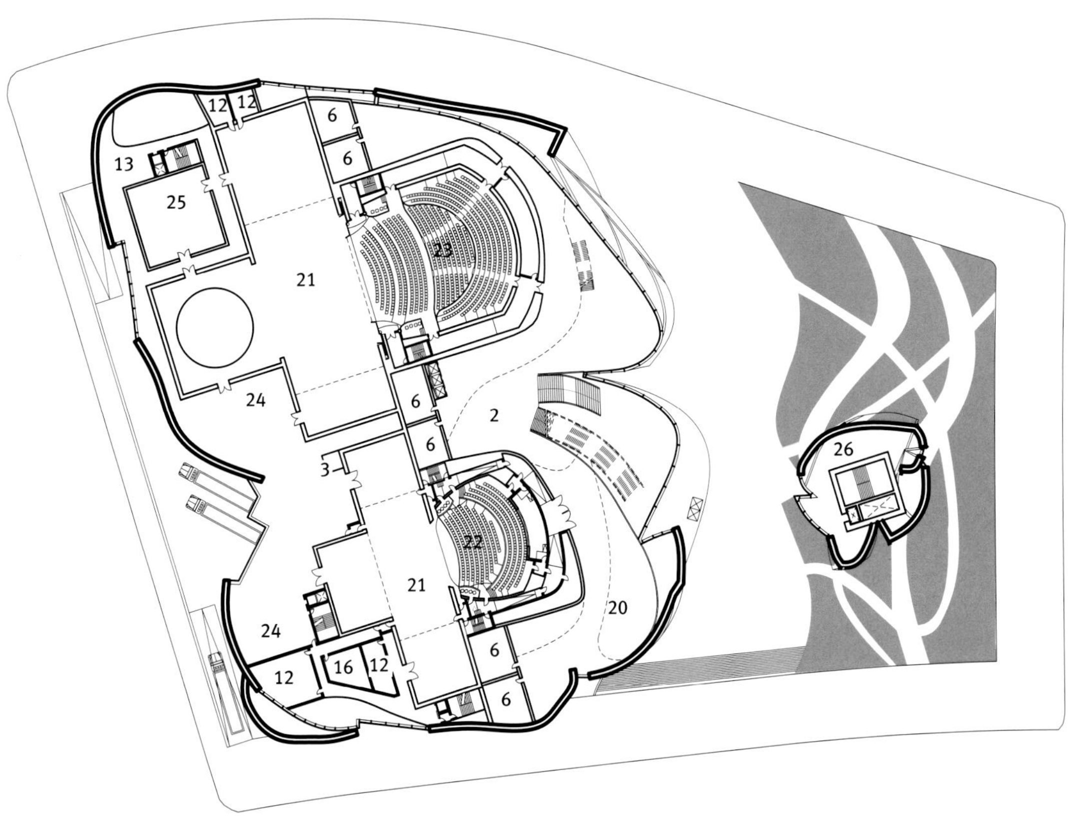

SECOND FLOOR

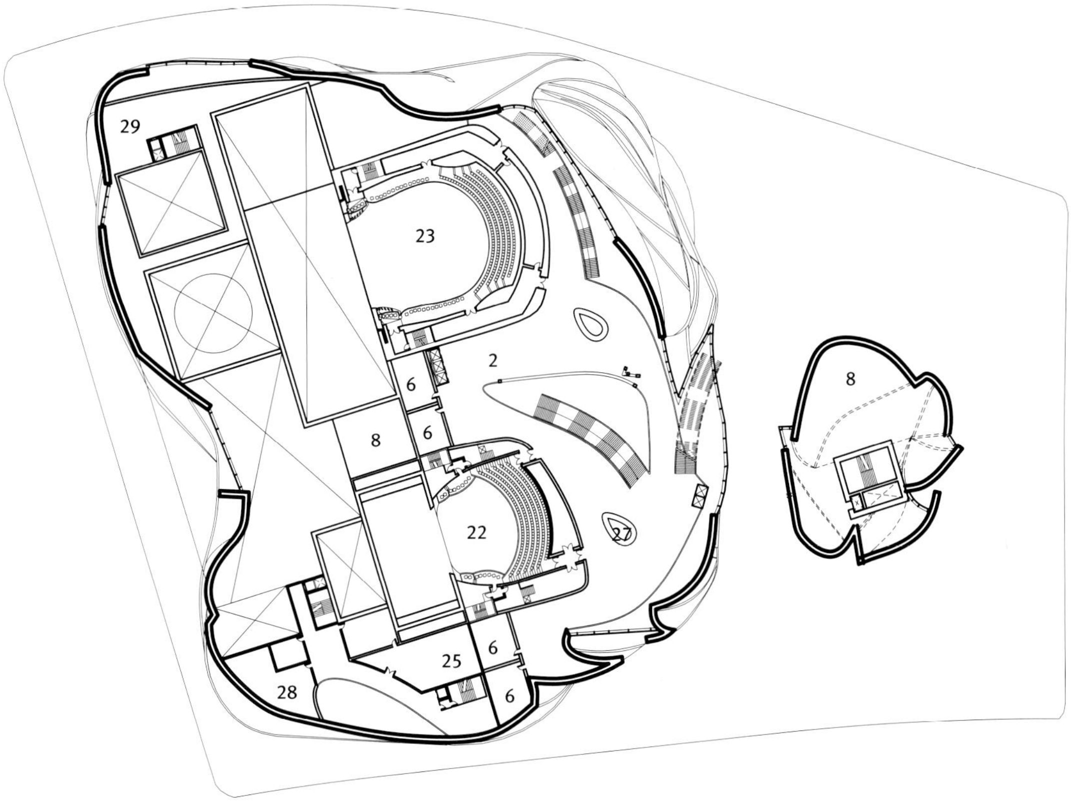

SIXTH FLOOR

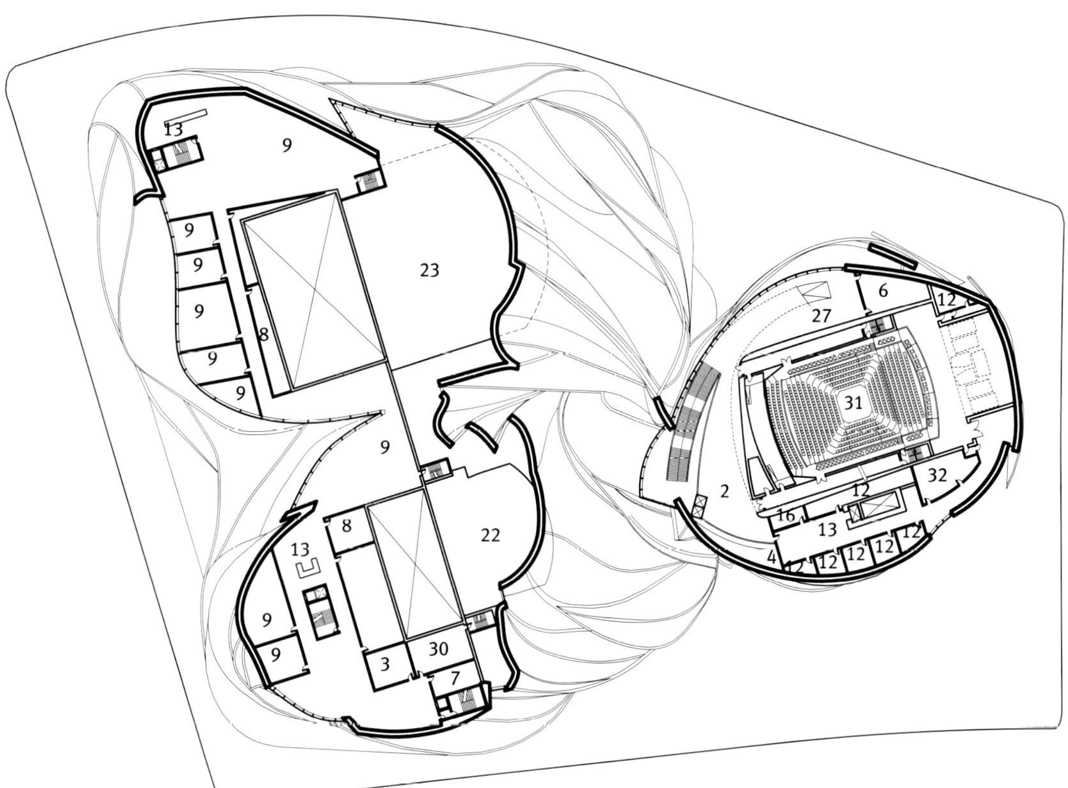

EIGHTH FLOOR

EAST ELEVATION

WEST ELEVATION

NORTH ELEVATION

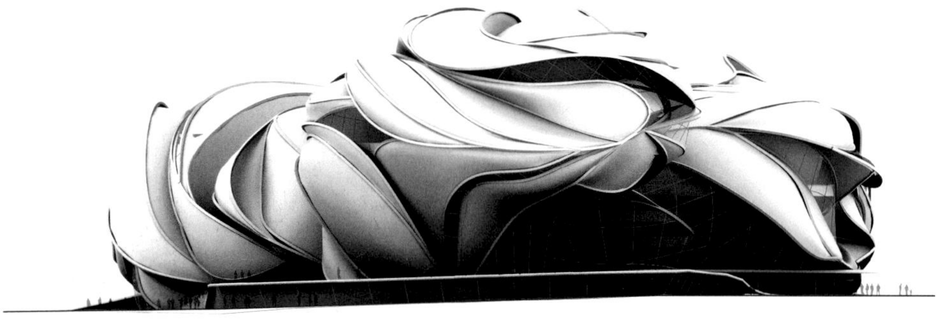

SOUTH ELEVATION

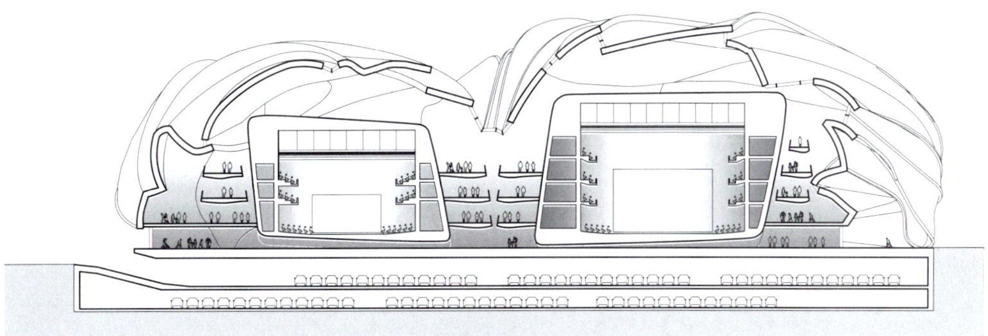

CROSS SECTION—PLAYHOUSE AND GRAND THEATER

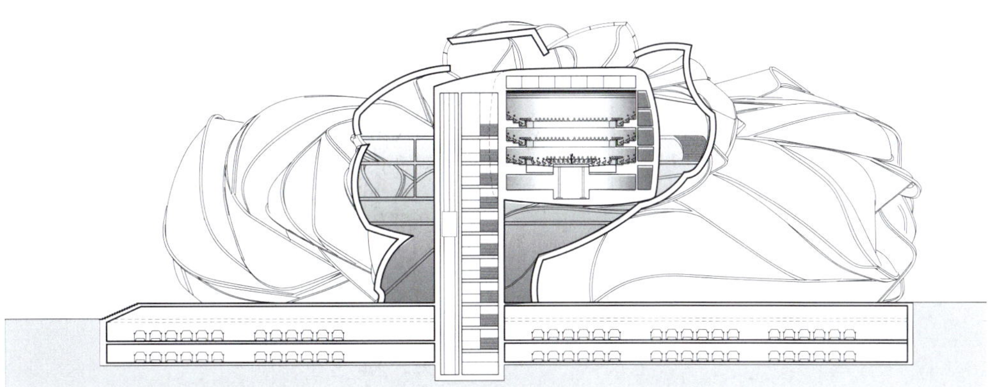

CROSS SECTION—MULTIFORM THEATER

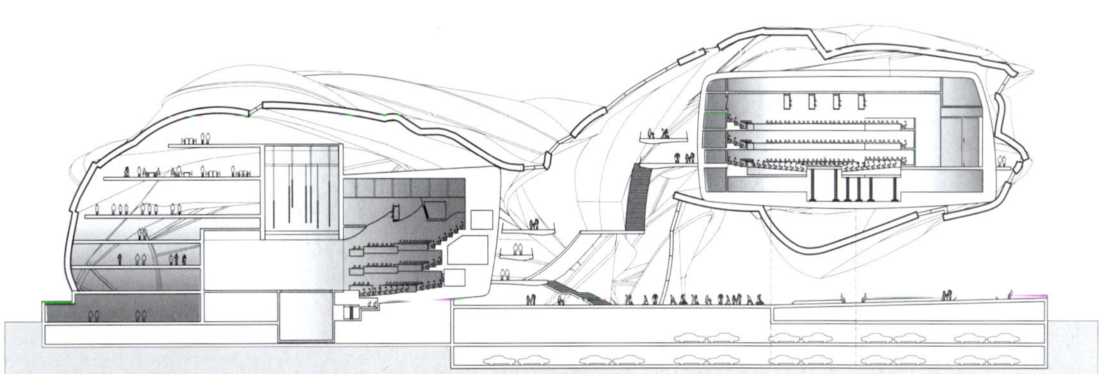

LONGITUDINAL SECTION—PLAYHOUSE AND MULTIFORM THEATER

306

The main priority was to design spaces specially adapted to the needs of Taiwanese dramatic arts while also remaining suitable for performances in various styles. The Grand Theater, with 1,500 seats and three levels, can put on operas, ballets, and orchestral concerts, as well as plays, dance pieces, multimedia events, percussion spectacles, martial art competitions, and even Zen meditation. The Playhouse was designed as a large proscenium auditorium, with 800 seats and two levels; the Multiform Theater, with 800 seats and two levels, has a stage that can be configured as required (in the center, in the front, or in the round).

The Grand Theater and Playhouse stand on the northern part of the lot, while the Multiform Theater is set to the south, raised slightly above ground level. In order to create a central space and a visual connection between the three volumes, the main foyer, which is covered with glass, gives rise to a large staircase leading to the entrance to all three theaters. The latter operate as independent buildings, each with its individual circulation, and they link up to the level of the central space. The general public can enter the area around the auditorium in each interior without having to see a show.

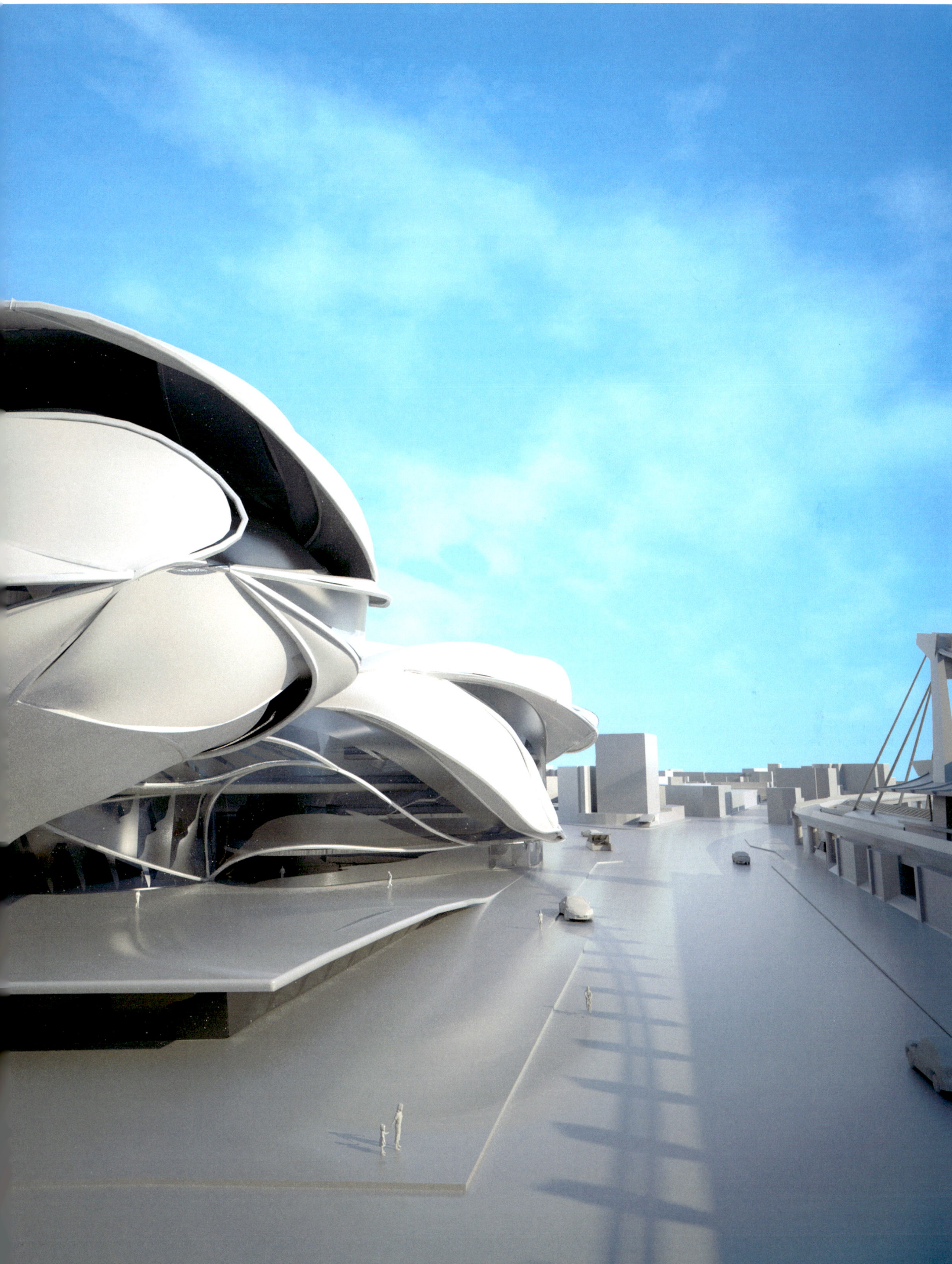

Backstage, the theaters are organized to cover the various requirements of different dramatic arts while also satisfying the needs of Taiwanese cultural forms. Each theater has its own stage door on one of the neighboring streets.

Low Rez / Hi Fi

HÖWELER + YOON ARCHITECTURE | WASHINGTON, DC 2007

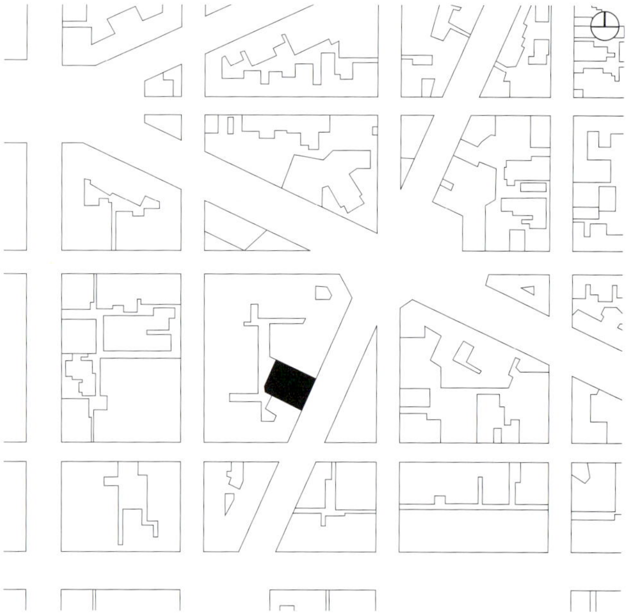

SITE PLAN

Low Rez/Hi Fi is an interactive installation designed to renovate the foyer of a building at 1110 Vermont Avenue in Washington, DC. It is made up of glass display cases with an LED (Low Rez) matrix and a grid of posts sensitive to the touch (Hi Fi). Each element follows the movement of passersby to program sound and lighting in real time.

The display cases in the Low Rez module are aligned perpendicular to the building's facade. Each one consists of 8,000 LED pixels supported by cables. These pixels were custom-made to be switched on and off individually. The display cases interact with each other to form a screen that can broadcast texts or low-resolution images. The screen normally displays the building address—1110—against a background of ones and zeros in movement. The changes on the screen attract pedestrians to the display cases, while a security camera takes a person's picture, adjusts the contrast, and sends a signal to the LED matrix. This process creates a digital shadow in real time that fits into the moving background.

The Hi Fi is an urban musical instrument, a space with stainless-steel posts that make a series of melodic sounds—composed by Erik Carlson—when they are touched.

TYPE OF PROJECT Permanent installation

SOUND Erik Carlson

TOTAL SURFACE AREA 3,300 sq. ft. (310 m²)

PHOTO © Höweler + Yoon Architecture, Alan Karchmer

This project, set just a few blocks from the White House, was originally intended as a temporary installation to activate the public space and attract the attention of pedestrians toward the entrance to the building at 1110 Vermont Avenue. It forces passersby to reconsider their usual relationship with constructed space and change from being a mere spectator to an active participant.

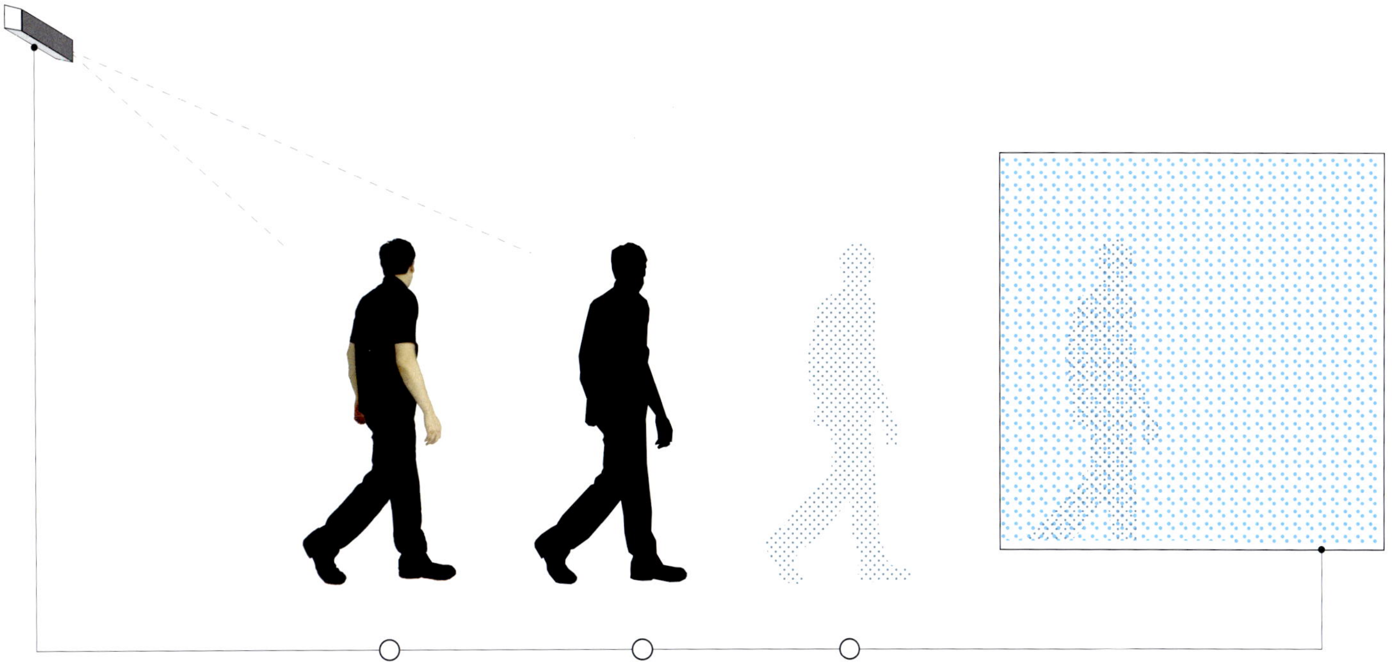

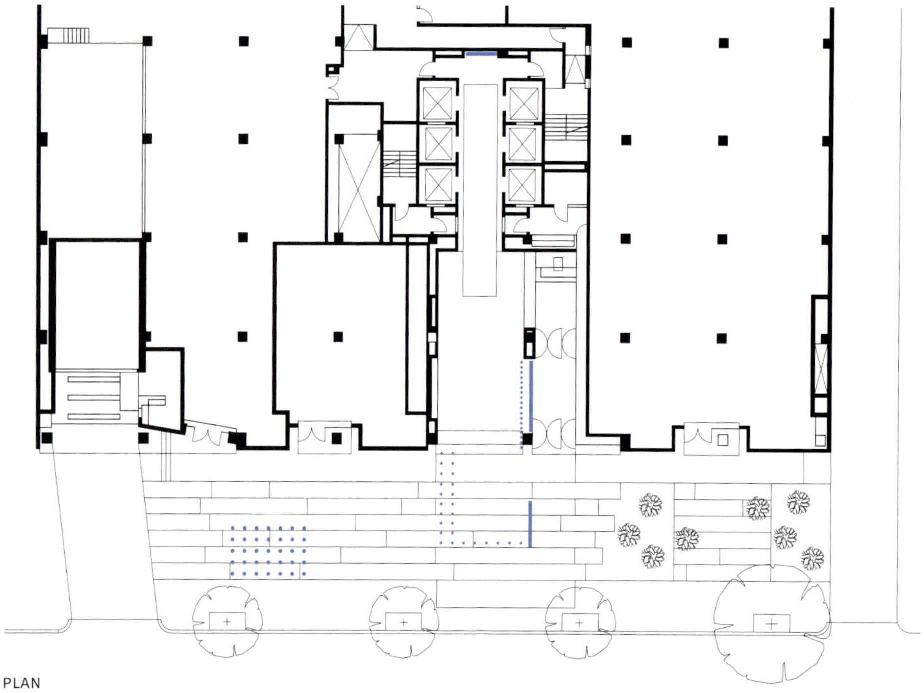

PLAN

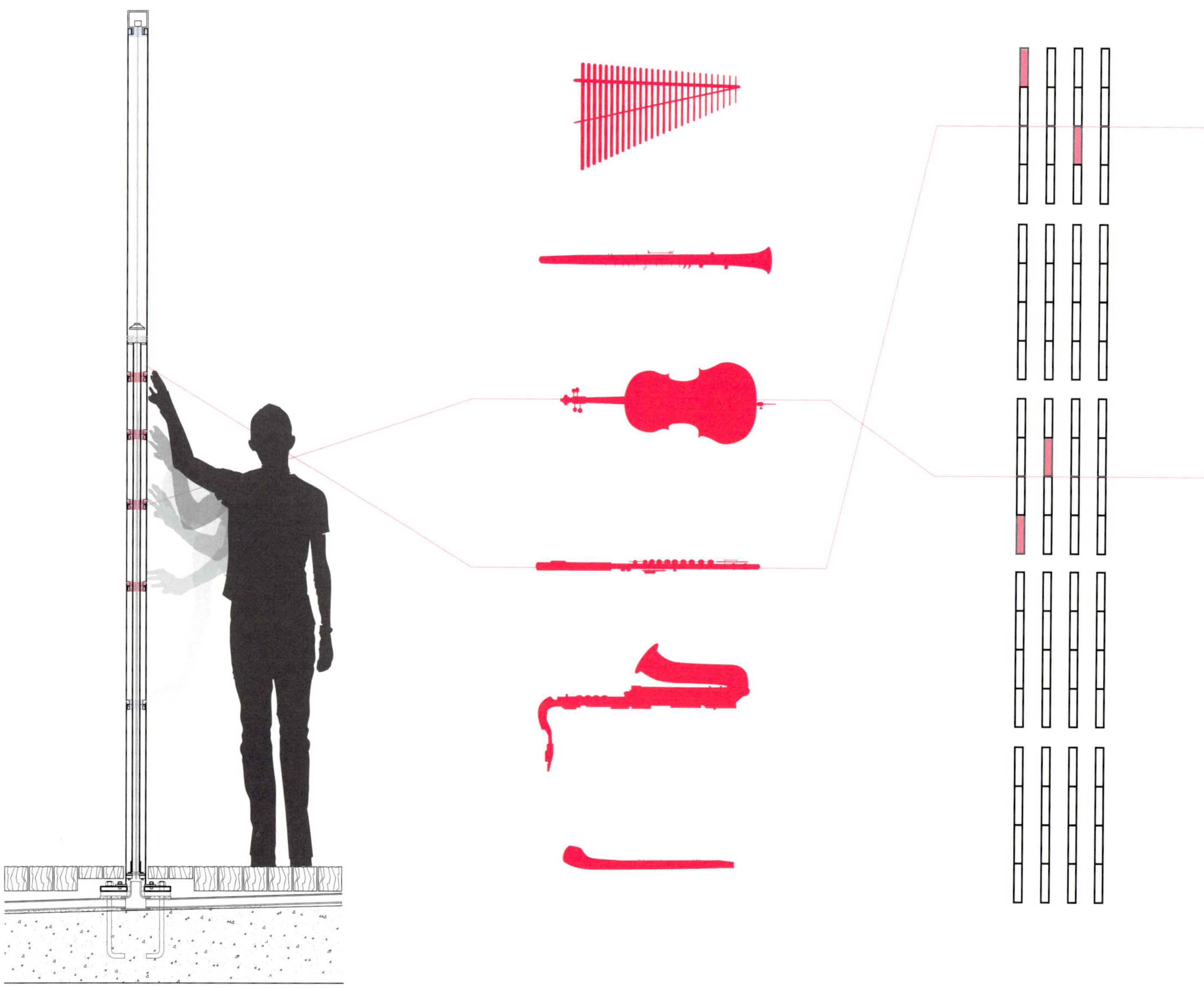

VARIABLE CONFIGURATION OF SOUNDS

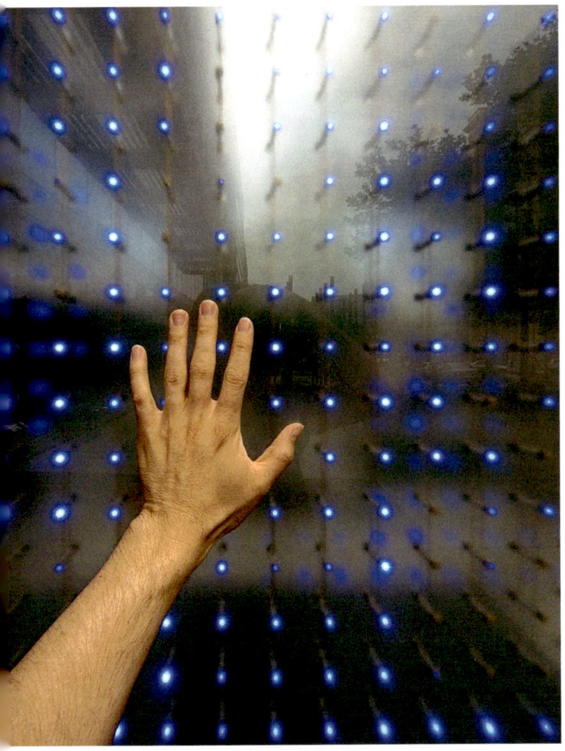

The Hi Fi module, also known as the "Sound Grove," is an interactive area with twenty posts sensitive to touch. This project is an evolution of the White Noise, White Light project created for the 2004 Olympic Games in Athens. The posts are lit by blue LED rings designed to link up with the Low Rez display cases.

Chant de bambous

N+B ARCHITECTES | CHAUMONT-SUR-LOIRE, FRANCE 2006

SITE PLAN

Every year the gardens of the Chaumont-sur-Loire Château, set 112 miles (180 km) from Paris in the Loire Valley, play host to the International Garden Festival, which has grown into a showcase for the latest trends in gardening and landscaping. In 2006, twenty-six projects were created to explore the theme established that year by the organization: playing in the garden. The firm of N+B Architectes came up with a structure of hanging bamboo poles that "sang" with the movement produced by visitors as they passed through the site. The result was a game that allowed both children and adults to transform the space and make their own sounds.

The architects of N+B are interested in developing projects that delve into the relationship between spirit and matter, between time and material. In the case of the play garden, they dreamed up the idea of a space that gave full rein to the senses and emotions. In the Chaumont-sur-Loire Festival, they sought to play with opposites: a fixed structure opposed to the hanging bamboo poles; the installation's flexibility as opposed to the solidity of the trunks; the sound of the wind blowing through the poles opposed to the sounds made by the poles as they bang against each other. Playing in the garden required players, so the *Chant de bambous* (Song of bamboos) invited its visitors to enter a maze and create noises, spaces, even images—an experience that involved all the senses and evoked the pleasure of exploration.

TYPE OF PROJECT **Temporary installation**

TOTAL SURFACE AREA **344 sq. ft. (32 m²)**

PHOTOS **© N+B Architectes**

ELEVATION FROM THE ENTRANCE

SOUTHEAST ELEVATION

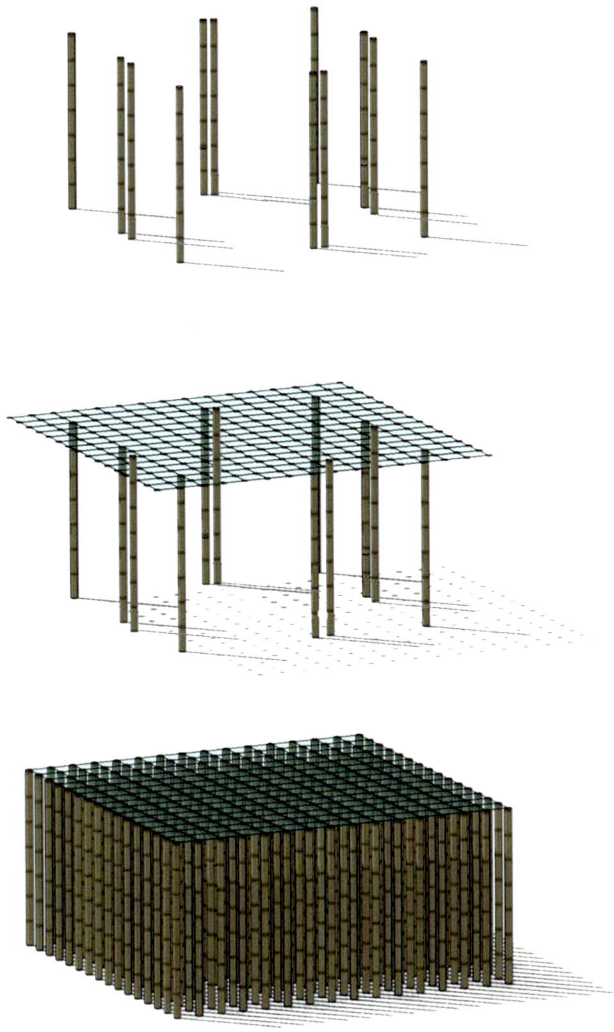

CONSTRUCTION AXONOMETRIC

DIAGRAM OF COLORS

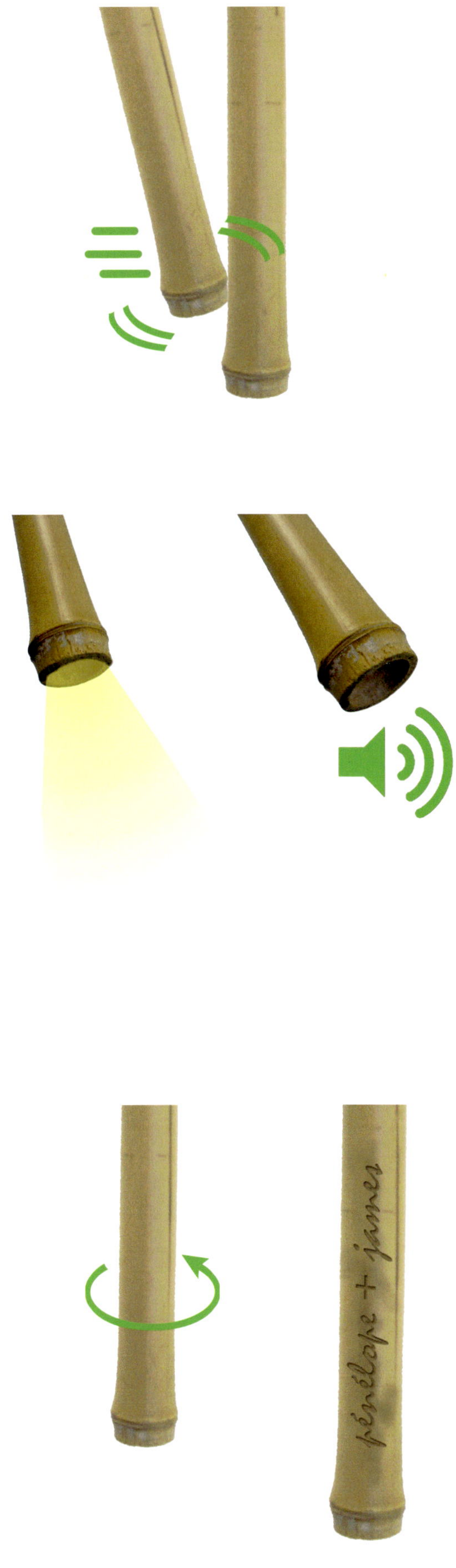

USES OF BAMBOO POLES

Kofmehl

SSM ARCHITEKTEN | SOLOTHURN, SWITZERLAND 2005

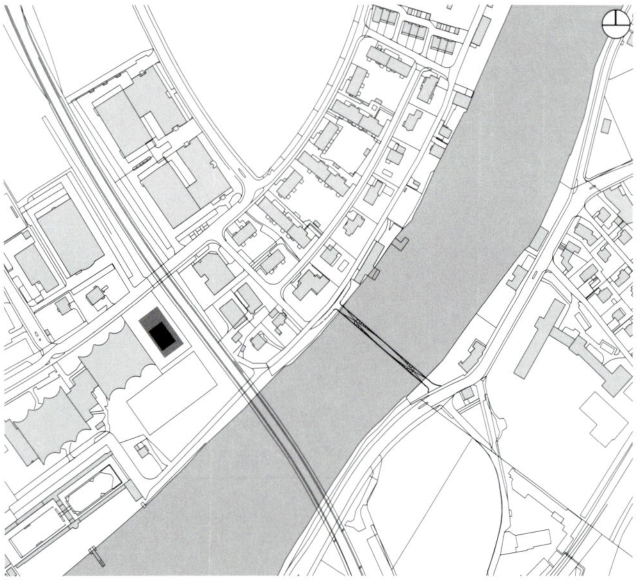

SITE PLAN

The Kofmehl is situated on the outskirts of a small Swiss town, Solothurn, in an area with an industrial tradition. The town boasts a wide range of cultural activities that attract visitors from all over the region, as well as an impressive array of Baroque and Renaissance buildings. But it is also known for its long-standing heavy industry. The Kofmehl, built to replace an old concert hall, was designed in an architectural idiom that emphasized this industrial context. The architects sought to integrate elements, such as colors and textures, that evoked the old structure as well as its surroundings; so, the interior was totally inspired by the old concert hall, while the exterior reinterprets the typical look of a factory.

The building was designed as a neutral place that could be transformed in an infinite number of ways. The end result was a cube set within another cube: the central volume is the concert hall, and the services are arranged around it. This buffer zone between the concert hall and the outer facades prevents noise from reaching the outside, in contrast to typical concert halls, which are kept out of reach of vibrations from the outside. The flow of sound was thus controlled through a measured interaction between physical and aural space. The design of the Kofmehl's prism, in proportions of 1:1.6:2.33, guarantees optimum acoustics and sound quality.

TYPE OF PROJECT Concert hall

TOTAL SURFACE AREA 18,500 sq. ft. (1,720 m²)

PHOTOS © Hansruedi Riesen

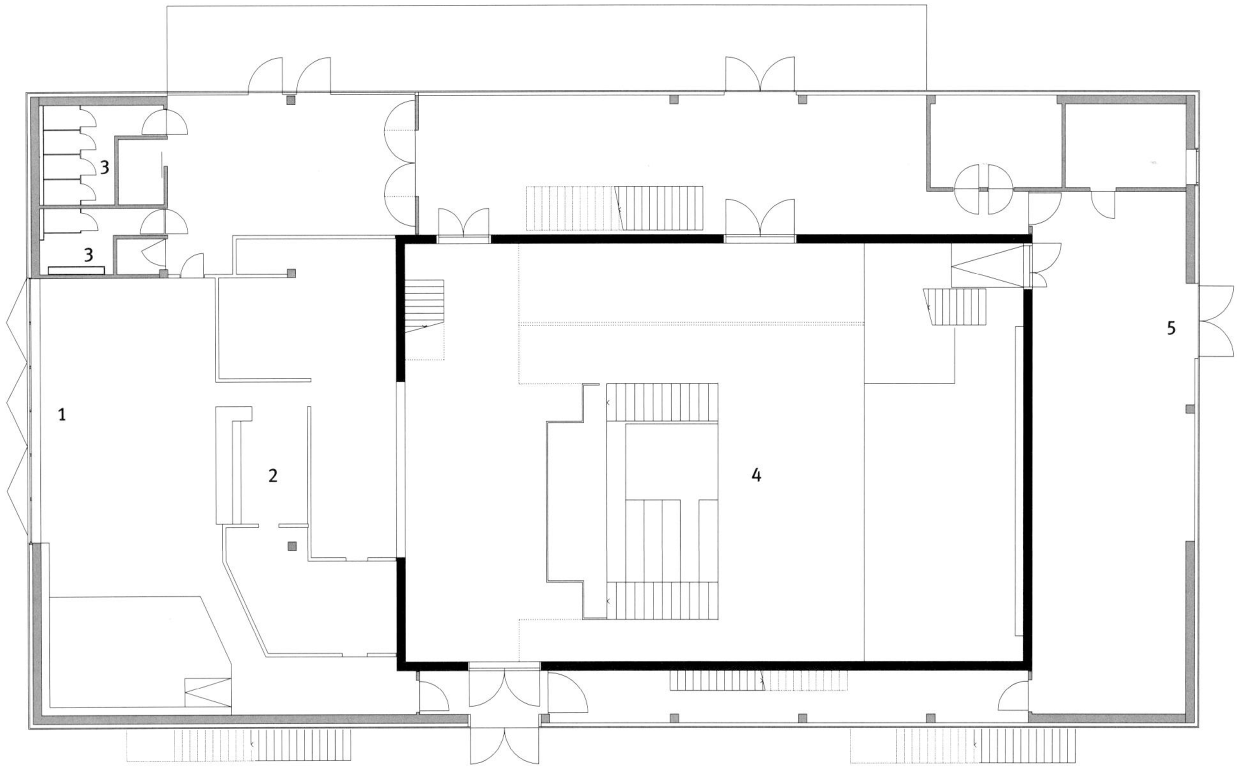

GROUND FLOOR

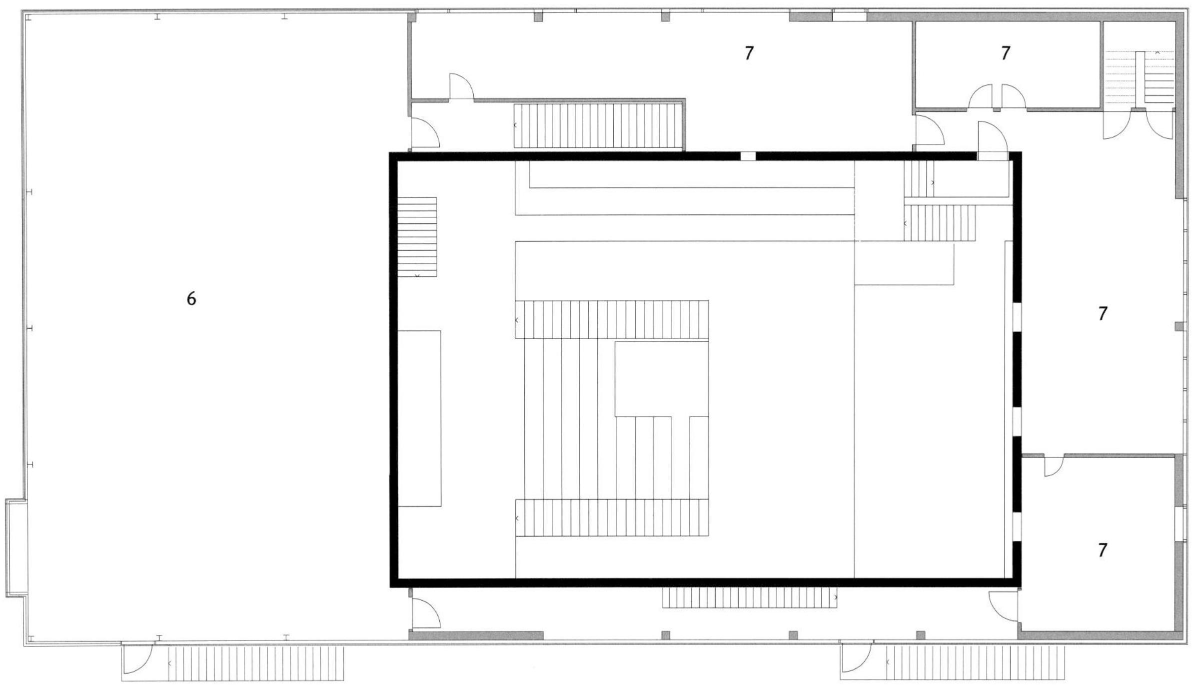

SECOND FLOOR

1. MAIN ENTRANCE
2. RAUMBAR (BAR)
3. SERVICES
4. MAIN HALL
5. STAGE DOOR
6. MEETING ROOM
7. OFFICES

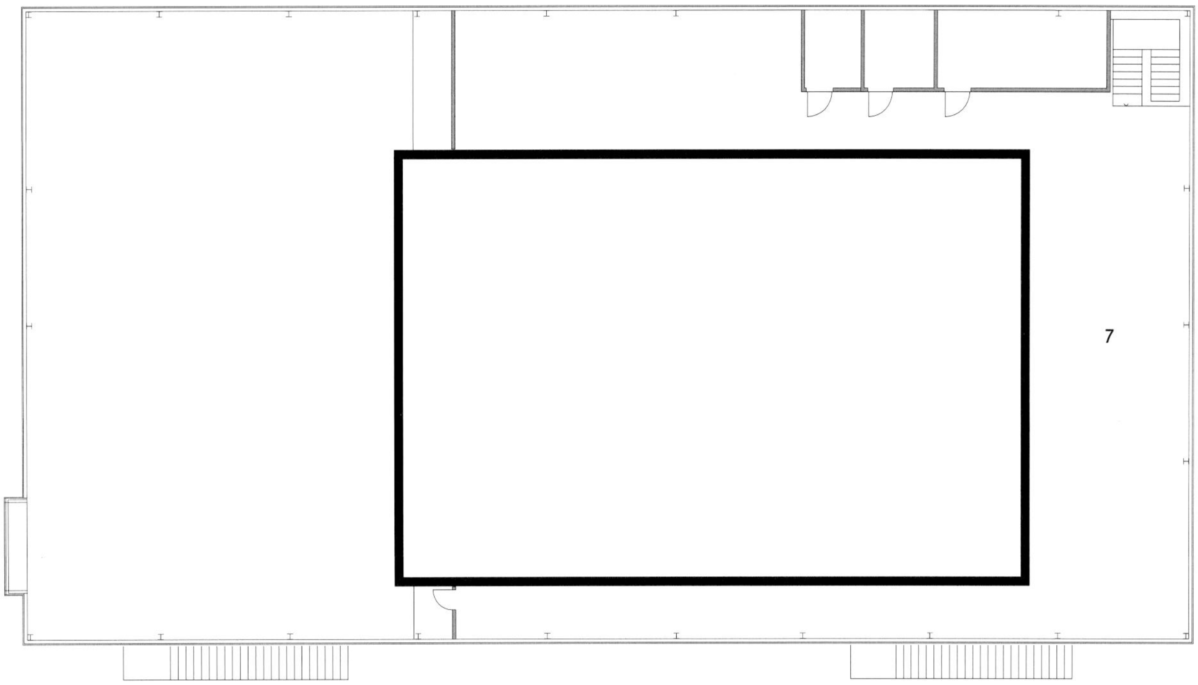

THIRD FLOOR PLAN

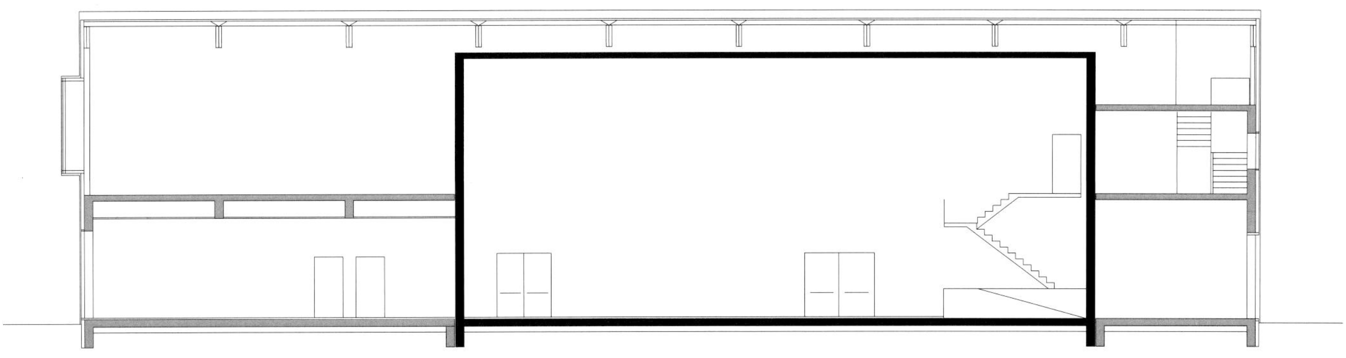

LONGITUDINAL SECTION

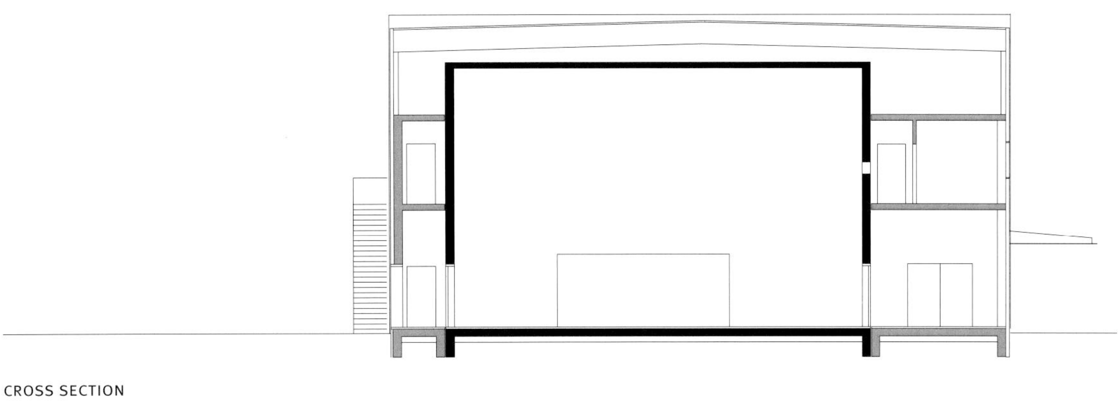

CROSS SECTION

The project sought to respond to cultural codes that would be familiar to young people in order to encourage them to participate in the building: the "little house," as it was nicknamed from the start of the construction process, was covered with graffiti shortly after it opened. The red-painted steel sheets on the facades seem to be old and well-worn, and the addition of unplanned urban art has only added to the building's character. So, the essence of an old concert hall was successfully implanted in an area usually devoid of passersby—an industrial estate—and the building has become a new urban reference point.

On the front facade, facing northwest, an extruded square window connects the building with the city and the Jura Mountains. To the northeast, an outbuilding protects the entrance to the foyer and the perforated metal sheets provide glimpses inside. Two metal staircases on the southwest facade echo the proportions within the building: one leads to the meeting room, the other to a corridor. The interior spaces are painted red, black, and yellow, just like the previous Kofmehl. The foyer, restrooms, and dressing rooms have an independent entrance, while the front of the building contains the Raumbar, a hall designed for small-scale events. Finally, the top floor plays host to offices and a meeting room.

LOKUS
LOKUS

Duttmann, Martina, ed.
Colour in Townscape
The Architectural Press
London, 1981

Lord, Peter, and Duncan Templeton.
The Architecture of Sound: Designing Places of Assembly
The Architectural Press
London, 1986

Minnaert, M.
The Nature of Light and Color in the Open Air
Dover Publications
New York, 1954

Moor, Andrew
Colours of Architecture: Coloured Glass in Contemporary Buildings
Mitchell Beazley
London, 2006

Moreno, Susana
Arquitectura y música en el siglo XX
Fundación Caja de Arquitectos
Barcelona, 2008

Pallasmaa, Juhani
The Eyes of the Skin: Architecture and the Senses
John Wiley
New York, 2005

Rasmussen, Steen Eiler
Experiencing Architecture
MIT Press
Cambridge, MA, 1964

Rossotti, Hazel
Color
Princeton University Press
Princeton, NJ, 1983

Speirs, Jonathan, et al.
Made of Light: The Art of Light and Architecture
Birkhäuser
Basle, 2006

Tornquist, Jorrit
Color and Light: Theory and Practice
Ikon
Milan, 1999

Treib, Marc
Space Calculated in Seconds. The Philips Pavilion, Le Corbusier, Edgard Varèse
Princeton University Press
Princeton, NJ, 1996

Xenakis, Iannis
Musique Architecture
Editorial Casterman
Tournai, 1976

References

ALEJANDRO ECHEVERRI RESTREPO
Calle 5G #32–103, Of. 604, Medellín, Colombia
T: +574 312 12 11
aecheverri@aearquitectos.com.co
www.aearquitectos.com.co

BRISAC GONZÁLEZ ARCHITECTS
7 Bermondsey Exchange, 179–181 Bermondsey Street,
London SE1 3UW, United Kingdom
T: +44 20 7378 7787
admin@brisacgonzalez.com
www.brisacgonzalez.com

B+U
834 S. Broadway Blvd #502, Los Angeles, CA 90014, United States
T: +1 213 623 2347
contact@bplusu.com
www.bplusu.com

CAMENZIND EVOLUTION
Samariterstrasse 5, 8032 Zurich, Switzerland
T: +41 44 253 9500
zurich@camenzindevolution.com
www.camenzindevolution.com

CHETWOODS ASSOCIATES
12–13 Clerkenwell Green, London EC1R 0QJ, United Kingdom
T: +44 20 7490 2400
laurie.chetwood@chetwoods-london.com
www.chetwoods.com

CHRISTIAN DE PORTZAMPARC
1, rue de l'Aude, 75014 Paris, France
T: +33 1 40 64 80 00
mail@portzamparc.com
www.portzamparc.com

CHRISTOPHER JANNEY
75 Kendall Road, Lexington, MA 02421, United States
T: +1 781 862 6413
phenom@rcn.com
phenomenarts.blogspot.com

HAL INGBERG
4844, av. Henri-Julien, Montreal H2T 2E1, Canada
T: +1 514 843 6578
ingberg@halingberg.com
www.halingberg.com

HÖWELER + YOON ARCHITECTURE
150 Lincoln Street, #3A, Boston, MA 02111, United States
T: +1 617 517 4101
info@mystudio.us
www.hyarchitecture.com

JULIANO DUBEUX ARQUITETOS ASSOCIADOS
Avenida Alfredo Lisboa 507 1º, Recife, PE 50030–150, Brazil
T: +55 81 3424 3796
julianodubeux@julianodubeux.com
www.julianodubeux.com

LAB[AU]
Lakensestraat 104, rue de Laeken, Brussels 1000, Belgium
T: +32 2 2196555
lab-au@lab-au.com
www.lab-au.com

METRO ARQUITETURA
Av. João de Barros, 1527 Sl. 701 Recife, PE 52021–180, Brazil
T: + 55 81 3426 5655
metro@metro.arq.br
www.metro.arq.br

MODULORBEAT
Hüfferstr. 20, D-48149 Munster, Germany
T: +49 251 2877670
info@modulorbeat.de
www.modulorbeat.de

MVRDV
Dunantstraat 10, 3024 BC Rotterdam, Netherlands
T: +31 10 477 28 60
pr@mvrdv.nl
www.mvrdv.nl

Directory of Architects

From the United States, drop the + sign; dial 011 instead of the + sign for international calls.

nARCHITECTS
68 Jay Street, #317, Brooklyn, NY 11201, United States
t: 718.260.0845 f: 718.260.0847
n@narchitects.com
www.narchitects.com

N+B ARCHITECTES
2 rue Saint-Côme, F-34000 Montpellier, France
T: +33 467 925 117
valerie@nbarchi.com
www.nbarchi.com

NEUTELINGS RIEDIJK ARCHITECTEN
P.O. Box 527, NL-3000 AM Rotterdam, Netherlands
T: +31 0 10 404 66 77
info@ neutelings-riedijk.com
www.neutelings-riedijk.com

NIETO SOBEJANO ARQUITECTOS
Talavera 4 L-5, 28016 Madrid, Spain
T: +34 915643830
nietosobejano@nietosobejano.com
www.nietosobejano.com

PÉRIPHÉRIQUES ARCHITECTES
4, passage de la Fonderie, 75011 Paris, France
T: +33 1 43 55 59 95
afja.peripheriques@club-internet.fr
www.peripheriques-architectes.com

PLATT BYARD DOVELL WHITE ARCHITECTS
20 West 22nd Street, New York, NY 10010, United States
T: +1 212 691 2440
pbdw@pbdw.com
www.pbdw.com

PTW ARCHITECTS
Level 17, 9 Castlereagh Street, Sydney, NSW, Australia 2000
T: +61 2 9232 5877
info@ptw.com.au
www.ptw.com.au

RCR ARQUITECTES
Fontanella, 26, 17800 Olot, Spain
T: +34 972 269 105
rcr@rcrarquitectes.es
www.rcrarquitectes.es

REALITIES:UNITED
Falckensteinstr, 47–48, D-10997 Berlin, Germany
T: +49 30 206466-30
info@realU.de
www.realities-united.de

SAMYN AND PARTNERS
1537 Chaussée de Waterloo, B 1180 Brussels, Belgium
T: +32 2 374 90 60
sai@samynandpartners.be
www.samynandpartners.be

SIMONE GIOSTRA & PARTNERS ARCHITECTS
55 Washington Street, Suite 454, Brooklyn, NY 11201, United States
T: +1 212 920 8180
info@sgp-architects.com
www.sgp-architects.com

SSM ARCHITEKTEN
Gibelinstrasse 2, Ch-4503 Solothurn, Switzerland
T: +41 32 625 24 44
mail@ssmarchitekten.ch
www.ssmarchitekten.ch

STEVEN HOLL ARCHITECTS
450 West 31st Street, 11th floor, New York, NY 10001, United States
T: +1 212 629 7262
nyc@stevenholl.com
www.stevenholl.com

UNSTUDIO
Stadhouderskade 113, P.O. Box 75381, 1070 AJ Amsterdam, Netherlands
T: +31 20 570 20 40
info@unstudio.com
www.unstudio.com